(SOME OF)
THE ESSENTIALS
OF FINANCE
AND INVESTMENT

By

RONALD J. GILSON
Charles J. Meyers
Professor of Law and Business
Stanford University, and
Professor of Law
Columbia University

and

BERNARD S. BLACK
Professor of Law
Columbia University

Westbury, New York
THE FOUNDATION PRESS, INC.
1993

(SOME OF) THE ESSENTIALS OF FINANCE AND INVESTMENT

PREFACE

This small book is a first, partial installment on what we expect will become, in a couple of years, a full textbook in *corporate finance and investment* for *law students*. It consists of the Chapters 1-7 of our book, *The Law and Finance of Corporate Acquisitions* (2d ed. forthcoming 1994 from Foundation Press). These chapters are being published separately for those professors who want to teach a serious course in finance, with more rigor and skepticism about such concepts as the Capital Asset Pricing Model and the Efficient Capital Markets Hypothesis than is available in the standard business school textbooks.

An important accompaniment to this book is extensive class notes for a 3-unit course in finance, together with homework problems (with solutions), and supplemental readings, available from Bernard Black, Columbia Law School, 435 West 116th St., New York NY 10027; (212) 854-8079; internet: bblack@lawmail.columbia.edu. These teaching materials were prepared in Wordperfect 5.1 and are available on disk as well as in hardcopy.

This book and the accompanying materials were prepared in the belief that a solid grounding in finance is an important tool for lawyers. Elements of finance theory affect many things that lawyers do. Almost every lawyer needs a solid grounding in the basics of valuation - discounting; the time value of money; computing *expected* return in an uncertain world; the value of diversification of an investment portfolio; tradeoffs between risk and return. Family lawyers must value marital assets; personal injury lawyers must be able to advise clients on the merits of a structured settlement with periodic payments over time; litigators must understand how the decision to take one more deposition or file one more motion affects the expected value of a lawsuit to their client.

Business lawyers -- corporate lawyers; tax lawyers; real estate lawyers; entertainment lawyers; etc. -- need more. *Finance is the theory of business.* To read business documents; to draft contracts and disclosure documents; to counsel clients on issues that mix business sense with legal constraints; to know when a less than fully honest client has put them into a practical and ethical minefield -- business lawyers need a solid grounding in finance. They need to understand the business realities of the transactions that they work on. They need to understand which contractual language gives meaningful comfort to the buyer of a business (or the seller), which language nobody really cares very much about, and *why*.

They need to be able to read, *really read*, financial statements and footnotes to financial statements, and financial projections, to find hidden problems that may affect a deal or call for special disclosure in a prospectus or other disclosure document. They have to find the mistakes that accountants and businesspeople make all too often. They have to find the hidden assumptions buried in a set of projections. Number crunchers are great at adding things up, but they don't always add up the right things. Sometimes, one side to a transaction has something to hide; the numbers deliberately camouflage a major problem. Lawyers are often the front line troops in ferreting out financial fraud and deception.

Our firm belief, grounded in our own experience, is that the best business lawyers -- the ones who add value to a transaction, instead of just being transaction costs -- are the men and women who can put themselves in the shoes of their clients, understand what's important to the client, and counsel the client on alternative ways to achieve a particular goal.

Finance theory also has important policy implications. For any serious debate about the merits or demerits of takeovers, leveraged buyouts, junk bonds, bank regulation, securities markets, the efficiency of large corporations, and many other topics, the language of modern finance theory is essential. To debate whether capital markets are efficient or not, one must understand what the claim that they are efficient means, what it doesn't mean, what the evidence in support of the efficient markets hypothesis is, and what the anomalies are. The same thing is true with regard to how expected risk, expected return and diversification affect optimal capital structure and the construction of an investment portfolio.

Many important recent changes in legal rules have been driven by the development of modern finance theory. Examples include integrated disclosure for securities offerings by public companies; the "fraud on the market" theory of liability for securities fraud; the move in trust law toward evaluating the prudence of a *portfolio* rather than the prudence of particular investments; and proposals for risk-based regulation of bank capital requirements or pension insurance.

In a course that is centrally about *finance*, we have to give something up, compared to a more traditional format. There are no cases in this book and only a few in the course that it forms a part of. There is little on the *law* of financial instruments like preferred stock and debt. The omission is regrettable, but necessary, we think. It is hard enough to offer a solid grounding in finance in a semester, starting as we do from the assumption of no prior background in finance.

At the same time, we have approached our subject with a rigor not commonly found in introductory business school texts. Assumptions are clearly laid out; cookbook approaches are avoided; complexities are mentioned even when they cannot be fully pursued; the limits of standard paradigms are explored. We provide as much analytical rigor as is consistent with the initial decision to limit the required mathematical background.

The target audience for the underlying course, as we conceive it, is someone whose last exposure to mathematics was taking (and disliking) algebra in high school, n yeara ago (n being a large number). The pace of the materials is deliberately slow at the beginning; more complex topics are introduced gradually. Students who have already had an MBA-level business school course in finance should not take a course taught from this book. Indeed, one probably shouldn't allow such students to take the course, because their presence will scare off others whom begin with less sophistication.

To learn finance, or any quantitative subject, one must do problems. This book includes problems at the back of every chapter; additional problems with solutions are available as noted above. Students should plan to purchase a basic business calculator - - which one doesn't matter. We urge teachers to assign regular problem sets. For many students, problems are the best way to learn much of the subject matter of this course, for others, they are a critical reality check on whether one really understands the material.

Ronald J. Gilson
Palo Alto, California

Bernard S. Black
New York, New York

August 1993

TABLE OF CONTENTS

Page No.

CHAPTER ONE: AN INTRODUCTION TO CORPORATE ACQUISITIONS AND TRANSACTION PLANNING

CHAPTER TWO: VALUATION UNDER CERTAINTY

CHAPTER THREE: VALUATION UNDER UNCERTAINTY--RISK AND DIVERSIVICATION

CHAPTER FOUR: THE RELATIONSHIP BETWEEN RISK AND RETURN--THE CAPITAL ASSET PRICING MODEL AND ALTERNATIVES

CHAPTER FIVE: THE EFFICIENT CAPITAL MARKETS HYPOTHESIS

CHAPTER SIX: EVENT STUDIES -- MEASURING THE IMPACT OF INFORMATION

CHAPTER SEVEN: THE OPTION PERSPECTIVE

CHAPTER 1: AN INTRODUCTION TO CORPORATE ACQUISITIONS AND TRANSACTION PLANNING

A. An Overview of This Book

This book is an effort to fuse several distinct innovations in corporate law scholarship and curriculum. The first, a transactional approach, treats as the focus of interest actual business activities that cut across several academic subject areas. This approach was pioneered by David Herwitz in his 1966 casebook *Business Planning: Materials on the Planning of Corporate Transactions*. Its insight lay in both its problem orientation and its integration of corporate, tax and securities law in a single book. The second innovation, pioneered by Victor Brudney and Marvin Chirelstein in their 1972 *Cases and Materials on Corporate Finance*, is the recognition that financial theory is centrally important to understanding corporate law issues. The third is the increasing importance of empirical evidence in corporate law scholarship. To assess the pros and cons of an active takeover market, for example, we must study the available evidence with a skeptical eye, and understand which questions the empirical evidence seems to answer and which it leaves open. This book builds on the premise that financial theory and empirical studies provide important insights not just for the familiar exercise of evaluating legal doctrine but, more importantly, for understanding the transactional process and, ultimately, for good lawyering.

Part I of the book (Chapters 2 through 7) provides the finance skills necessary to analyze corporate acquisitions. Chapter 2 introduces the idea of discounting and present value. Chapters 3 and 4 introduce the core of modern portfolio theory and capital asset pricing, including discussion of the Capital Asset Pricing Model's success in explaining how risk affects expected return. Chapter 5 examines the Efficient Capital Market Hypothesis with emphasis on the multiple meanings of market efficiency. It explores when we should, and should not, expect to find a reasonable level of market efficiency, the evidence for and against market efficiency, and the factors that lead toward or away from efficient pricing.

Chapter 6 introduces an important empirical technique for measuring whether a particular event alters the market value of a security -- the event study. This chapter is the most technically demanding in the book, but the payoff is large. Event studies form the core of much of the empirical literature examining whether corporate acquisitions result in gains to investors in the acquirer or the target. Understanding the event study technique is critical to evaluating the fit between theory and empirical evidence concerning gains from acquisitions. Moreover, students need to understand the uses and misuses of statistical data, independent of the value of that understanding for the particular subject of corporate acquisitions.

1

Part I ends with Chapter 7, an examination of option pricing theory. Many common securities and business relationships can be characterized as options. Understanding what factors determine the value of an option can highlight the incentives of the parties to an acquisition or other business transaction.

The material in Part I should be understandable to readers who have had no prior exposure to financial theory. It requires no mathematical skills beyond high school algebra. Students need to understand the insights underlying each aspect of financial theory covered, but do not need to master the formal techniques in a computational sense. The book reflects the belief that lawyers must understand and, through advance planning, structure the incentives of the parties to the transaction. The financial theory covered in Part I can illuminate these incentives and suggest ways of dealing creatively with them. Using financial theory in this way requires conceptual understanding; it does not require mastery of the technical apparatus.

New to this edition are problems at the back of the chapters in Part I and selected chapters in part II. Our experience is that solving problems, even relatively simple ones, aids one in understanding the financial concepts developed in the text. Problems are also a good reality check -- does one really understand the concepts?

Building on the skills imparted in Part I, Part II (Chapters 8 through 15) evaluates in separate chapters the commonly offered explanations for acquisitions: operating synergy; financial synergy or antisynergy (diversification versus deconglomeration through divestitures and bust-up takeovers); replacing inefficient management; the management incentives, debt constraints, and concentrated ownership that characterize leveraged buyouts; tax savings; boosting financial statement earnings and thus share price through choice of accounting method; mispricing of the target company's stock that creates an opportunity for an acquirer to pay a premium over market and still make a bargain purchase; and wealth transfers to shareholders from creditors or employees. For each explanation, the text describes why it might provide a motive for an acquisition, and evaluates its fit with the financial theory developed in Part I, and its consistency with the available empirical evidence. The chapters on financial accounting and tax motives for acquisitions also provide an opportunity to survey the financial accounting and tax aspects of acquisitions, with which *all* business lawyers need to be generally familiar.

We think it important to examine at length the alternative explanations for why acquisitions take place for several reasons. First, without a systematic analysis of the multifaceted phenomenon of takeovers, it is impossible to formulate sensible policy prescriptions. Second, lawyers need to understand how their clients expect to gain from a transaction. Third, the analysis of motives in Part II illustrates the importance of empirical evidence in formulating legal arguments and public policy. To evaluate the evidence, students must understand the empirical methodology well enough to evaluate the academic studies with an appropriate level of skepticism, something the original investigators sometimes have not done.

Part III (Chapters 16 through 19) considers corporate and securities law planning considerations in friendly acquisitions. It begins our consideration of what can be called the public ordering role of the business lawyer: Structuring a transaction to minimize the cost of the potentially applicable regulatory apparatus. Chapter 16 examines, from the perspective of a planner, the alternative acquisition techniques available and such issues as what vote should be necessary to approve a negotiated acquisition, who should be allowed to vote, and the de facto merger doctrine. Chapter 17 addresses the corporate and securities law concerns of the target company, focusing on issues created by the sale of control. Chapter 18 considers the concerns of the acquiring company, focusing on discouraging competing bids, freezing out minority shareholders, and compliance with the Williams Act rules for tender offers if a tender offer forms part of the chosen transaction form. Registration requirements under the Securities Act of 1933 for non-cash transactions are covered only briefly, on the assumption that they will be addressed in a securities regulation course. Chapter 19 explores the special issues involved in leveraged buyouts, including going private rules, and how the target's board can respond when managers sit on both the buyer's and seller's sides of the negotiating table.

Part IV (Chapters 20-22) considers the special corporate law concerns of target and acquiring firms and strategies in hostile takeovers. Chapter 20 considers the target's defenses, both self-help and those provided by state antitakeover laws. Chapter 21 considers the bidder's weapons, alternatives, and legal concerns. Chapter 22 addresses proxy fights as an alternative means to transfer corporate control, or as part of an overall acquisition strategy. The financial theory developed earlier in the book is used to evaluate the desirability and effectiveness of particular offensive and defensive tactics.

Part V (Chapters 23-24) covers other legal aspects of corporate acquisitions. Chapter 23 considers the Hart-Scott-Rodino Premerger Notification Act. Chapter 24 considers the acquiring company's ability to shed or limit its exposure to the target's preexisting liabilities, including hazardous waste cleanup liability, products liability, and collective bargaining and pension obligations. These areas of law fall within the subject matter boundaries of other law school subjects; however, each is usually given scant attention in the survey course covering that subject.

Part VI (Chapter 25) is an effort to integrate the perspective of financial theory with the task of drafting an acquisition agreement. It illustrates how a "standard" form of acquisition agreement can solve a series of problems inherent in valuing a complex asset such as a business. The value of a business depends on the expected cash flows and the riskiness of those expected returns. Standard financial theory, however, builds on a set of perfect market assumptions, such as homogeneous expectations, common time horizons, and costless information, which are obviously not valid in the real world.

Chapter 25 builds on this fact to develop two related ideas. The first is that part of the role of the business lawyer is to create a transactional structure which allows the parties to act more nearly *as if* the perfect market assumptions were valid. The second is that many elements of an acquisition agreement can be understood from this perspective.

The end result of the analysis is to present the business lawyer as a transaction cost engineer whose task is to formulate the transaction structures as near to "perfect" as possible. Looking at the lawyer's role in an acquisition in terms of financial concepts can affect how lawyers negotiate acquisition agreements -- seeing representations as a means of reducing information asymmetry changes the lawyer's task from one of distributive bargaining to one of joint problem solving -- and improve their ability to respond creatively to new problems. Once one understands the transactional problems posed by asset pricing in an imperfect world, many seemingly new problems may turn out to be manifestations of the same problem in different contexts.

Having said something about the subjects the book covers, we should also say something about the manner in which those subjects are covered. This book does not hide the ball; our views on the issues considered are made apparent, sometimes insistently so. We have taken this approach, in contrast to the traditional agnosticism typified by a series of unanswered questions at the end of a section, for two reasons -- one pedagogic and one substantive. The pedagogic reason for giving the book an explicit point of view is that integrating different bodies of law, plus a broad range of financial theory and an extensive empirical literature, is hard enough as it is. Our views are hardly the only ones possible (and alternatives are also discussed) but they illustrate the way in which the various elements interact and what matters must be considered in reaching normative judgments. They can serve both as an example and as a target, each of which can be a useful pedagogic tool.

The substantive reason for the book's normative bent is the absence in the literature of an integrated treatment of the full range of legal issues raised by corporate acquisitions. The need for such a treatment is apparent in the recent performance of the Delaware Supreme Court and the state legislatures. The furious development in the 1980s of sophisticated hostile acquisition techniques and equally sophisticated defensive tactics subjected the Delaware courts to a seemingly unending stream of difficult corporate law issues that left little time for contemplation, for stepping back to see how the individual problems fit together. Like a law professor launching a Socratic attack on a beleaguered corporations student, transaction planners almost immediately gave the courts back their own justifications, but now taken just another step forward.

Each new decision was reflected in the tactics of the next transaction; the Chancery Court often had to confront the "next case" on a motion for preliminary injunction soon after the initial decision. This drastic telescoping of the common law process makes careful reconsideration of prior doctrine quite difficult. The demands of individual cases for prompt resolution (lest delay alone resolve the outcome of a transaction) are also inconsistent with careful development of the common law. This book can hopefully provide some of the perspective, and perhaps a reconceptualization, that courts have not been able to undertake themselves.

As for the legislatures, their often frantic rush to enact a new statute to prevent a particular transaction is a caricature of how legislative policy should be made. Few academics think that all hostile takeovers are bad, or that corporate managers should be able unilaterally to decide whether a takeover bid may proceed, but that is the premise on which state legislatures often seem to act. We need to understand the special interest pressures that lead state legislatures to act this way, but we also need to criticize the legislative actions, in the hope that the tide may be stemmed in a calmer moment or in another forum.

B. The Professional Setting: Value Creation by Business Lawyers[1]

We begin here an inquiry, set in the context of corporate acquisitions, into what business lawyers *really* do. By and large, critical study of the legal profession has displayed a myopic fixation with litigation -- its frequency, complexity, expense and unequal availability -- and what can be done to "improve" it: clinical training, methods of delivering legal services, procedural reforms. Careful analysis of the function of the rest of the profession -- business lawyers -- has been absent.

Lawyers as a group are often criticized as non-productive actors in the economy. Engineers, it is said, make the pie grow larger. Lawyers only rearrange the slices, shrink the pie, and take some for themselves in the process.[2] The criticism, though, doesn't distinguish among the tasks that lawyers do. This book explores how business lawyers can add value as participants in corporate transactions. Lawyers are necessary, but are they merely a necessary evil? It is surprising and just a little embarrassing that there seems to be no coherent answer to the question of what business lawyers *really* do.[3] That is not, of course, to say that answers have not been offered; lawyers have

---

[1] This discussion draws heavily on Ronald Gilson, *Value Creation by Business Lawyers: Legal Skills and Asset Pricing*, 94 Yale L.J. 239 (1984).

[2] See, e.g., Kevin Murphy, Andrei Shleifer & Robert Vishny, *The Allocation of Talent: Implications for Growth*, 1991 Q.J.Econ. 503; Derek Bok, *The President's Report to the Board of Overseers of Harvard University for 1981-1982*, reprinted in 33 J.Leg.Educ. 570 (1983); Akio Morita, *Do Companies Need Lawyers? Sony's Experiences in the United States*, 30 Japan Q. 2 (Jan.-Mar., 1983); Stephen P. Magee, *The Optimum Number of Lawyers: Cross-National Evidence*, (Univ. of Texas, Dept. of Fin., working paper, 1992).

[3] The work of William Klein is an important exception. In *Business Organization and Finance* (1980) and *The Modern Business Organization: Bargaining Under Constraints*, 91 Yale L.J. 1521 (1982), he has made a major effort to use finance theory to understand consensual business arrangements.

offered a number of familiar responses at one time or another. The problem is that none of them is very helpful.

Clients have their own, often quite uncharitable, view of what business lawyers do. In an extreme version, business lawyers are perceived as evil sorcerers who use their special skills and professional magic to relieve clients of their possessions. Kurt Vonnegut at least makes the point in an amusing way. A law student is told by his favorite professor that, to get ahead in the practice of law, "a lawyer should be looking for situations where large amounts of money are about to change hands":

> In every big transaction [the professor said], there is a magic moment during which a man has surrendered a treasure, and during which the man who is due to receive it has not yet done so. An alert lawyer will make that moment his own, possessing the treasure for a magic microsecond, taking a little of it, passing it on. If the man who is to receive the treasure is unused to wealth, has an inferiority complex and shapeless feelings of guilt, as most people do, the lawyer can often take as much as half the bundle, and still receive the recipient's blubbering thanks.[4]

Clients frequently advance another, more charitable but still quite negative view of the business lawyer that also should be familiar to practitioners. Business lawyers are just a transaction cost, part of a system of wealth redistribution from clients to lawyers; legal fees are a tax on business transactions. All too often, lawyers are also deal killers whose continual raising of obstacles, without a commensurate effort at finding solutions, kills otherwise viable transactions. A lawyer turned journalist has captured the criticism nicely:

> What happens between lawyer and client today goes something like this: The lawyer sits at the elbow of the businessman while contracts are being negotiated, that is, while a deal is being made. Then, once the principals feel an agreement has been concluded, the lawyers assure them it has not. After further negotiation, the lawyers "draft a contract" -- *reduce the deal to written law* -- and pass it back and forth accompanied in each passage by increasingly minute argumentation (e.g., "We believe in all fairness that the law of Luxembourg should govern in the event of non-performance under Para. V(e)(ii)" etc., etc.). Once they have decided that neither party can be further hoodwinked or bullied, the typist prepares many copies to make "doubly sure" (making doubly sure in this special fashion is 28 per cent of law practice), and the clients sign all of them. Then they smile at each other and shake hands, while glancing sidelong at their lawyers, who are still scowling (it's part of the fee-action). This little

---

[4] Kurt Vonnegut, *God Bless You, Mrs. Rosewater* 9 (Dell ed.1965).

6

drama, in numerous manifestations, is the beginning of law -- perhaps, even, the final heart of it as well.[5]

Lawyers, to be sure, do not share these harsh evaluations of their role. When this question -- what do business lawyers *really* do -- is put to business lawyers, the familiar response is that they "protect" their clients, get them the "best" deal. In the back of their minds is a sense that their clients neither perceive nor understand the risks that lawyers raise, and that, as a result, clients do not recognize that it is in their best interests when lawyers identify the myriad of subtle problems unavoidably present in a typical transaction.

The academic literature offers a more balanced view. Here the predominant approach is functional. The lawyer is presented as counselor, planner, drafter, negotiator, investigator, lobbyist, scapegoat, champion, and, most strikingly, even as friend. Certainly the list of functions identified rings true enough. An experienced practitioner can quickly recall playing each of these roles.

These characterizations of what business lawyers do share an important similarity and a common failure. The unfavorable view ascribed to clients reflects the belief that business lawyers *reduce* the value of a transaction, while both the favorable view held by business lawyers themselves, and the more neutral but still positive view offered by the academic literature, implicitly assume that business lawyers *increase* the value of a transaction. But both sides agree on the appropriate standard by which the performance of business lawyers should be judged: *Is the transaction worth more, net of legal fees, as a result of the lawyer's participation?* This same question can, of course, be asked for other professionals, including investment bankers and accountants, who participate in a business transaction. The critical failure of all of these views is not their differing conclusions. Rather, it is the absence of an explanation of *how* the activities of business lawyers and other professionals affect transaction value.

One goal of this book is to understand the relationship between what business lawyers do and transaction value, to develop analytical techniques that identify what activities can create value, and to explore approaches that make business lawyers better at achieving this potential. We will explore the two critical aspects of business lawyers' involvement with clients: the *public* ordering and *private* ordering aspects of business transactions. The public ordering aspect of business transactions arises because, in our mixed economy, complex business transactions are affected by multiple regulatory regimes. Tax law, corporate law, securities law, antitrust law, financial accounting rules, environmental law, tort law, labor law, and pension law all can affect the form of

---

[5] Bazelon, *Clients Against Lawyers: A Guide to the Real Joys of Legal Practice*, Harper's Mag. 104 (Sept.1967) (emphasis in original).

a particular acquisition. As a result, a transaction that is private, in the sense that the government is not a party, has important elements of public ordering resulting from the need to comply with regulatory requirements and emanating from the public policy concerns that gave rise to the regulations.

The most important part of the public ordering aspect of private transactions is not merely passive compliance -- structuring a business transaction to meet the terms of seemingly applicable regulations. Rather, business lawyers often must actively design the structure of the transaction to minimize the number of rules that apply and the cost of complying with those that do. Regulation determines the structure of the transaction but, for the client, the goal may be minimizing cost, not maximizing compliance. From this perspective, it is critical that most regulatory systems express the boundaries of their application and the detail of their requirements in formal terms: Transactions that take a particular outward form are covered. So, for example, Subchapter C of the Internal Revenue Code treats corporate acquisitions that take the form of a statutory merger differently from those that take the form of a sale of assets, and a similar distinction is drawn by many state corporation laws.

This approach to regulation invites a planning response. As will be developed in Part I, the subject of most acquisitions can be described as a collection of assets and people with a particular potential for generating future income and with a particular level of risk. If cash flows and risks are not altered, the formal trappings of the acquisition can be manipulated extensively without altering its financial substance. Thus, the parties can often structure transactions so that their form falls outside the terms of at least some otherwise applicable regulatory schemes. This regulatory eternal triangle is completed by the courts which, in the end, must determine whether to credit the form in which the parties cast a transaction, or to look beyond form to purpose and financial substance. This tension -- between voluntary selection of transactional form and regulatory purpose -- is a central dilemma for business law. The form versus substance and step transaction doctrines in tax law and the de facto merger doctrine in corporate law are among the familiar examples.

The opportunity thus exists for business lawyers to create value by structuring a transaction to minimize the cost to the client of the variety of complex, sometimes conflicting regulatory systems that might otherwise touch on the transaction. Much of this book is directed at this opportunity: to understand the regulatory systems that apply to corporate acquisitions and the public policy that gave rise to them, and to develop the facility to manipulate them to achieve a client's goals.

In addition to the public ordering aspects of business transactions, there are also important *private* ordering aspects: matters bearing on transactional structure that would be important even in a world with *no* regulation. To examine the lawyer's role with respect to these aspects of business transactions, however, it is important to be more specific about what it means to create value. Imagine that a client has the good fortune to retain a very talented business lawyer, while the other party to the transaction is represented by a dullard. This may alter the allocation of gains from the transaction between the parties. The transaction is worth more to the talented lawyer's client than if that lawyer had not participated.

One reaches a quite different conclusion, however, if the transaction is viewed from the perspective of *both* clients. Then the lawyers' participation doesn't increase the value of the transaction; rather, resources have been expended to alter the *distribution* of joint gains. And for purposes of evaluating whether business lawyers can increase transaction value, the appropriate perspective is not that of the client with the more talented lawyer, but the joint perspective of both clients.

As in many other areas, evaluating whether a practice is beneficial, in this case participation by business lawyers, depends on whether the issue is evaluated *ex ante* or *ex post*. If the evaluation is *ex post* -- that is, if it has already been determined that both sides will retain a lawyer -- then a business lawyer whose bargaining skill results in his client receiving a larger portion of the gain from the transaction has increased the transaction's value to *that* client. If, however, the evaluation is *ex ante* -- before either side has decided whether to retain a lawyer -- the result is quite different. Both clients would determine jointly whether to retain lawyers for the transaction, recognizing that if either retained a lawyer, so would the other to avoid being at a bargaining disadvantage. In this situation, if all business lawyers provide is skillful distributive bargaining, the clients' joint decision would be to hire *no* lawyers because, net of lawyers' fees, the surplus from the transaction to be divided between the clients would be *smaller* as a result of the participation of lawyers. Only a client who believed that its lawyer would systematically be better than the other party's, by enough so that the expected gain from better distributive bargaining exceeded the cost of *both* lawyers, would still use lawyers in the transaction. Given any reasonable assumption about the availability and distribution of legal talent among lawyers serving commercial clients, this disparity is unlikely to exist with any frequency.

Our focus with respect to the business lawyer's private ordering function thus will be on identifying how, regulation aside, a business lawyer can help private parties order their relationship in a way that increases the size of the entire pie, rather than merely increasing the size of one party's piece at the expense of the other's. This question is most prominent in Part II, where we examine motives for acquisitions; in Part III, where we consider friendly acquisitions; and in Part VI, where we examine a standard corporate acquisition agreement to see if it evidences techniques that hold the promise of creating value, and whether these techniques fit a general pattern that can help explain how business lawyers can create value through skill in designing the transaction structure.

9

The discussion thus far has focused on *value*. The central question is how business lawyers can increase the value of a transaction. But how can we determine whether a transaction would have been more valuable if a lawyer had participated or, conversely, would have been worth less had legal counsel not been hired? A truly empirical approach to measuring the impact of a business lawyer's participation seems impossible for a number of reasons. It is unlikely that we could find data covering both a sample of transactions in which a business lawyer did participate and a control group of equivalent transactions which were accomplished without a lawyer. Even if the data-collection problem could somehow be solved, serious methodological problems would remain. We might know the dollar value attached to particular transactions by the participants, but we would face overwhelming problems in determining whether the transactions were really comparable so that any difference in value could be ascribed to the business lawyer's participation.

There is, however, an alternative approach to determining the potential for business lawyers to add value to a transaction. The first step is to understand how a transaction is valued in the absence of a business lawyer's participation. If the factors that generally determine transaction value can be identified, the second step is relatively straightforward. By understanding the relationship between these factors and the business lawyer's activities, it should be possible to frame hypotheses that directly link the application of legal skills to transaction value.

We begin this analysis by recognizing that the subjects of business transactions are typically capital assets: assets whose value is determined solely by the income, whether in cash flow or appreciation, they are expected to earn.[6] A corporate acquisition can be seen as the transfer of a capital asset from one party to another. Characterizing transactions as transfers of capital assets is important because, over the last 30 years, financial economists have begun to develop a body of theory to explain how capital assets are valued or, as a financial economist would put it, "priced." If asset pricing theory can identify the factors that determine transaction value, then we can examine whether business lawyers can influence these factors in ways that alter transaction value. And if the systematic application of legal skills can affect transaction value, then two important results follow. First, we should be able to examine what business lawyers do and determine if their activities bear on transaction value. That is, it would be possible to inquire positively into the efficiency of the common business "lawyer." Second, and more important, we should be able to make normative statements about what business lawyers *should* do to increase the value of a transaction. Here the

---

[6] This definition, while standard, is limited. Any asset that has consumption value -- i.e., its owner holds it for reasons other than (or in addition to) its potential for generating income -- falls outside the definition. For example, the psychic value of being your own boss may explain why many owners of small businesses continue in their vocation even though the businesses earn less than the market value of their owners' services plus a return on invested capital.

prospect is really quite exciting: Theory will have been brought to bear not merely to criticize doctrine or urge public policy reform, but as a tool to improve the quality of legal practice.

On a more prosaic level, corporate acquisitions are transactions where, as Vonnegut put it, "large amounts of money are about to change hands;" and large legal fees are hardly possible when *small* amounts of money change hands. Thus, corporate acquisitions are an important source of business for major law firms. Students aspiring to be business lawyers obviously can gain from an introduction to a significant area of their prospective employers' practice.

The effort to understand what business lawyers do, and to learn how better to do it, must begin with study of modern financial theory. Part I of the book introduces this theory. Part II applies the theory to evaluating the various reasons why clients might *think* corporate acquisitions are a useful activity. Understanding how the client hopes to gain from a transaction is a prerequisite to making the transaction more valuable (and to keeping the client happy). Moreover, if some reasons makes sense (e.g., synergy) and others (e.g., financial statement alchemy) do not, business lawyers can add value by structuring transactions so that the real values are preserved, when these values come in conflict with less sensible reasons for acquisitions. Parts III through V review the various regulatory systems that bear on the opportunity to create value in connection with corporate acquisitions. We return to purely private ordering concerns in Part VI.

C. The Historical Setting

With the potential for business lawyers to create value in mind, the next step is to explain the choice of corporate acquisitions as a context. It is, of course, criticial to look at the value creation in context. Bringing theory to bear on practice requires its careful application in a *real* setting so that its relevance can be evaluated. In our case, the theory to be applied is modern financial theory, with special emphasis on how capital assets are valued. Corporate acquisitions are a particularly appropriate setting for applying this theory for three important reasons.

First, a corporate acquisition is centrally the transfer of a capital asset. Indeed, valuation of corporate securities -- the indicia of ownership of a corporation -- has dominated the empirical tests of modern financial theory. Moreover, a large body of empirical literature now exists that measures the impact of both corporate acquisitions generally, and of the techniques and alternatives associated with corporate acquisitions, on the security holders of both acquiring and target companies. Thus, there is a body of both theory *and* data against which both clients' beliefs about the private value of acquisitions, and public beliefs about the social impact of acquisitions can be assessed.

11

Second, despite extensive regulation, corporate acquisitions still provide substantial opportunity for private ordering. They thus allow examination of the potential for business lawyers to create value both by manipulating the regulatory regimes bearing on acquisition transactions and by structuring the private arrangement between the parties. And because the private ordering function is often difficult for outsiders to observe, acquisitions are a particularly useful setting in which to study what business lawyers do. A business lawyer's principal charge in the transaction is to negotiate and prepare the acquisition agreement. Thus, a fairly complete record of the lawyer's activity is created as a matter of course.

Third, corporate acquisitions are centrally important objects of study without regard to what they may tell us about how to be a business lawyer. In the 1980s, acquisition activity reshaped the structure of the American economy. Critics claim that takeovers exact a huge cost in jobs and financial stability. Others argue that corporate acquisitions are a critical element of the overall corporate governance structure, that helps to ensure corporate management keeps the goal of profit maximization firmly in mind. Moreover, corporate acquisitions may be a primary means by which changes in the economic environment affect the structure of individual companies and industries.[7] Numerous Congressional hearings have been held on the question of whether particular types of corporate acquisitions, or acquisitions generally, should be curtailed, and significant changes in the corporate income tax during the 1980s were motivated by concern over the level of acquisition activity, rather than issues of tax policy.[8] Developing a detailed understanding of so controversial an activity is thus justifiable in itself.

Despite the continued controversy, takeovers are not a new phenomenon. Apparent waves of acquisition activity, and controversy concerning them, have been a feature of the American economy since the late 1800's. But the character of the activity has changed dramatically over time, and understanding current transactional forms and legal rules is aided by understanding something of the history of corporate acquisitions in the United States.

---

[7] See Ronald Gilson, *The Political Ecology of Takeovers: Thoughts on Harmonizing the European Corporate Governance Environment,* 61 Ford.L.Rev. 161 (1992).

[8] For example, the original legislation concerning taxation of corporate acquisitions that became part of the Tax Equity and Fiscal Responsibility Act of 1982 was introduced by Representative Stark, in H.R. 6295, 97th Cong., 2d Sess. (1982), as The Corporate Takeover Tax Act of 1982. Martin Ginsburg describes the legislation as responding to the public impression "of a nation overwhelmed by a spreading rash of enormous corporate acquisitions motivated and financed in significant part by extraordinary tax avoidance." Martin Ginsburg, *Taxing Corporate Acquisitions,* 38 Tax L.Rev. 171, 216 (1983). With respect to the motives of the Tax Reform Act of 1986, see Myron Scholes & Mark Wolfson, *Taxes and Business Strategy: A Planning Approach* ch. 23 (1992).

MALCOM SALTER & WOLF WEINHOLD,
MERGER TRENDS AND PROSPECTS FOR THE 1980s
2-27 (1980)

A Brief History of Corporate Mergers and Acquisitions in the U.S.

Economists and students of industrial organization have identified three major merger waves which swept the American economy between 1890 and 1975. Figure 1-1 . . . outlines the scope and magnitude of these cycles. Each cycle has been well documented with extensive economic literature and policy debate.[7] To help put current merger and acquisition activity into proper perspective, it is useful to briefly review these three waves.

The first peak in merger and acquisition activity just prior to 1900 was reached in a period of rapid economic expansion following two decades of economic stagnation (industrial production, for instance, grew 100%). The wave of mergers between 1895 and 1905 involved an estimated 15% of all manufacturing assets and employees, and accompanied major changes in the nation's social and technological infrastructure. An important characteristic of this merger wave was the simultaneous consolidation of producers within numerous industries. These mergers, mostly horizontal integrations, were often made in search of market dominance. Many of today's industrial giants, including U.S. Steel, the several descendents of Standard Oil, General Electric, Westinghouse, United Fruit, Eastman Kodak, American Can, American Tobacco, U.S. Rubber, DuPont, PPG, International Harvester, and U.S. Gypsum, among others, trace their origins in this period. The tailend of this merger wave in 1903-1904 coincided with a severe economic recession and the *Northern Securities* decision which established that mergers could be successfully attacked under then existing antitrust law.

While George Stigler has characterized the first wave as "merging for monopoly," other economists have not been so bold. Many have noted that this merger wave accompanied a frenzied stock market and aggressive promotional activities by bankers and brokers. J.P. Morgan, for example, is estimated to have earned over $60 million for his efforts in the consolidation of U.S. Steel. Others have argued that many of the consolidations failed in the following recession and that others did not even lead to market dominance. Nevertheless, as Markham concluded, "The conversion of approximately 71 important oligopolistic or near-competitive industries into near

---

[7] Jesse Markham, *Survey of the Evidence and Findings on Mergers*, in *Business Concentration and Price Policy* (NBER 1955); Peter Steiner, *Mergers: Motives, Effects, Policies* (1975); *The Corporate Merger* (William Alberts & Joel Segall eds.1966); F.M. Scherer & David Ross, *Industrial Market Structure and Economic Performance* (3d ed.1988); and Jesse Markham, *Conglomerate Enterprise and Public Policy* (1973), all provide excellent commentary on these merger waves.

monopolies by merger between 1890 and 1904 left an impact on the structure of the American economy that fifty years have not yet erased."

Figure 1-1
Number of Manufacturing and Mining Firms Acquired, 1895-1978

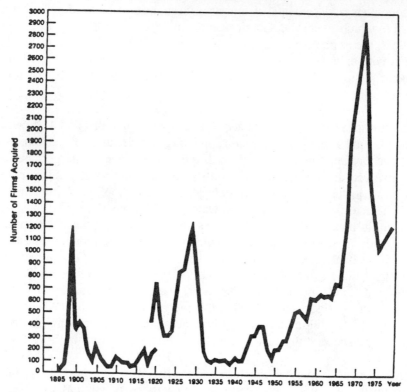

Source: Malcolm Salter & Wolf Weinhold, *Diversification Through Acquisition: Strategies for Creating Economic Value* (1979)

The two decades following the 1903-04 market crash were relatively quiet ones in terms of merger activity. Only two notable combinations arose, General Motors in 1909, and International Business Machines in 1911. Much more important, however, was a relatively wide scale legal attack on the trusts formed in the previous wave. The year 1911 was the landmark, with the Supreme Court ordering the breakups of the Standard Oil and American Tobacco Companies. Market monopolies were clearly established as illegal. However, further judicial decisions, such as the 1920 U.S. Steel Decision, established that dominant firms would be subject to antitrust attack only if they abused their market position through aggressive and predatory attacks on their rivals. Since the Sherman Act only addressed issues of substantial monopoly power, Congress

14

passed the Clayton Act in 1914 whose stated purpose was "to arrest the creation of trusts, conspiracies and monopolies in their incipiency and before consummation."[12] The Federal Trade Commission was also established at this time to better control unrestrained corporate power. For the first time in antitrust history, specific business actions were declared illegal.

The second wave of merger and acquisition activity occurred during the 1920s and peaked in 1928. As with its predecessor, it too rode a period of economic growth and a stock market boom. All told, an estimated 12,000 firms disappeared during this period. Its impact on market structure, however, was much less noticeable for several reasons.

First, over one-third of this activity was in the banking and public utility sectors. Most significant was the rise of the giant utility holding company pyramids in the gas, electricity and water sectors, pyramids which were to collapse in the following depression. Since these sectors were already regulated, increased market concentration had little or no impact on economic power. Second, since the Clayton Act prevented large scale stock consolidations in search of market power, but not asset acquisitions, merger activity in the manufacturing sector was primarily limited to either small market share additions or to vertical integration. Worthy of special note, however, was the formation of strong "number two companies" in numerous industries previously dominated by one giant firm. The consolidations of Bethlehem Steel, Republic Steel and Continental Can all date from this era. This advent of oligopoly in many industrial sectors led George Stigler to characterize this period of merger activity as "merging for oligopoly."

It was outside the previously consolidated heavy manufacturing industrial sectors where much of the merger activity was occurring. Mergers in the still fragmented food processing, chemicals, and mining sectors comprised 60% of all merger activity in manufacturing. Extensive vertical integration (in mining) and product extension moves (in food processing and chemicals) led to many major industrial enterprises. Kennecott, Anaconda, and Phelps Dodge, Allied Chemical and DuPont (in chemicals outside explosives), and General Mills, General Foods, and Kraft all trace their emergence to this period.

While the merger wave of the 1920s was clearly as large or larger in absolute terms than the 1890-1904 wave, its relative impact was much less. In total, it apparently involved less than 10% of the economy's assets rather than the former wave's over 15%. Furthermore, in most industries, mergers embraced only a small proportion of the

---

[12] S. Rep. No. 698, 63d Cong. 2d Sess. at 1 (1914).

competing firms. Only in the food processing, metals, and chemicals sectors was industry structure substantially altered. . . .

The 1920's merger wave did, however, have several similarities with that of 1890-1905. Both occurred during a period of economic prosperity and a booming stock market. And, as before, it came to an end with a stock market crash and a severe economic slowdown. Internally, stock promoters once again seemed to have been a major driving force. Perhaps rightfully recognizing stock promotions as the principal avenue of abuse in this merger wave, legislation in the following years was aimed at securities regulation rather than at more rigorous antitrust controls.

The onset of a worldwide depression in 1929 brought merger activity to a halt. Throughout the 1930s and into World War II, acquisition activity remained at its lowest levels of the century. As the war ended, an upsurge in merger and acquisition activity began, once again accompanying economic prosperity and rising stock prices. The Federal Trade Commission, in its landmark 1948 report, concluded:

> No great stretch of the imagination is required to foresee that if nothing is done to check the growth in concentration, either giant corporations will ultimately take over the country, or the government will be impelled to step in and impose some form of direct regulation.[13]

Something was done, however, with the Celler-Kefauver Amendment substantially strengthening the anti-merger provisions of the Clayton Act in 1950. . . . [But by] the mid-1950s, a third merger and acquisition wave had begun. Table 1-1 . . . detail[s] this growth in acquisition activity. . . . This wave, which would prove to be longer and larger than either of the two preceding waves, was of an entirely new sort. This wave did not, in general, involve either large acquisitions or large acquirers. . . . What arose was a strategy of corporate diversification into new product markets.

---

[13] Trade Commission, *The Merger Movement: A Summary Report* 25, 68 (1948). [Later studies challenge the FTC's conclusion that industrial concentration was increasing. See Philip Areeda, *Antitrust Analysis* 844 n.16 (2d ed.1981) (collecting studies showing industrial concentration roughly constant after 1909). Eds.]

Table 1-1
Acquisition Activity, 1950-1971

Year	Number of Acquisitions				Value of Assets Acquired	
	Total Recorded	All Manufacturing and Mining (M&M)	Large M&M Acquisitions*	Large M&M Acquisitions by 200 Largest Firms**	Large M&M Acquistions	Large M&M Acquisitions by 200 Largest Firms
1950	NA	219			186	20
1951	NA	235			204	149
1952	NA	288	15		361	196
1953	NA	295	26	16	839	581
1954	NA	387	38	16	1,465	942
1955	NA	683	69	33	2,179	1,217
1956	NA	673	59	25	2,076	1,440
1957	NA	585	50	23	1,363	843
1958	NA	589	45	22	1,242	831
1959	NA	835	62	30	1,947	1,277
1960	1,345	844	64	32	1,279	1,013
1961	1,724	954	60	25	2,356	1,565
1962	1,667	853	70	33	2,448	1,301
1963	1,479	861	83	41	3,148	2,051
1964	1,797	854	91	38	2,728	1,248
1965	1,893	1,008	91	29	3,845	1,928
1966	1,746	995	101	35	4,171	2,468
1967	2,384	1,496	168	73	9,091	6,287
1968	3,932	2,407	207	94	13,297	8,209
1969	4,542	2,307	155	52	11,353	5,543
1970	3,089	1,351	98	30	6,346	2,672
1971	2,633	1,011	66	19	2,544	989

* Acquired firms with assets of $10 million or more.
** Ranked by 1970 total assets.
N.A. = not available.

Source: Federal Trade Commission, Bureau of Economics, *Current Trends in Merger Activity, 1970 and 1971,* Statistical Rep. Nos. 8 (Mar.1971) & 10 (May 1972).

This concept of unrelated diversification was pioneered by Textron, Litton, and ITT, and led to high rates of corporate growth. These fast-growing firms, known as "conglomerates," [began as] small- to medium-sized companies that emphasized acquisition activity outside their traditional areas of interest. Furthermore, their acquisitions were also of typically small- to medium-sized firms operating in either fragmented industries or on the periphery of major industrial sectors. As the stock market soared in the mid-sixties, this concept became more and more popular with both investors and corporate executives. [Earnings per share] growth and synergy were the bywords of this period. The dramatic increase in the number of companies following a diversification strategy during this period is seen in Figure 1-2, where "unrelated business" is roughly synonymous with conglomerate. Since this merger wave brought corporate growth but not increased market concentration, we have labeled this wave, to paraphrase George Stigler, "merging for growth."

Figure 1-2
Estimated Percentage of Fortune 500 Companies in Each Category

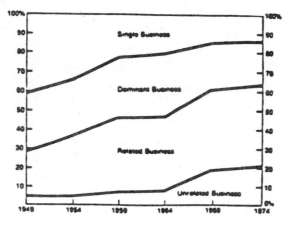

Source: Richard Rumelt, *Diversity and Profitability* (UCLA working paper 1977)

At its peak in 1967-1969, several conglomerates were selling at 100 times earnings and were using their stock to devour acquisitions, often at the rate of one per week. Over 10,000 independent companies were acquired in the 1967-69 peak (over 6,000 in mining and manufacturing alone) and over 25,000 firms disappeared over the course of the entire wave (1960-1971). . . . [A]t the wave's peak over 70% of these acquisitions were conglomerate in nature and over 30% [were] totally unrelated to the acquirer. Total assets acquired in the mining and manufacturing sectors exceeded $70 billion, or approximately 7-8% of all corporate manufacturing assets.. . . . The 200 largest manufacturing firms accounted for approximately one-half of all acquired assets during this period and among these 200, the 25 most active acquirers accounted for 59% or a total of $20.2 billion. Of these 25, there were at least 17 companies actively following a strategy of unrelated diversification. . . .

As with the two previous merger waves, this wave was also accompanied by aggressive stock promotion and rose and fell with the stock market. For conglomerates, the wave ended with the collapse of their stock prices following lowered earnings in the mild 1969-70 recession. For other acquirers it came to an end in 1973 with the advent of the nation's severest economic recession and stock market collapse since the 1930s.

At this stage it is useful to review what we know about the three merger waves that have occurred so far in U.S. history. Four similarities, all previously identified by Jesse Markham in 1955, apply to each of the three waves.[14] Briefly stated, these similarities are:

1. Contrary to popular opinion, relatively few mergers seem to have had market monopolization as their goal. Market power was most evident in the first wave but declined in each of the next two. The conglomerate wave of the 1960s had virtually no effect on either market concentration or aggregate economic concentration;

2. The most striking single motive for merger at each peak seems to have been the search for promotional profits. All three waves occurred during sustained periods of economic prosperity and rapidly rising levels of stock prices. Each merger wave peaked with the stock market and then quickly receded as stock prices fell and each wave was followed by a serious economic recession (the 1903-04 crash, the 1929-37 Great Depression and the 1974-75 recession). As each wave progressed, speculative stock activity and the formation of less viable enterprises became more evident. Stock promotion, of one form or another, eclipsed economic reality as each wave peaked. Thorp's comment on the 1920s wave is just as relevant to the other two waves: " . . . one businessman regarded it as a loss of standing if he was not approached once a week with a merger proposition. . . . A group of businessmen and financiers in discussing this matter in the summer of 1928 agreed that nine out of ten mergers had the investment banker at its core;"[15]

3. Many mergers were simply ordinary business transactions among entrepreneurs. Mergers and acquisitions provide one of the best means for entrepreneurs to exit an industry while reaping the maximum benefits of their work; and

4. Many mergers accompanied or were stimulated by massive changes in the economy's infrastructure. Typically, these radical changes in the economy lead to new market definitions and/or new production and distribution technologies. For example, the first wave followed rapid rail building, the advent of electricity and the rise of coal. The second was accompanied by automotive transportation and the radio. The last wave was accompanied by aircraft, television, and the use of liquid hydrocarbons. Whether a cause-and-effect relationship exists or whether it is coincidence has not been established.

---

[14] Markham (1955), supra note 7, at 180-82.

[15] Willard Thorp, *The Persistence of the Merger Movement,* Am.Econ.Rev. 86 (Supp.1931)

The differences between the waves are surprisingly few. In essence, they concern the relative impact of each wave on the economy and their primary focus. While each wave was larger than the ones before it in both the number of companies involved and assets acquired, they consumed increasingly smaller proportions of the total economy. Either the size and diversity of the economy outgrew the capacity of corporations to grow through merger or, as some cynics have suggested, fewer and fewer attractive assets were left to acquire. In either case, relatively effective antitrust measures changed the focus of corporate merger and acquisition activity from that of market domination in the first wave to one of product market diversity in the third. Nevertheless, the fear of unrestrained market power, established in the public's mind in earlier years, still continued to influence economic and political debate on corporate mergers and acquisitions.

Merger and Acquisition Activity Since 1975

Since 1975 the characteristics of merger and acquisition activity have continued to evolve. Table 1-2 . . . provide[s] a comparative profile of acquisition activity during this most recent period, based on data compiled by the Federal Trade Commission. . . . In contrast to the surge in small- to medium-sized acquisitions during the 1967-1973 period, the number of large and very large acquisitions has increased dramatically since 1975. This is even more striking in light of the fall in the rate of acquisition activity to one-half of its earlier level. . . . [The trend toward diversifying acquisitions has continued, and] many of the recent large and very large acquisitions have been unrelated diversification moves by the country's largest firms. . . .

Table 1-2
Trends in Acquisition Activity, 1951-1978

Year	All Acquisitions			Mining and Manufacturing Acquisitions		
	Number of Acquisitions	Number over $10 million	Number over $100 million	Number of Acquisitions	Number over $10 million	Number over $100 million
1951-55	NA	NA	NA	378/yr	30/yr	2/yr
1956-60	NA	NA	NA	705/yr	48/yr	1/yr
1961-66	1514/yr	NA	NA	920/yr	63/yr	5/yr
1967-69	3403/yr	NA	NA	2070/yr	150/yr	27/yr
1970	2854	NA	NA	1351	91	12
1971	2303	NA	NA	1011	59	5
1972	2758	NA	NA	NA	60	6
1973	1919	137	28	697	64	7
1974	1276	129	26	505	62	11
1975	889	112	16	355	59	11
1976	1081	159	23	461	81	14
1977	1182	195	38	619	99	19
1978	1350	260	45	NA	NA	31

Source: Salter & Weinhold (1979), supra

Table 1-3 helps place the most recent upsurge in merger and acquisition activity in much broader perspective. While total acquired assets in 1977-1979 exceeded the 1967-1969 peak in book value terms, the amount of acquired assets relative to *existing assets* was just approaching the average acquisition rate for the 1960-1966 period and still far below that of the frenzied 1967-1969 period. In fact, background data suggests that 1955-1956 and 1963-1971 as having as high or higher rates of merger and acquisition activity, relative to either new investment or total existing assets, than the more current 1977-1979 period. . . .

Table 1-3
Comparison of Large Acquired Assets to New and Existing Investments for Manufacturing and Mining Companies

Year	New Investment ($ billions)*	Acquired Assets ($ billions)*	Acquired Assets as Percent of New Investment	Acquired Assets as percent of Existing Assets
1948-1953	$10.6/yr.	$0.3/yr.	2.8%	.18%
1954-1959	14.82/yr.	1.7/yr.	11.4	.80
1960-1966	20.2/yr.	2.9/yr.	14.5	.92
1967-1969	31.2/yr.	11.6/yr.	37.2	2.47
1970	33.8	6.6	19.5	1.14
1971	32.2	3.1	9.8	.51
1972	33.8	2.7	7.9	.41
1973	40.8	3.6	8.7	.50
1974	49.2	5.1	10.4	.69
1975	51.7	5.5	10.7	.68
1976	56.5	6.9	12.2	.79
1977	65.5	9.6	14.7	1.02
1978	73.2	12.3	16.8	1.19

* Total expenditures for new plant and equipment by manufacturing and mining firms.
** Acquired firms with assets of $10 million or more.

Source: Salter and Weinhold (1979), supra

The upswing in merger and acquisition activity beginning in 1975 has led many observers to announce a fourth wave of corporate marriages. This announcement reflects the fact that the aggregate annual value of all acquisitions in the late 1970s reached or exceeded the levels seen during the conglomerate wave of the late 1960s (though the total number of acquisitions was much lower). . . .

Whether or not another major merger movement was launched in the late 1970s will only become possible to determine with the passage of time. Nevertheless, we feel that current merger activity can usefully be placed in an historical context. But this must be done with some care. An analysis based on gross comparisons between the total number of acquisitions made or the total asset values acquired will not be particularly enlightening. Both are static measures and fail to recognize the dynamic nature of the U.S. economy with its ever-growing size and complexity. In an expanding economy, comparisons based upon such static data will tend to suggest greater levels of merger activity than actually exist. Furthermore, rapid rates of inflation (such as what the U.S. has experienced over the last 15 years) will further distort any comparisons of merger activity based upon asset or market values. To establish reasonably consistent and truly comparable comparisons between current merger activity and that of earlier periods, the data on merger activity normally reported must be refined. Two adjustments are especially important: (1) merger volume should be measured in terms of constant or inflation adjusted dollars; and (2) merger activity should be measured in terms of the assets acquired *relative* to the total assets of the economy. . . .

Table 1-4 looks at recent merger and acquisition activity on a constant dollar basis. . . . What this analysis shows is that a substantial portion of recent acquisition activity reflects the high rates of inflation that have occurred over the last decade. In real terms, current acquisition activity is only running at about two-thirds of the rate of the 1967-69 peak in conglomerate acquisitions.

Table 1-4
Inflation Adjusted Consideration Paid in Acquisitions, 1967-1979

Year	Total Consideration ($ billions)	GNP Implicit Price Deflator (1972 = 100)	Constant Dollar Consideration (1972 $ billions)
1967	18.0	$79.0	22.8
1968	43.0	82.6	52.1
1969	23.7	86.7	27.3
1970	16.4	91.4	16.9
1971	12.6	96.0	13.1
1972	16.7	106.0	16.7
1973	16.7	105.8	15.8
1974	12.5	116.0	10.8
1975	11.8	127.1	9.3
1976	20.0	133.7	15.0
1977	21.9	141.7	15.5
1978	34.2	152.1	22.5
1979	43.5	165.5	26.3

Source: W.T. Grimm & Co., based upon all reported acquisition offers where purchase price was available. . . .

Table 1-5 measures current acquisition activity . . . relative to all other assets in the economy. This approach recognizes that the U.S. economy is continuing to grow and that what might be a high level of merger activity at one period in time may amount to only a modest level of activity a decade or two later. This data suggests that despite the extremely high aggregate value of acquisition payments made during 1975-79, it was not as great as in the mid-1960s relative to the market value of all other corporations.

Table 1-5
Consideration Paid Relative to the Market Value of all U.S. Equities

Year	Consideration Paid ($ billions)	Total Market Value of all Equities ($ billions)	Consideration Paid ÷ Market Value of all Firms %
1967	$18.0 Est.	868	2.1%
1968	43.0	1,034	4.2
1969	23.7	914	2.6
1970	16.4	906	1.8
1971	12.6	1,060	1.2
1972	16.7	1,198	1.4
1973	16.7	947	1.8
1974	12.5	675	1.8
1975	11.8	891	1.3
1976	20.0	1,106	1.8
1977	21.9	1,039	2.1
1978	34.2	1,086	3.1
1979	43.5	1,244	3.5

Source: W.T. Grimm & Co., based upon all reported acquisition offers where purchase price was available. . . .

What we can see, then, is that merger activity in the 1975-79 period has indeed been significant when looked at in absolute terms. However, relative to the size of the economy or the level of merger activity during the 1960s, the size and magnitude of the current merger activity is much less impressive. The 1970s witnessed rapid inflation and a growing economy, both of which served to diminish dramatically the relative impact of a given level of merger and acquisition activity. Table 1-6 summarizes current acquisition activity in comparison to the previous three merger waves. When viewed in terms of constant dollars or as a percent of total assets, merger and acquisition activity within the mining and manufacturing sectors during the 1975-1979 period does not look as significant as that during earlier periods.

Table 1-6

Estimated Impact of Merger Activity on the U.S. Mining and Manufacturing Sectors: 1975-79 vs. the Three Previous Merger Waves

	1895-1902	1919-1929	1960-1970	1975-1979*
Total Mining and Manufacturing Acquisitions	2,600+	8,000	12,000	3,100
Total Mining and Manufacturing Assets Acquired ($ billions)	6.4+	12-15	70+	50
Assets Acquired in constant dollars ($ billions)	26+	24-30	69	30
Assets Acquired as a % Total Mining & Manufacturing Assets	15+	7-9	10+	6

* The current merger wave is not yet over so these estimates will necessarily grow . . . .

Note: This table is based upon authors' estimates. . . . [It] does not reflect the increasing importance of service-based industries (and acquisitions within the service sector) in the post-WWII economy.

In addition to characteristics relating to the number, size, and diversity of transactions, other distinguishing characteristics of the current merger movement are emerging. Eight important ones stand out and are discussed below.

1. In contrast to the conglomerate buying spree of the 1960s, many of the acquiring companies in the late 1970s were well-established, conservative, old line giants. These acquirers typically had most of their assets concentrated in one or a few closely related businesses. More often than not, these conservative giants were also facing maturing product markets in their major lines of business. General Electric, Johns Mansville, Mobil, Continental Group, Atlantic Richfield, R.J. Reynolds, Allied Chemical, United Technologies, and N.L. Industries all fall into this category.

This is not to say that these conservative giants were highly active acquirers during 1975-79, or that the conglomerates were not active acquirers. Both inferences are, in fact, misleading. . . . [T]he most active acquirers, in terms of the number of acquisitions made during the period, were companies following a strategy of either conglomerate diversification or companies within industries where environmental and competitive conditions were leading to substantial consolidation. On the other hand, the so-called conservative giants generally limited their merger activity to one or, at most, two acquisitions during this period. The important difference between these two groups, however, lies in the size of the acquisitions being made by the conservative giants. Despite little acquisition experience, they were the companies making the $300 million deals. . . . Ironically enough, in several instances, entire conglomerates (Eltra and Studebaker-Worthington) were themselves swallowed up by old line, conservative giants (Allied Chemical and McGraw Edison).

Virtually all of these large-scale acquisitions (outside continued consolidation within the petroleum sector) were unrelated to the acquirer in either classic economic or judicial senses. This pursuit of unrelated acquisitions undoubtedly reflects the antitrust constraints faced by most large U.S. companies. Their size and resource base virtually foreclosed either entry or expansion by acquisition in any market where they were a competitor or where they were perceived as a potential competitor. . . .

2. Unlike the conglomerate merger movement of the 1960s where virtually every sector of the economy was affected, merger and acquisition activity since 1975 has been more severe in certain sectors than in others. The most active sectors -- finance, bank, insurance, general services and wholesale and retail trade -- are all service industries. Together they encompass over 30% of all acquisition activity. This activity reflects the increasing importance of services in the U.S. economy as well as the fact that these industries have a history of fragmentation. . . .

3. The second sector where significant acquisition activity has occurred is the natural resources area. This sector has witnessed relatively few acquisitions, but acquisitions which often dwarfed those done in any other industry. In 1979, the 5 largest participants have been the large oil companies which have acquired both additional oil reserves as well as companies with other natural resources reserves. At the same time, many industrial companies have also acquired natural resources companies as a way of securing a known set of inflation resistant, irreplaceable assets. Perhaps the most dramatic example of this strategy was General Electric's $2.1 billion acquisition of Utah International, a major coal producer with smaller activities in copper, uranium and other metals. Similarly, International Telephone and Telegraph, a pioneer of the conglomerate movement (which had been quiet since the antitrust proceedings following its 1968 acquisition of Hartford Insurance), acquired both a coal and an oil company. It is worth emphasizing that companies with their resource base in the United States or other safe, stable political environments have been those primarily sought after.

4. Another distinct characteristic of 1975-79 merger and acquisition activity is the widespread use of cash as a principal means of payment. During the 1960s, by far the principal payment medium was common stock or equivalents such as convertible debt, convertible perferred, or debt plus warrants. The proliferation in the use of these common stock equivalents at the height of the conglomerate craze led many to call them

"funny money" or "Chinese paper." Only rarely was a cash payment used during this acquisition spree; when used, it was usually as a sweetener to an already complicated package of securities.

In contrast, cash or a package of cash and equivalents was the payment medium in over [50] of the transactions from the mid-1970s onward. Figure 1-3 shows how the relative importance of cash, common stock, or a package of securities as the payment medium has changed over the last 10 years. It is worth noting that the use of cash for payment has had an inverse relationship to the general level of stock prices. Cash usage surged in 1973-74 as stock prices fell by over 40%. . . .

Figure 1-3
Payment Medium Used in Corporate Acquisitions, 1964-1979

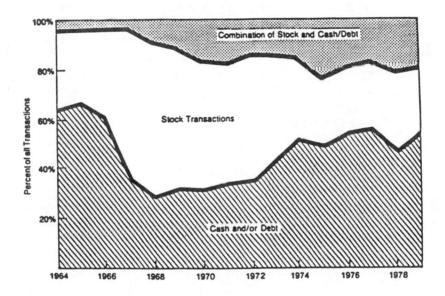

Source: W.T. Grimm & Co.

An additional observation about the "packaging" of acquisitions in 1975-79 is important. Since an acquisition may lead to a taxable transaction for both the buyer and the seller, tax considerations play an important part in structuring any deal. Marginal tax rates, the magnitude of capital gains, and the strength of the economy and the stock market are all significant forces in selecting an attractive securities package. Reflecting recent tax reforms and an unstable economy, many recent acquisitions have been structured to provide both taxable and tax free alternatives. In these cases, taxable cash payments are limited to less than half of the acquisition's purchase price. A package of common stock, preferred stock, convertible preferred, or debt instruments is then designed to preserve the transaction's tax status (generally tax-free or tax deferred to the seller) while meeting the acquirer's cash flow, tax and control requirements.

5. Closely linked to the use of cash as the primary payment medium for acquisitions during the 1975-79 period was the increase in the size of the average acquisition premium over market value. During the conglomerate merger wave of the 1960s, premiums on the order of 10% to 20% were common and only rarely did one exceed 40%.[20] However, in the merger movement of the late 1970s, premiums of 100% or more were not uncommon. Acquisition offers which were successful had an average premium over market of about 50%. . . .

The relative magnitude of the premium in a successful acquisition has been inversely related to the level of stock prices over this time period. The highest average premiums occurred in 1973-74 as the stock market reached its lowest level in a decade. That successful offers have higher premiums during periods of relatively poor stock price performance is quite natural. In this environment, investors will remember the recently higher values of their holdings and tend to consider their stocks "temporarily depressed." For an acquisition offer to be successful in this psychological context it must be at a premium that more than compensates for the stock's currently depressed value. . . . It is also worth noting that large acquisitions have also tended to have relatively large tender premiums. . . .

6. One of the principal reasons for the increase in the average size of successful acquisition premiums during this period is that hostile or unwelcome takeovers have been much more common than before. Though there were only half as many acquisitions made in 1975/76 as in 1968, there were almost twice as many hostile tender offers. This trend toward hostile takeovers has continued. . . . In addition to these visibly hostile takeovers, it is probable that many outwardly friendly mergers are, in fact, the vestiges of, or reactions to, undisclosed hostile overtures.

The number of hostile corporate takeovers became so numerous during the late 1970s that an entire supporting infrastructure grew up around it. Specialists on each side, with well-developed strategies and competitive tactics, are brought in at the slightest indication of a takeover. If the unwanted suitor cannot be driven off through adverse publicity or exhaustive litigation, the goal then shifts to extract the maximum purchase price possible. Often the target's incumbent management brings in a "white knight," or a company that is more friendly to its interests. Bidding wars and legal battles between

---

[20] S. Hayes and R. Tausig, *Tactics of Cash Takeover Bids*, Harv.Bus.Rev. 135 (Mar.-Apr. 1967), John Shad, *The Financial Realities of Mergers,* Harv.Bus.Rev. 133 (Nov.-Dec. 1969).

the unwelcome suitor and the "white knight" then decide who wins. A classic example of this intercorporate warfare was the attempted takeover of Babcock & Wilcox by United Technologies in 1977. Following United's opening bid, J. Ray McDermott acquired stock in the open market and became a second unwanted suitor. As events unfolded, Babcock & Wilcox decided that McDermott would be the lesser of two evils. In the ensuing bidding battle, won by McDermott, the final price of Babcock and Wilcox was driven up by $200 million over United's initial overture, a bid which was itself at a $100 million premium over market value. In several other instances, three or even four corporate bidders entered the fray for a particularly desirable property. The 1979 divestiture of oil rich General Crude by International Paper saw Gulf, Mobil, Tenneco and Southland Royalty as bidders. International Paper took its proceeds (over $800 million) and, in turn, won a bidding battle with Weyerhaeuser for timber rich, privately owned Bodcaw.

Other takeovers were even more hostile than the General Crude situation. Two offers, one in late 1978 and the other in early 1979, set new standards for unlimited corporate warfare. The first was Mead Corporation's rebuff of Occidental Petroleum. Mead's counterattack was so thorough and complete in its exposure of Occidental's business affairs that it led to an investigation and censure by the SEC. Failing in the acquisition attempt, Oxy's president resigned and Armand Hammer, Oxy's chairman, commented that "had we known of the bloodshed . . . we never would have gone into it." In early 1979, fireworks erupted with American Express' billion dollar offer for McGraw Hill. McGraw Hill's response spared no punches. Even the ethics and morals of American Express' top management was openly challenged in the business press. Leaving no stone unturned or word unsaid and implying self annihilation if unsuccessful in its defense, McGraw Hill's counterattack gave rise to what is now known in the trade as a "scorched earth" policy. . . . American Express backed down.

The exact level of hostility in merger and acquisition activity is impossible to measure. Still, the hottest topic in the business press as the 1970s ended was not how to do a takeover, but rather how to defend/protect yourself (and, consequently, your company) from one. Many of the most vocal supporters of legislation aimed at limiting large-scale corporate acquisitions were not economists nor consumer activists, but rather corporate executives of middle-sized, prosperous companies that were quickly becoming the most attractive targets. It is somewhat ironic that many of these vocal critics of corporate takeovers, 1979 style, were themselves aggressive acquirers a few years earlier.

7. A very distinctive and important characteristic of merger and acquisition activity in the late 1970s is that approximately one-half of all corporate acquisitions were also corporate divestitures. In contrast, during the conglomerate merger wave of the 1960s, divestitures made up only 10% to 15% of all acquisitions. Figure 1-4 details the ratio of divestments to acquisition activity over this period. The significance of this

increased divestment activity is that a substantial portion of acquisition activity merely resulted in the "swapping" of assets by different companies. . . .

The peak in divestment activity occurred in 1975-76 as many companies, both diversified and nondiversified, pruned their businesses following the severe 1974-75 recession. Product lines, operating units, and entire divisions were sold or shut down as companies attempted to rid themselves of weak or low potential units. N.L. Industries, for example, divested over 60 businesses . . . Many of these divestitures were businesses acquired during the conglomerate era of the 1960s, businesses that often had little relationship to the mainstream of the company's activities or whose financial and management needs were out of proportion with their performance. Others, such as General Motors' 1979 divestiture of Frigidaire, were of long-standing businesses that no longer fit the corporate image or which continued to absorb valuable assets. Finally, several companies such as W.R. Grace and Allegheny Ludlum, in a constant search for the "perfect" portfolio of businesses, developed divestiture programs that were almost as active as their acquisition programs.

Figure 1-4
Corporate Divestitures as a Percent of Total Acquisition Activity 1969-1979

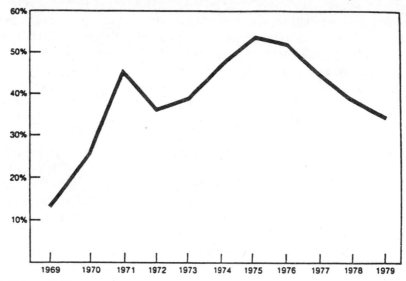

Source: W.T. Grimm & Co.

8. In contrast to the modest increase in the number of acquisitions in the 1975-1979 period, there was a noticeable increase in the number of acquisitions of publicly held companies. This is shown in Table 1-7. . . .

Table 1-7
Acquisitions of Publicly Held Companies, 1974-1979

| Year | Public Companies | | Total Acquisition Announcements | Public Acquisitions as Percent of all Acquisitions |
	Announcements	Completed or Pending		
1974	133	68	2,861	4.7%
1975	174	130	2,297	7.6
1976	232	163	2,276	10.2
1977	267	193	2,224	12.0
1978	325	260	2,106	15.4
1979	343	248	2,128	16.1

Source: W.T. Grimm & Co.

There are three major links between the increased number of public acquisitions and the characteristics previously identified. First, publicly held companies tend to be several orders of magnitude larger than privately held companies and, therefore, it is only natural that the increasing number of public company acquisitions went hand in hand with the increasing size of acquisitions during the late 1970s. Second, since management and ownership are generally separated in public companies while closely linked in private companies, it was only natural that there were more tender offers involved in order to reach directly the public companies' owners. In addition, the so-called "hostility" surrounding these acquisitions was generally much higher since management had a limited ownership interest and any takeover would have severely affected its prerogatives. Third, since publicly held companies have a liquid market for their stock, their stockholders do not generally have as low a tax basis as shareholders in private companies for the stock. Payment packages for the acquisition of publicly held companies, therefore, tend to be biased toward the use of cash or cash equivalents, especially during periods of poor stock price performance, such as was the case during the 1970s.

Apart from these characteristics, an aspect of merger activity during the 1975-1979 period that has received considerable attention in the business press and in public policy debates is the purported preference of today's acquirers for "well-managed" companies. Corporate executives are often quoted as saying that they have neither the managerial resources nor the time to successfully undertake a turnaround. In contrast, many of the conglomerates of the 1960s argued that they brought new management talent and sophisticated management techniques to bear on poorly run companies. Whether or not this preference for well-managed companies is a real and distinctive characteristic of the current merger movement is not entirely clear.

It may be that the apparent emphasis on good management is merely coincidental with the increasing scale of many acquisitions being made today. Many large companies, by virtue of their age and experience, have often established themselves as market leaders. And while market leadership and good management often go hand in hand, they are often confused by outside observers. On the other hand, the high proportion of divestments and the fact that several conglomerates (such as Gulf + Western Industries and Tyco Labs) have continued to acquire low performing companies with underutilized assets suggests that substantial opportunities for "turnarounds" still exist. Thus, it is not at all clear that current acquisition activity is as sharply focused on well-managed companies as many commentators would lead us to believe. What is more clear is that many highly visible, large public companies have been acquired, that these companies are often leaders in one or more product markets, and that due to their age, size, and market position, many have well-established, solid managements. Yet, it is also apparent that a large proportion of current merger activity involves divestitures of unwanted divisional operations whose performance does not meet the standards of the divesting parent. Thus, in the presence of conflicting suppositions we feel that it is inappropriate to state that the acquisition of well-managed companies is a distinctive characteristic of current merger activity.

Acquisitions in the 1980s: Characteristics of the Fourth Wave

Salter & Weinhold remark that "whether or not another major merger movement was launched in the late 1970s will only be possible to determine through the passage of time." By 1992 it was clear that the increased acquisition activity observed in the 1975-1979 period had begun a fourth wave of takeovers that lasted through the 1980s. It had four primary characteristics, three of which Salter & Weinhold noted with respect to the 1975-1979 period.

First, the nominal size of transactions continued to grow, culminating in Kohlberg Kravis Roberts' 1989 acquisition of RJR Nabisco for $24.7 billion. This can be seen Tables 1-8 and 1-9, which set out the number of acquisitions over $100 million from 1968 through 1991, and the number and total value of acquisitions over $1 billion from 1982 through 1991.

Table 1-8
Acquisitions over $100 Million, 1968-89

Year	Number	Year	Number
1968	46	1980	94
1969	24	1981	113
1970	10	1982	116
1971	7	1983	138
1972	15	1984	200
1973	28	1985	270
1974	28	1986	346
1975	14	1987	301
1976	39	1988	369
1977	41	1989	328
1978	80	1990	181
1979	83	1991	150

Source: Mergerstat Review

Table 1-9
Acquisitions over $1 Billion, 1982-89

Year	Number	Value ($ millions)
1982	10	19,440
1983	6	9,111
1984	19	55,179
1985	26	61,459
1986	31	67,932
1987	30	62,176
1988	42	96,399
1989	35	117,477

Source: Mergers and Acquisitions, May/June 1990, at 57.

Second, the trend toward hostile transactions continued, both directly and indirectly through friendly transactions undertaken in anticipation of a possible hostile transaction. Third, deconglomeration became a major theme of 1980s transactions. Fourth, a new transaction form, the leveraged buyout transaction form developed. More generally, many acquisitions and take over defenses relied heavily on debt financing, often through high-yield or "junk" bonds.

Volume of Activity. Table 1-10 sets out, for each year from 1980 through 1991, the number of transactions, their nominal value and, to control for price changes and growth of the economy, the value of, acquisitions as a percentage of real GNP. Table 1-11 restates Salter & Weinhold's Table 1-4 using 1982 (instead of 1972) to calculate constant dollar consideration and extends the period covered through 1991.[9]

Table 1-10
Total Acquisition Activity, 1980-1991

Year	No. of Deals	Value ($bil)	Real GNP ($ bil) 1982 dollars	No. of deals per $ bil real GNP	Value as percent of real GNP
1980	1558	34.8	3187	0.49	1.1%
1981	2328	69.5	3249	0.72	2.1%
1982	2298	60.7	3166	0.73	1.9%
1983	2395	52.7	3279	0.73	1.6%
1984	3175	126.1	3501	0.91	3.6%
1985	3486	146.0	3619	0.96	4.0%
1986	4448	205.8	3722	1.20	5.5%
1987	4015	178.2	3847	1.04	4.6%
1988	4001	236.4	4024	0.99	5.9%
1989	3846	249.7	4144	0.93	6.0%
1990	3851	170.0	4188	0.92	4.1%
1991	2117	98.0	4589	0.46	2.1%

Sources: M&A Series, Department of Commerce, Bureau of Economic Analysis (GNP data).

---

[9] Because of differing data bases, the value of transactions differ between Tables 1.10 and 1.11.

Table 1-11
Inflation Adjusted Value of Acquisitions, 1967 - 1991

Year	Total Consideration ($ billions)	GNP Implicit Price Deflator (1982 = 100)	Constant dollar Consideration (1982 $ billions)
1967	18.0	35.9	50.1
1968	43.0	37.7	114.1
1969	23.7	39.8	59.6
1970	16.4	42.0	39.1
1971	12.6	44.4	28.4
1972	16.7	46.5	35.9
1973	16.7	49.5	33.7
1974	12.5	54.0	23.2
1975	11.8	59.3	19.9
1976	20.0	63.1	31.7
1977	21.9	67.3	32.5
1978	34.2	72.2	47.4
1979	43.5	78.6	55.3
1980	44.3	85.7	51.7
1981	82.6	94.0	87.8
1982	53.7	100.0	53.7
1983	73.1	103.9	70.4
1984	122.2	107.7	113.5
1985	179.8	110.9	162.1
1986	173.1	113.9	152.0
1987	163.7	117.7	139.1
1988	246.9	121.3	203.5
1989	221.1	126.3	175.1
1990	108.1	129.7	83.4
1991	71.2	123.7	57.5

Source: W.T. Grimm & Co. The 1967-1979 figures are identical to those used by Salter & Weinhold.

The continued growth in number of acquisitions appears from comparing where Salter and Weinhold's Table 1-4 ends and Table 1-10 begins. Table 1-4 shows the number of acquisitions rising from 1,081 in 1976 to 1,350 in 1978. Table 1-10 shows the number acquisitions reaching 1558 in 1980, peaking at 4,448 in 1986, and still at 3,851 in 1990. A similar pattern appears in Table 1-11. The total consideration paid in acquisition transactions increased dramatically over the 1980s, peaking in constant dollars in 1988 at almost four times the 1979 level.

The data thus demonstrate the existence of a fourth merger wave that ran through the 1980s. However, to compare the size of this merger wave to that of the previous three, acquisition activity must be measured relative to the size of the economy. Figure 1-5 shows for the period 1895 through 1985 the value of assets transferred through acquisitions as a percentage of real GNP. Figure 1-6 shows for the same period the number of acquisitions per billion dollars of real GNP. Both figures are extended through 1991 in the last two columns of Table 1-10. The data show that while the number and value of acquisitions in the 1980s were still relatively modest compared to the merger waves of the 1890s and 1920s, the 1980s wave was larger than that of the 1960s in dollars and comparable in number of transactions.

Figure 1-5
Value of Assets Acquired Relative to GNP, 1895-1985

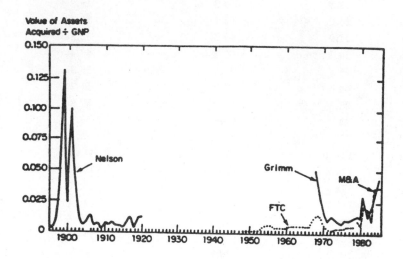

Source: Devra Golbe & Lawrence White, *A Time-Series Analysis of Mergers and Acquisitions in the U.S. Economy*, in *Corporate Takeovers: Causes and Consequences* 265 (Alan Auerbach ed. 1988)

Figure 1-6
Number of Mergers per Billion Dollars of GNP, 1895-1985

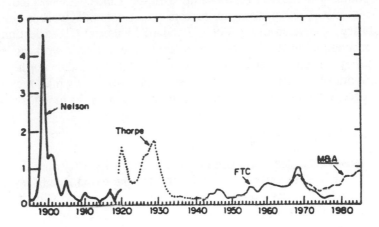

Source: Devra Golbe & Lawrence White (1988), supra.

Deconglomeration. Table 1-12 shows, for each year from 1966 through 1991, the number of divestitures and the percentage of that year's acquisitions represented by divestitures. Between 1965 and 1969, divestitures represented from 11% to 13% of all acquisitions. The range was from 34% to 54% between 1975 and 1980, and from 35% to 45% during the 1980s.

Table 1-12
Divestitures, 1966-1991

Year	Number	Percent of Transactions	Year	Number	Percent of Transactions
1966	264	11%	1979	752	35%
1967	328	11%	1980	666	35%
1968	557	12%	1981	830	35%
1969	801	13%	1982	875	37%
1970	1,401	27%	1983	932	37%
1971	1,920	42%	1984	900	36%
1972	1,770	37%	1985	1,218	41%
1973	1,557	39%	1986	1,259	38%
1974	1,331	47%	1987	807	40%
1975	1,236	54%	1988	894	40%
1976	1,204	53%	1989	1,005	45%
1977	1,002	45%	1990	940	45%
1978	820	39%	1991	849	45%

Source: W.T. Grimm & Co., Mergerstat Review

The increased frequency of divestitures reflects an important shift in United States industrial organization. After becoming more diversified during the 1960s and 1970s, American companies became less diversified in the 1980s. Liebeskind & Opler show that over the 1980-1989 period, the percentage of a firm's workers employed in its largest industry, measured using 4-digit Standard Industrial Classification (SIC) codes, increased on average by 10.6%, and the percentage of a firm's workers employed in its 2-digit industry group increased by 16.8%.[10] Similarly, during the 1980s, public companies reduced significantly the number of industries in which they participated.[11] Divestitures were a principal means medium by which this shift in industrial organization took place.

Leverage. The deconglomeration of American industry that occurred over the 1980s was closely tied to another phenomenon: the increased role of leveraged buyouts ("LBOs") and other highly leveraged transactions.[12] The growth in LBOs is shown in Table 1-13. The table begins in 1984 because before that, LBOs were too new to be separately reported. The first leveraged buyout of a public company was Houdaille Industries in 1979. Five years later, deals of this type numbered in the hundreds, and were a significant percentage of all acquisition activity.

Leveraged transactions took several forms. The first form of leveraged buyout occurred when a large company voluntarily divested a division. The sale was often to the division's managers who lacked access to capital to finance the transaction. In that setting, the divesting company would loan the acquiring managers most of the purchase price, or provide enough equity financing to secure a loan from an outside lender.

---

[10] Julia Liebeskind & Tim Opler, *The Causes of Corporate Refocusing*, (working paper 1992). The higher the number of SIC digits, the more specialized the classification measured. A 4-digit classification is relatively precise while a 2 digit classification reflects a more general industry segment.

[11] *See* Robert Comment & Gregg Jarrell, *Corporate Focus, Stock Returns and the Market for Corporate Control* (working paper, Managerial Econ. Res. Ctr., Simon Sch. of Business, Univ. of Rochester 1992); Frank Lichtenberg, *Industrial De-Diversification and its Consequences for Productivity*, 18 J. Econ. Behav. & Org. 427 (1992).

[12] Leveraged buyouts as a transactional form are considered in depth in Chapter 11 *infra*.

Table 1-14
Leveraged Buyout Transactions, 1984 - 1991

Year	No. of Deals	Buyouts as % of All Deals	Value ($	Value as % of
1984	237	9.8%	$18,718	15.4%
1985	238	8.6	19,670	14.0
1986	330	8.7	45,160	22.5
1987	270	8.6	36,228	21.1
1988	378	11.4	47,100	20.2
1989	371	12.1	66,800	27.4
1990	241	7.6	15,900	9.7
1991	112	5.3	5,500	5.6

Source: Mergers & Acquisitions

The second form of leveraged transaction -- the hostile bust-up takeover -- arose following an innovation in the capital markets: the development of a public market for non-investment grade debt, called "high yield debt" or "junk bonds" depending on the orientation of the observer. This new form of debt provided financing to a new group of takeover entrepreneurs whose function was largely brokerage. Companies were acquired with borrowed funds and more or less broken up, the pieces being sold to pay down the debt with the acquirer keeping either the profits or the pieces of the business it thought it could most efficiently operate. A number of studies have directly linked this type of transaction to deconglomeration. For example, Randall Morck, Andrei Shleifer & Robert Vishny concluded "that the source of bust-up gains in the 1980s is the reversal of the unrelated diversification of the 1960s and 1970s."[13]

A closely related type of leveraged transaction was the management buyout or "MBO"of an entire company. These were largely friendly transactions, although often in response to an existing or anticipated hostile transaction. In an MBO, the "target's" management, often joined by an LBO firm -- a firm specializing in leveraged transactions like Kohlberg, Kravis, Roberts -- acquired the target. In addition to its leverage, this form of transaction was characterized by a large increase in management's equity investment in the company and the continuing oversight role played by the leveraged

---

[13] Randall Morck, Andrei Shleifer & Robert Vishny, *Do Managerial Objectives Drive Bad Acquisitions*, 45 J.Fin. 31 (1990); see Sanjai Bhagat, Andrei Shleifer & Robert Vishny, *Hostile Takeovers in the 1980s: The Return to Corporate Specialization*, Brookings Papers on Econ. Activity: Microecon. 1990, at 1 ("By and large, hostile takeovers represents the deconglomeration of American business and a return to corporate specialization."); Amar Bhide, *The Causes and Consequences of Hostile Takeovers*, J.Applied Corp.Fin. 36 (Summer 1989).

buyout firm. The combination was said to provide managers with both greater performance incentives than they previously had and more intense monitoring of management performance, by both the LBO firm and debt holders.

The End of the Fourth Wave. The fourth merger wave peaked in dollar value in 1988 and 1989, and was clearly over by the first quarter of 1991, when acquisition activity receded to its lowest level since the first quarter of 1980. The trend clearly appears from Figure 1-7.

The full explanation for the end of the fourth merger wave remains speculative, although a number of factors seem relevant. The demise of the junk bond market, said to have resulted from the elimination of the central figures in junk bond financing, Michael Milken through criminal prosecution and his firm, Drexel Burnham, through bankruptcy, is one possible factor. One principal source of financing for acquisitions in the later part of the 1980s became less available.

A second explanation looks to a different external source: regulation. By the end of the 1980s, most states had adopted anti-takeover laws that made hostile acquisitions more difficult and, in some states, may have made them impossible.[14]   With the diminished liklihood of a hostile takeover, the number of anticipatory friendly transactions also declined.

Others argue that the wave had simply run its course. From this perspective, the fourth merger wave, like earlier waves discussed by Salter & Weinhold, served an economic function. If the 1980s takeover wave was fueled by deconglomeration, as Morck, Shleifer & Vishny argue, then at some point deal makers would run out of companies that could be successfully broken up. By the end of the decade the best deals were said to have been done[15] and acquisition activity accordingly dropped. An increase in acquisition activity then would have to wait for another idea, an explanation for why widespread ownership changes of capital assets would increase the assets' value.

The drop in both value and activity may also have reflected the economic downturn which began in 1990. The recession, accompanied by economic uncertainty, poor consumer confidence and lack of job security, forced buyers and sellers to remain cautious when considering acquisitions.

---

[14] *See* Mark Roe, *Takeover Politics*, in *The Deal Decade: What Takeovers and Leveraged Buyouts Mean for Corporate Governance* 321 (Margaret Blair ed.1993).

[15] See William Long & David Ravenscraft, *Decade of Debt: Lessons from LBOS in the 1980s*, Brookings Discussion Papers in Econ. No. 90-6 (Dec.1991).

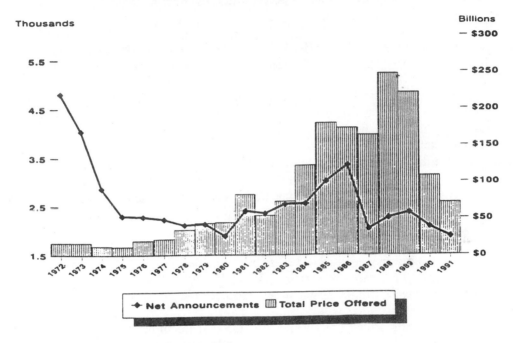

Figure 1-7
Trends In Mergers And Acquisitions, 1972-1991

Source: W.T. Grimm & Co., *Mergerstat Review*

D. The Modern Transactional Setting

Until 1975, no major investment banking firm would participate in a hostile takeover attempt. But once Morgan Stanley, the most conservative of the leading firms, legitimized hostile takeovers by participating in a hostile tender offer for International Nickel in 1975, the conduct of parties to acquisitions moved farther and farther from the image of "gentlemen" conducting business in a restrained and courteous fashion. Increasingly, the dominant metaphor was war: "battle" replaced "transaction" as a description of the event; "sneak attacks" by an offerer and "scorched earth" tactics by a target replaced "negotiation" as a description of the parties' activities. Moreover, as the 1980s progressed, the parties grew ever more sophisticated in using the new techniques. The changed character of many transactions appears from the following account of one of the major deals of the decade: Time Incorporated's successful friendly acquisition of Warner Communications in the face of Paramount Communications' hostile offer for Time. The account touches many of the subjects explored in this book, including important judicial opinions growing out of the Time-Paramount contest, that are considered later in this book. But the business story of the transaction -- its planning, the strategies forged and abandoned, and the role of lawyers and investment bankers -- gives a rich introduction to what corporate acquisitions have become.

BILL SAPORITO, THE INSIDE STORY OF TIME WARNER
Fortune, Nov. 20, 1989

Around six o'clock on the evening of June 6, [1989,] Time Inc. CEO J. Richard Munro walked into the office of President N. J. "Nick" Nicholas Jr. holding a fax message in his hand and a blank stare of disbelief on his face. Munro is normally outgoing, excitable, and expressive, but his stunned look told Nicholas all he needed to know. "He did it," Munro said to his friend Nicholas. "Martin Davis did it."

Davis is the CEO of Paramount Communications. And what he did was waltz by Time's dream house with a pail of gasoline and a flame thrower, torching the company's long-planned merger with Warner Communications and touching off one of the most ferocious corporate clashes in a decade chock-full of them. The battle provoked tremendous controversy and touched every bare-wire business issue of the age: long-term vs. short-term value, shareholder rights, the significance of corporate culture, executive compensation, business ethics, management practice, and merger and acquisition tactics.

Paramount's offer to buy Time for $175 a share in cash hit barely two weeks before Time stockholders were set to vote on the planned merger with Warner, the diversified entertainment and media company run by Steven J. Ross. To hold off Davis and hold on to its independence, Time instead acquired Warner for $13.1 billion in cash and securities.

No one disputes that Time and Warner are an excellent fit. The combined company is an American giant in an age when global behemoths rule the media planet. Time Warner makes movies, television programs, records, tapes, books, and magazines, including this one, and can sell virtually all of these things around the world. It sells pay TV through Home Box Office and Cinemax to 23 million subscribers, and owns cable TV systems serving six million households across the U.S. "It is awesome how impressive this company will become," says Munro, now co-CEO of Time Warner with Ross. Sales in 1989 will approach $11 billion, and the underlying assets are worth some $25 billion. All that and Bugs Bunny, too. Awesome indeed.

But agreement about the combination ends there. Davis too wanted to walk in the land of the giants and saw a combination with Time as a perfect way to get there. In launching his bid Davis acknowledged Munro's logic but chose as a weapon a rather basic fact of arithmetic: $175 is more than $120. The first figure was Paramount's initial offer for each share of Time; the second was the maximum value Paramount and its investment adviser, Morgan Stanley, figured Time Warner's stock would reach if the original merger went through. Davis assumed that given the choice, shareholders would take the cash. He was probably right. They generally do. He was definitely wrong in assuming that they would get the choice.

Time and Warner managers view the acquisition as a perfect combination that would have sailed through in its original form had it not been for that spoilsport Davis. But he couldn't let it sail through, they say, arguing that the debt-free, tax-free merger would have left Paramount too small to compete with a media and entertainment powerhouse such as Time Warner. In this view Davis looked at a no-lose situation and jumped in: He might succeed in buying Time cheaply, or he might break up the deal, or he would at least saddle the new company with debt, making it less competitive. Davis says that notion is ridiculous.

Davis charged in the Paramount lawsuit to prevent Time from buying Warner that Munro and Nicholas sold the shareholders out to preserve their own empire. He said they did this on the pretense that Time's editorial independence and culture demanded it. Munro and Nicholas insist that notion is ridiculous. Says Munro, 58, who will retire as co-CEO next year after ten years of running Time: "This is my legacy. I did not work here 33 years to bust the company up." He and Nicholas, 50, own loads of company stock, he points out. If they had just wanted to get rich, they would have sold the company to Davis or the highest bidder -- and cleared many millions of dollars each.

Steve Ross, 62, Warner's affable, high-profile chairman and CEO, demonstrated once again that in the music of deals he has perfect pitch. Ross orchestrated a great short- and long-term bargain for his shareholders and flattened a persistent boardroom antagonist. He now will share the CEO's job for five years at a company twice the size of Warner. He also retains a compensation package so abundant in dollars that, should the oilman fail to show this winter, Ross can shovel money into his furnace and have plenty left over in the spring.

THE STRATEGY EMERGES

Publishing is a wonderfully profitable business. Basically it comprises a bunch of people and a bunch of trees that eventually run into each other at a printing press. The product of this union is sold to readers and to advertisers who wish to communicate with them. Publishing can offer a high return on assets and terrific margins. Time's magazines, which include Time, FORTUNE, Life, Sports Illustrated, Money, and People, plus a score more wholly or partly owned, are doing just swell, thank you.

But over the past decade Munro, Nicholas, and Time vice chairman Gerald M. Levin came to believe that the magazine division was not growing fast enough. Revenue gains in the division have averaged about 5.7% a year since 1985, and when the Warner deal was announced in March Time's investment bankers could not project anything beyond 6% for the future. Time already has about 22% of the U.S. magazine advertising business, more than twice the share of its nearest competitors, and 33% of magazine profits. Says Munro: "We have two huge engines that drive that division, People and Sports Illustrated. So I would say that the growth there is a little bit limited."

While Time's soul is in publishing, the company tried for decades to find another leg to hold up the financial body. Magazine publishing is a cyclical business hitched to the U.S. economy, and Time Inc. has suffered through several profit swings. The corporation has bought and sometimes sold newspapers, television stations, and forest-products companies in several unavailing efforts to diversify profitably.

Successful diversification did not come until the company happened on cable television and pay channels early in the game, and . . . they took off. Time had picked up a few cable systems in the Sixties, and in the early Seventies a free-spirited entrepreneur named Charles Dolan had briefly joined the company and started something called the Green Channel, soon renamed Home Box Office. By 1974, after years of losses and frustration, these ventures were about to start spouting money, and the executives in charge happened to be three young men named Munro, Nicholas, and Levin. With less than ten years' TV experience among them, they faced the best problem a manager can have: struggling to handle all the growth. Time's future was getting tuned in to a new channel. Today the video side and the magazine side are approximately the same size, $2.1 billion and $1.9 billion, respectively, in sales.

That was terrific, but as of the mid-Eighties Time's top executives still saw three large problems with the corporate structure.

Problem No. 1: Time didn't own any significant copyrights in the fastest-growing sector of the media business, video. Copyrights are a central concept in media. When a film, book, or magazine is produced, distributed, and sold, the copyright owner makes a big chunk of the money. With its cable and pay TV operations Time owned entertainment distribution channels, but it didn't own any entertainment. That stuff had to be bought on the open market, and prices were getting steep.

Problem No. 2: The media industry is increasingly diversified and global, and as Munro and Nicholas saw it, Time was sufficiently neither. While foreign companies such as Bertelsmann, Hachette, and Rupert Murdoch's News Corp. inhaled properties through the mid-Eighties, Time's management thought of these companies as collectors paying crazy prices. Gradually, as prices continued to spiral and Time watched from the sidelines, another thought took hold.

Nicholas understood that not only would the prices continue to increase, but the very mass of these new empires also offered security from business risks. In addition, mass offered more protection from the appetites of the acquisitive. In a rapidly consolidating media industry, it was eat or be eaten -- and Time sincerely, intensely wished to avoid being eaten.

In pursuing this wish Time lacked a powerful weapon available to most of America's other great publishing enterprises: a separate class of nonvoting stock, which a company's founding family would sell to outside investors while retaining control of the voting stock. New York Times Co., Dow Jones, Washington Post Co., Times Mirror, all had created these two classes of stock, and all had remained independent. Failing to create such stock was, Nicholas says, one of founder Henry R. Luce's few big mistakes.

Besides being tough to take over, the newly forming media empires had another advantage, a capacity for laying off risk. Says Nicholas: "The idea is a very simple one. You get some businesses where you can spread your overhead. You've got to be able to control or have relationships with enough distribution channels to know you've got a great shot at amortizing the fixed costs." In other words, the $35 million price tag of a movie like Batman looks less chancy when a company knows it can get its money back by showing the movie in the U.S., then showing it abroad, selling the videocassette, selling the soundtrack on records, compact discs, and tapes, showing it on pay TV, and perhaps selling related books or producing related TV programs, all using the company's own resources. This year Warner's Batman opened the way for sales of videos, record albums, books, and even comic books (where the character originated) -- all owned by Warner.

Problem No. 3: Wall Street was not in love with Time Inc. and traded the stock at a fraction of its theoretical breakup value. Investors didn't like the variability of Time's earnings. With increasing frequency the stock would rise on rumors that Time was about to be taken over, but this was not Munro's idea of good news.

In the mid-Eighties Munro saw a way to attack all three problems: Hook up through merger or acquisition with another media giant. Allen Neuharth, chief of Gannett Co. and self-described S.O.B., came calling in 1985. Gannett's newspapers and broadcast division might have fit well with Time, but its management wouldn't. Munro had a cast-iron condition for any potential combination: Time Inc. would run the show or would share top-level authority equally. Neuharth scoffed at the idea.

CBS chief Tom Wyman also chatted with Munro about a merger in 1985, when Ted Turner was quixotically attacking CBS, but the talks led nowhere. In the fall of 1988, Warren Buffett came by with his friends from Capital Cities/ABC, in which he was a major investor. Munro and Nicholas met with Buffett and Cap Cities CEO

Thomas Murphy and President Daniel Burke. The meetings continued into December, until, according to Nicholas, Murphy mentioned that in any deal there should be one or two more Cap Cities directors than Time directors. Munro says he told Murphy, a good friend, thank you very much but Time Inc. is not for sale. A Cap Cities source says the two men couldn't agree on who would be boss.

Munro and Nicholas in 1987 began speculating about combining with a film and video producer. Disney had an excellent studio, but 60% of its revenues are from theme parks, a business in which Time had no expertise. Columbia Pictures, MCA, Fox -- each had charms but lacked size, strategic fit, or management. Only two companies looked right: Paramount (then called Gulf & Western) and Warner.

Warner was more profitable and a better strategic match than Paramount. Importantly, at a time when foreign markets offer the brightest growth opportunities, 40% of Warner's revenues come from overseas, vs. less than 10% of Time's (and only 16% of Paramount's). In movies and television both Warner and Paramount produced outstanding returns, but only Warner owned 100% of its movie distribution business. Additionally, Warner had 1.6 million cable subscribers who could combine nicely with the 4.3 million of Time's American Television & Communications, already America's No. 2 cable company (after Tele-Communications Inc.). Paramount's publishing division, Simon & Schuster, would also have fit well at Time, but the company wasn't looking to expand in book publishing. Instead Time got big eyes for Warner's wildly profitable record business, which accounts for about half the company's operating income.

NICK DROPS A DIME

One day in May 1987, Nick Nicholas found himself with an unexpected free afternoon. Citizen Nick had planned to spend the day on jury duty in state supreme court in Manhattan but was dismissed early. From the courthouse lobby he punched the digits for Warner Communications and asked for Steve Ross. Did Ross have some time that afternoon to discuss a couple of things? If Ross didn't have time, he soon made some available.

Nicholas knew Warner's cable operation well -- he had once negotiated, unsuccessfully, to sell Time's Manhattan Cable to it -- and he was interested in a joint cable venture. Ross was also interested because Warner was at a crossroads in cable -- "too big to be small and too small to be big," says Ross. In 1986 Warner had bought its partner American Express out of joint ownership in a cable television company that held systems Time coveted. A joint venture offered a way for Time to get co-ownership of those systems.

Ross took the idea one step further. During several subsequent meetings that summer he developed the notion that Time should throw in its HBO unit, while Warner would contribute its Warner Brothers studio. Such a combination would create a vertically integrated entertainment venture.

The egos in the media corporations that cluster around Manhattan's Sixth Avenue are as big as the buildings, and that was the problem the two sides grappled with in a sit-down at the Helmsley Palace Hotel on November 4, 1987. From Time came Munro, Nicholas, Levin, and HBO Chairman Michael Fuchs. The Warner group included Ross, Deane F. Johnson from Warner's office of the president, and Warner Brothers studio bosses Robert A. Daly and Terry S. Semel. There were no Indians among these chiefs, making the subject of just who would report to whom a touchy one. Ross wanted Warner Brothers left alone; Time felt the same way about HBO. Both sides agreed the cable systems could be jointly run.

As the talks progressed a number of hurdles sprang up. There were questions of how much money each partner could take out of the venture, serious tax problems within the new company, and a need to develop a divorce agreement should the two parties, like those in so many other joint ventures, decide they didn't like each other after all. Against that formidable stack of problems a simple solution occurred to several of the people involved: Just merge the companies.

Nicholas, with Munro's agreement, popped that merger question in early June 1988, after a year of trying to work out a joint venture. Ross thought about it for a week and agreed to begin negotiating.

In the original joint venture proposal, Munro and Ross would have been co-CEOs of the enterprise, with HBO reporting to Munro, Warner Brothers reporting to Ross, and the cable companies reporting jointly. This structure carried over into the merger talks. The two sides spent the better part of the summer divvying up the reporting relationships and hammering out the roles of the chief executives.

The concept of a co-CEO is not foreign to Ross. He shared the title at Warner with William Frankel from 1967 until Frankel's death in 1972. At one meeting he brought along a FORTUNE article that discussed Unilever, invariably described as the "Anglo-Dutch consumer products company." Unilever is essentially two companies and has two CEOs, one in the Netherlands and one in Britain, who run what Ross called a staple corporation. The two are joined at the bottom line.

Without much debate, Ross and Munro agreed to make Nicholas their successor. Ross had no logical No. 2 to compete for the spot, and over the months of negotiations he had become increasingly impressed with Nicholas. Ross says, "If he weren't with

Time I would have made overtures to have him with us. I think he is extremely capable and very knowledgeable. So we never had a problem."

A culture clash, however, has the makings of a problem.

THE CULTURE

Above all other considerations in any merger, Munro felt compelled to defend the Time culture. He sincerely believes, as do many employees, that working for Time isn't like working for, say, Amalgamated Spark Plugs. The executives and employees consider Time Inc. a kind of public institution and believe working for it confers special status.

The most famous feature of Time's culture is the separation, both psychic and structural, of church and state. Time founder Luce decreed that the editorial side of the business (church) would report directly to the editor-in-chief rather than to the publishing side (state), as it does in nearly every other journalistic enterprise in the world. The arrangement gives editors freedom to report and analyze the news without influence or interference from the business side and its advertisers.

The benefits of separating church and state are obvious: It attracts top journalists, it increases a magazine's value to readers, and it makes a magazine more valuable to advertisers, even though they may occasionally take their licks in the editorial pages. But the idea of dual hierarchies reaching all the way to the board is unknown at most companies, including Warner. Jason McManus, 55, Time Inc.'s editor-in-chief and church's high priest, took a philosophic view toward Warner. He was part of the tradition -- he had worked for Luce -- but believed that if Time didn't merge it would be taken over, with who-knows-what effect on the magazines' independence. "There was a nostalgia for Time Inc. as it was imagined to be," he says, "but the people who felt 'Gee, if we hadn't done anything we'd have been fine' were living in a dream world." . . .

To preserve the church-state structure, Warner acknowledged -- not that Time considered the matter negotiable -- the corporate hands-off policy regarding Time's magazines. Editorial operations would report only to editor-in-chief McManus, who is one of Time's four inside directors (the others: Munro, Nicholas, Levin). McManus reports only to the board. It exercises its responsibility for editorial operations through a committee of six outside directors, with four seats going to people who were on Time's board before the merger. Warner demanded the same protection for its creative output. Time agreed to an entertainment committee, controlled by directors who had been on Warner's board, to oversee Warner's movie and record businesses.

The Time directors came up with another method to ensure cultural survival: They authorized Levin, 50, to negotiate long-term contracts for Munro, Nicholas, and himself. Says Munro: "We told the board that we didn't want contracts, but they insisted."

Munro had long said that by age 60 he would step aside both as CEO and as a director. Working out the merger terms, he changed his mind in order to smooth the transition and be available should Ross be incapacitated. Munro's contract makes him co-CEO with Ross until he steps down next year. After that he will be chairman of the board's executive committee until 1994 and an adviser for five years more. He will be paid at least $1.5 million annually in salary and bonus as co-CEO. From 1990 until 1999 he will be paid at least $750,000 a year. He will later get another $4,275,000 in deferred compensation. Nicholas also signed a roughly comparable ten-year contract, making him co-CEO with Ross as soon as Munro resigns, and sole CEO in five years.

In theory the board could undo these arrangements, subject to restrictions in the contracts. But to the extent it was possible, Time had ensured that its cherished culture would have advocates at the top of Time Warner for a decade. The contracts put Munro in the position of explaining to employees, including hundreds of journalists, that he and Nicholas accepted the extraordinarily handsome agreements to protect them. . . .

JERRY'S DEAL

The task of negotiating the merger's financial terms fell to Levin from Time and to Oded Aboodi for Warner. Aboodi, 48, is neither a Warner officer nor a director, nor an investment banker in the usual sense, though he is sometimes called one. But Ross wouldn't make a move without him. A Jerusalem-born accountant, Aboodi handled some Warner transactions while a partner at Arthur Young & Co. Technically astute, he loves the creative aspects of dealmaking, and in Steve Ross he found a soul mate. Says Levin: "He reads the psychological set of the people he deals with."

Levin, an attorney by training and Time's chief strategist and planner, insisted from the beginning of negotiations in early 1988 that Time had to be the acquiring entity. Says he: "There was never a discussion of the acquisition of Time by Warner. We were interested in an acquisition -- where the Time culture, the Time institution, the Time tradition prevails."

That was fine with Aboodi. He had an imperative of his own: Ross's demand that the deal be erected not as a cash buyout but as a merger in which only stock changed hands. Ross wanted Time to issue millions of new shares with which to buy Warner from its stockholders. Time executives had hoped to borrow billions in good old cash and buy Warner that way, preserving greater assets and earning power for each Time share. On this issue Time gave in early. Says Ross: "They threw in the sponge because they knew finally that I wasn't going to do anything but a stock deal."

One reason Ross insisted on this form of merger was that it would let the merged company treat the deal as a pooling of interests, a now rarely used accounting method that combines the assets of the merging enterprises as if they were never apart. Most mergers use purchase-price accounting, a technique with an insidious cost. Acquired companies are generally worth far more than the value of the hard assets shown on their balance sheets. The difference between the price paid and an acquired company's updated asset value is called goodwill. Under purchase-price accounting this amount is amortized over a long period, with the amount amortized each year deducted from reported profits, even though no cash loss is involved. In the Warner deal goodwill amounts to $10 billion to $12 billion, or something like $300 million to $400 million a year for 30 years. Ross did not want such a hit to earnings.

So the deal would be an exchange of stock -- but at what ratio? By the end of June 1988, the talks focused on that question. Aboodi was in the driver's seat because Warner had a better bottom line and a higher market value than Time. In 1988 Warner earned $423 million after taxes on sales of $4.2 billion. Although Time had sales of $4.5 billion, its net profit was $289 million. Main reason: Warner enjoys a lower tax rate resulting from accumulated tax credits.

Warner's sales and earnings growth were outpacing Time's. Had the two companies remained independent, Warner's sales would have overtaken Time's this year. Aboodi argued further that Warner's stock price would rise faster and carry a higher earnings multiple because Wall Street liked its business mix better. He also noted that Time was supporting its own stock price, having bought back 10% of the shares, while Warner was not. Finally, and most important, Warner had to be accorded a takeover premium.

Time indicated it was willing to pay a premium for the right to take Warner out. The price of Warner's stock had been about 35% of Time's over the previous 12 months. Adding to that a premium of around 10 percentage points, Levin figured to get a deal at a ratio of 43% to 45% -- or, as the negotiators say, .43 to .45. He started at .40; Aboodi talked .50. They would not get any closer that year.

THE $193 MILLION MAN

A far more delicate challenge also awaited Levin, Munro, and Nicholas: how to sell Steve Ross to the Time board. Ross's contract was as lush as that of any CEO in America. In 1987, following a wild board meeting ending in a 9-to-6 vote, Ross took home a ten-year employment contract that guaranteed him base pay of $1.2 million a year. That's not unheard of, but the contract included a bonus that would pay an average $14 million a year for ten years if Warner stock appreciated 10% a year. It has.

Under his amended ten-year contract with Time Warner, Ross is due $193 million at the close of the deal for stock-based compensation he had coming at Warner: $70 million in cash and $123 million in deferred payments. He also gets the same $1.2 million annual salary and deferred compensation he did at Warner plus a minimum bonus of 0.4% of Time Warner's earnings before taxes and some amortization and depreciation. And he receives options on 1.8 million shares of stock at a minimum price of $150 a share. After 1999 he will collect $750,000 a year for five years as an adviser.

Time's management convinced the board that Ross's contract was his reward for founding the company in the 1960s and successfully nurturing it. Curiously, Ross owned only about 1% of his baby's stock, which is where most founders get their reward. Very few Time directors liked Ross's contract, but they viewed it as part of Warner's price. Says director Donald S. Perkins, a former CEO of Jewel Cos., a supermarket chain: "It just comes down to a cost of doing business. It was part of the price of the deal." Says another, who prefers to remain nameless: "I've made a lot of guys rich who didn't deserve it. The deal is what's important."

Ross patched Warner together initially by grafting a rental car business onto his father-in-law's funeral parlor business. He added parking lots and took the company public as Kinney National Service in 1962. In 1969, Kinney bought Warner Brothers-Seven Arts, then a broken-down relic of a Hollywood studio, for a reported $400 million in stock. But Warner also had real estate, a film library, a great record company, and good executives, such as Ahmet Ertegun of Atlantic Records. Warner is the ultimate people business, and it fit Ross's schmoozing style. A big guy's big guy, Ross lives the high life and makes no excuses for it. His longstanding friendships with Hollywood glitterati -- Clint Eastwood, Barbra Streisand, Steven Spielberg -- are counted as corporate assets.

Ross combined an uncanny sense of the future, a genial manner, and shrewd dealmaking skills to lift Warner onto the FORTUNE 500 in 1971. He put someone he could trust in charge of each business, left him alone, and paid handsomely if the division performed. The pay included stock appreciation rights. The deal with Time will enable about 700 Warner employees to cash in options totaling more than $600 million.

Retired Time president James Shepley, who died in November 1988, made no attempt to hide his belief that Ross and Warner were unsavory partners. In the early Eighties, Time lost three cable television franchise battles to Ross in Pittsburgh, Cincinnati, and the New York City borough of Queens, and Shepley was sure Warner had played dirty. Dick Munro had led the battle in Pittsburgh. He remembers: "We had the champagne all ready to pour. And then the word came that Warner had been picked. We couldn't believe we'd lost. They must have paid somebody off." Time sued Warner and the city of Pittsburgh, charging improper bidding procedures. The two sides eventually settled out of court.

TIME'S BOARD HOPS ON

Munro told Time's board in June 1988 that his team was talking to Warner about a merger, but he gave no details. . . . During the next few weeks Munro spoke with each director privately to explain his vision of Time Inc.'s future and ask for approval.

Events of the Eighties had affected several of Time's 12 outside directors in various ways that would directly influence their view of any deal. After he retired, Donald Perkins watched American Stores take over his Jewel Cos. and unhinge the organization he helped create. Edward S. Finkelstein, chairman of R.H. Macy & Co., had taken the retail merchandiser private when it became raider bait. James F. Bere, chairman of Borg-Warner, took his company private in a leveraged buyout to fend off raids by Irwin Jacobs and GAF.

A key player was director Michael D. Dingman, who [was] chairman of Henley Group. An astute shuffler of corporate assets, Dingman had done more deals in a few years than most executives do in a career. He knew leverage, he knew shareholder value, he sure as hell knew mergers and acquisitions -- and he knew as of late July 1988 that among Time directors Munro's merger plan with Warner was dead. Says he: "It was damned controversial. If you ran a board vote on it, it would have failed."

Levin was also keeping score, and it wasn't looking good. His handwritten notes revealed the tally: Bere was unenthusiastic, Perkins lukewarm, ditto Clifford J. Grum, CEO of Temple-Inland. Another director, Henry C. Goodrich, former chairman of Sonat, an Alabama energy company, was down as a flat no. John Opel, chairman of IBM's executive committee, was skeptical but open-minded. David T. Kearns, chairman and CEO of Xerox, was signed on, as was Finkelstein. Levin had no read on the board's two academics: Matina S. Horner, president of Radcliffe College, and Clifton R. Wharton Jr., former chancellor of the State University of New York and now chairman of Teachers Insurance & Annuity Association/College Retirement Equity Fund.

Director Arthur Temple's name did not appear on the list. Nor did that of director Henry Luce III, son of Time founder Henry R. Luce. There was no need. Arthur Temple would no sooner get in bed with Hollywood than he would climb a loblolly pine naked.

Director Henry Luce III wasn't wild about Hollywood either, but more fundamentally he did not yet buy the strategy. He had worked at Time for 30 years, including tours as publisher of FORTUNE and Time, then retired in 1981 to run the Henry Luce Foundation, which controls about 3.5% of Time's stock. For years he had approved company expansion into other media with mixed emotions. He accepted that Munro's strategy might be valid but felt it was not necessarily the only effective one. Says he: "I expressed disagreement to Dick and his colleagues. They made all their points that it was an important strategic move, but they left me unpersuaded." And like Temple, Luce was appalled by the rich employment contracts for Munro, Nicholas, and Ross.

Luce also believed that his father, Harry, would not have approved the Warner deal. In late July 1988, he sent Munro a note that quoted his father's will: " 'Time Inc. is now, and is expected to continue to be, principally a journalistic enterprise, and, as such, an enterprise operated in the public interest.' " Luce III continued: "In the spirit of the above, and in view of many other specific factors, I don't believe I could vote for the proposition . . ." Luce instead urged Munro to go after McGraw-Hill, the undermanaged publishing house two doors down Sixth Avenue from Time. . . .

ROSS TAKES A HIKE

If anyone held fears of a boardroom showdown, they were dispelled on August 11, 1988, when Ross pulled out of the talks after an emotional meeting at his Park Avenue apartment with Munro, Levin, Nicholas, Aboodi, and attorneys. . . . Some Time directors felt relieved. Although many of the so-called governance issues had been worked out, the Time board had insisted that Ross accept a finite term as co-CEO and the assured succession of Nick Nicholas as sole chief. "We didn't want another Armand Hammer," explains one director. Lawyers for Time kept referring to Ross's tenure as transitional. The language grated on Ross. He felt unwanted and unloved by the Time board, and worse yet feared being locked into a lame duck status, which would undermine his authority.

The last thing Ross wanted was another contentious board. At Warner he was living with an archenemy in Herbert J. Siegel, the Chris-Craft Industries chief who as a director controlled 17% of Warner stock and who often clashed with Ross over strategy.* . . .

Once again Dingman stepped into the deal, this time to explain to Ross how things work in the Time & Life Building. Toward the end of 1988 the two met for dinner at Ross's apartment, and Dingman told Ross that he had put Munro and Nicholas

---

* And Steve Ross's pay. [Eds.]

in a bad position with the Time board over the governance issue. The Time executives had talked up Ross, but if the merger was ever to get back on track the Time directors needed to know that Ross had no designs on a power grab, and they needed it in writing.

Ross relented. He says, "I realized that I've got to decide what I want to do -- take off those deal blinders and say, Okay, Steve, you've been guiding the company, enjoying working with your people. You enjoy long range planning, you enjoy dreaming of tomorrow and seeing what you can do. But there's one thing you don't enjoy doing, and that's running a business on a day to day basis . . . So I said to myself, Maybe this is an opportunity." He told Dingman he would agree to retire as co-CEO in 1994 and retain the chairmanship another five years, through 1999, to give Nicholas whatever strategic help was necessary.

Dingman reported back to Munro that Ross was ready to deal again. Time's directors had viewed his reluctance to set a date for his retirement as the last roadblock to an agreement in principle. Levin and Aboodi resumed negotiations in January 1989, and over the next month closed the gap. On March 2 Ross was summoned from a Warner board meeting to a session with Aboodi, Levin, and Nicholas. They had a ratio: .465 shares of Time to be exchanged for each Warner share.

TIME FOR A COUNTERATTACK

Dick Munro felt certain that Martin Davis would not move against Time. He believed he had secured a firm promise that Davis would respect Time's independence. A few days before Davis announced his bid, Munro found out that Davis was to lunch with Joseph Flom, the famous M&A lawyer from Skadden Arps Slate Meagher & Flom who is a Time attorney. Munro, not exactly thrilled to learn that one of his attorneys was breaking bread with a potential enemy, sent word to Flom to feel Davis out one more time. According to depositions, Flom asked Davis if he knew anything about a raid on Time. Davis said something on the order of "Time? It's 12:30. I'll have the soup." Munro understood that the road to the deal wasn't mined.

Neither of Time's investment advisers, Bruce Wasserstein of Wasserstein Perella and J. Tomilson Hill of Shearson Lehman, was all that surprised by the Paramount raid. From the beginning they considered the all-stock merger a risky piece of dealmaking because it could be easily upset by a higher cash bid like Davis's. Neither Wasserstein nor Shearson was willing to recommend the deal without a commitment that Time would complete it for cash if the merger fell through.

Despite their concerns, Time's investment bankers had believed it was an auspicious time to try the merger. With the market set to digest the huge amounts of junk bonds being floated in early May in the RJR Nabisco takeover, buyers for newer issues might be scarcer, and the political environment was growing increasingly anti-buyout. These factors could discourage potential raiders, who might try to finance their attacks by issuing junk. Says one [Wasserstein Perella] staffer: "We thought the usual crazies would lie low. We went down the roster. We all knew these people and their predilections."

Still, Time's stock had begun to climb, from $110 in early March to about $135 by May 30, in anticipation of a raider's play. The investment bankers picked up Paramount's trail in late March, and it led to Morgan Stanley, the investment banking house. Morgan Stanley had marked Time for two years before the Warner merger, occasionally sharing its information with Paramount. Soon after Time and Warner announced their merger, Morgan sent Paramount a business-by-business analysis of Time Inc. with an estimate of what a potential acquirer might expect to pay for the company. And incidentally, if Paramount was interested, Morgan was ready and able to assist said potential acquirer to make the purchase. Morgan wasn't alone. Salomon Brothers smelled blood, too, and made a similar presentation to Paramount.

That Paramount was talking to Morgan Stanley did not seem all that threatening. Time's investment bankers assumed Davis was lining up a partner should someone else try to break the Time-Warner deal. He might then step in as a white knight, or buy one of the pieces. In fact, Paramount was getting calls from Bass and other interested parties about making a joint run at Time.

Davis, Munro, and Nicholas had circled one another for years. HBO signed a deal long ago to show Paramount movies and renewed the arrangement last year. The three men chatted occasionally, and several times they gathered for breakfast at the Ritz-Carlton Hotel on Central Park South, between Time's and Paramount's headquarters. Says Nicholas: "The discussions about doing things together probably lasted no more than five minutes, and they were initiated by Martin Davis, and he made comments like, 'You know, we're a great fit.' And then he would say, 'Gee Dick, you're retiring and then I can run it, and then Nick, you're younger and you can eventually run it.' That's about as substantive as it got." Davis also shared a lunch with Hollywood-hating Arthur Temple to get to know such an influential Time director a little better.

It is Munro's distinct recollection that Davis told him several times that Paramount would never attack Time. "I never asked Martin if he would make a hostile attempt to take over Time," says Munro. "He volunteered that on at least two or three occasions -- that he would never do anything hostile, period." In testimony for his lawsuit, Davis agrees with Munro on one point: They did meet. Memories diverge after that. Davis says Munro told him that Time Inc. was not interested in the motion picture business and wanted to remain just as it was.

By the end of May Paramount had hired Morgan Stanley to prepare for a raid on Time, with Paramount wheeling in the financial ammunition. Paramount paid Citibank to issue a "highly confident" letter stating that Paramount could secure the credit needed to take Time over.

Davis decided on Friday, June 2, that he would pull the trigger, and he sent relevant information to his directors so they could consider the matter over the weekend. He sounded out a small group of lieutenants but spent hours thinking by himself. Paramount's board met the following Tuesday, June 6, and Davis got the go-ahead then. The merger that had been all wrapped up and ready for delivery suddenly wasn't.

RAINMAKERS

The Time-Warner-Paramount battle brought together a monsoon's worth of Wall Street rainmakers. The Time lineup included Cravath Swaine & Moore, one of the company's law firms for more than 60 years, led by senior partner Samuel Butler and merger ace Allen Finkelson. Takeover titan Joe Flom was also on hand, as were Bruce Wasserstein, who has had a finger in nearly every big takeover pie, and Tom Hill, Shearson Lehman's top merger mogul.

Some of the bills were shocking. Cravath and other law firms jacked up their normally stiff hourly rates because of the difficulty of the assignment. Time's bill for Cravath and Skadden is $14 million and rising. Warner's fees, to be paid by Time Warner, include well over $25 million due the firm of Wachtell Lipton Rosen & Katz.

Warner's legal team included Arthur Liman of Paul Weiss Rifkind Wharton & Garrison. Liman, a legendary litigator, last made headlines as one of Ollie North's interrogators in the Senate's Iran-contra hearings. Warner also had Herbert Wachtell and Martin Lipton of Wachtell Lipton, the firm that virtually created all modern corporate defense strategies. As investment adviser, Ross had another old friend, Rohatyn of Lazard, assisted by three partners.

Paramount was outmanned but not outgunned. Davis's team included his inside counsel, Donald Oresman, a former partner at Simpson Thacher & Bartlett, Paramount's outside counsel and the law firm that represented Kohlberg Kravis Roberts in the RJR fight. Paramount often worked with Lazard and Wasserstein, but their dance cards were obviously filled. So Davis went with Morgan Stanley. Stephen Waters, ex-Shearson merger specialist and no stranger to the takeover wars, led Morgan's group.

The M&A experts are like the Pharaohs: few, rich, powerful, and incestuous. They are also hired guns, and many of them had met a few months earlier at the battle for RJR, or in even more recent business. Rohatyn had worked for RJR's special committee of the board, prominently including Martin Davis. Shearson had banked Ross

Johnson's losing hand in the RJR game. Wasserstein's was one of four banking houses employed by KKR; Morgan Stanley was another. Paramount retained Wasserstein for a year, until February, 1989, to review acquisition strategies. Lazard had represented Paramount in the recent sale of its Associates subsidiary; a Lazard partner sits on Paramount's board.

The sides chosen, the gang was ready to play again, and for big money: $16 million each for Shearson and Wasserella. Morgan signed on for pocket change, $2.5 million, but stood to gain more than $100 million in fees if Paramount's bid succeeded.

THE ACQUISITION SOLUTION

"We will not make a decision this week." Time's board convened on Thursday, June 8, to those words from Munro. The decision not to choose a response to Davis's hostile offer had several purposes, the first being to see if any other players were going to jump out of the wings. The second was to take some heat off the board and minimize the chance of committing a tactical error under pressure. The third and most important was to give the board time to carry out its strict legal duty of carefully deliberating over its next step.

Munro, livid and convinced that Davis had snookered him, sent the Paramount chief a so's-your-old-man letter flooded with invective and hyperbole. "You've changed the name of your corporation but not its character: it's still 'engulf and devour,'" he wrote. "Hostile takeovers are a little like wars: it's impossible to tell where they may end."

If Munro wanted the head of Martin Davis, an in-your-face, Pac-Man counterattack could deliver it. Just buy Paramount. Director John Opel asked the advisers for a detailed analysis of the pros and cons of Time making a counterbid for Paramount, the so-called Pac-Man defense. The company was, after all, No. 2 on Time's short list of merger-acquisition candidates, and it would be cheaper to buy than Warner.

The problem with Pac-Man attacks is that they seldom succeed, and the tactics are messy. There was, however, one intriguing potential outcome: Once Time turned the tables on Paramount, Davis might be amenable to a mutual disengagement. But then again he might not, and the strategy would be a step removed from the real goal of merging with Warner. So Time renounced Pac-Man.

Instead, Time attacked Paramount's bid on two fronts, price and conditions. Mack Rossoff of Wasserstein Perella appraised Time's value at $238 to $287 a share, a range some directors thought far too low. Later, however, Wasserstein lowered it a bit. Even by that measure, Paramount's $175-a-share offer didn't get into the ballpark. The

Time board cited the low bid as a reason for refusing to negotiate with Paramount. The advisers figured that if Paramount owned Time, Paramount's stock price might double in a year. Wasserstein and Shearson's analysis of Paramount indicated that it could afford at least $225 a share.

Paramount attached a large number of conditions to the deal. Time had the usual poison pill defenses that Paramount wanted rescinded. As part of the original merger deal with Warner, the two companies had also agreed to exchange a small amount of each other's stock. Such a swap would increase the price Paramount would have to pay, and Davis wanted the obstacle removed.

Davis's offer had a standard "financing out" condition, a technical way of saying, "If we can't get the money, the deal's off." More important, the offer was contingent on Paramount's obtaining approvals from cities and towns across the U.S. for the transfer of cable television licenses from Time to Paramount. "If theirs was such a great offer," asks Ross, "why were there 27 conditions to it?"

Rossoff, Levin, and ATC Chairman Joseph J. Collins argued at one Time board meeting that Paramount's bid had to be discounted because the company needed at least three months and more likely a year to get approvals for the cable franchise transfers. Cable franchises generally carry a right to renewal, but Collins explained that it goes out the window in any change of ownership that is not first approved by the governing municipality. Furthermore, he said, no hostile acquirer had ever asked for franchise transfers; maybe some wouldn't be granted at all. Wasserstein noted that at a discount of 1% per month compounded -- the rate of return Time shareholders expect on their investment $175 four months down the road is worth $170 today. If the payoff is a year away, the present value is only $155.

In addition to the franchise transfers, Paramount also had to obtain license transfers from the Federal Communications Commission for such things as microwave relays and radio operating permits associated with cable transmission. That too would take a while. So Paramount asked the FCC to let it establish a voting trust, run by former Defense Secretary Donald Rumsfeld, that would hold Time shares while the company pursued the license transfers. Since Paramount's offer prevented the company from buying shares until it got FCC license and cable transfers, the company planned to have the trust pay Time's shareholders immediately. Collins told the Time board the trust was probably illegal.

In response, Time launched a guerrilla attack to delay the transfer approvals. Lawyers for Time and ATC told officials in many cities and towns that Paramount's plan to set up a trust for the shares violated franchise agreements. Should city fathers be as horrified as Time Inc. at this state of affairs, Time would help them sue Paramount for illegally interfering with the franchise. Time sent to officials of about a dozen large cities all the legal papers necessary to file suit -- just fill in the blanks -- and told a couple of cities it would even pay the legal costs and indemnify the plaintiffs against countersuits by Paramount. The company also challenged Paramount's application to the FCC to set up a voting trust. ATC sued Paramount in Connecticut for illegally interfering with its business.

Such civic-mindedness is hardly the type of behavior that usually characterized the preppies of Time Inc. This is big league, sharpen-your-spikes-and-slide-in-high type stuff. Asked by Paramount's lawyers if the legal ambush was an ethical business practice, Munro was clearly uneasy: "I would have a little trouble with that. I'm not sure it's right or it's wrong, but it's marginal." (Not to director Finkelstein. He says: "One pursues the tactics that one thinks are in one's own interest. Both sides do that.")

During meetings on June 8, 11, 15, and 16, the Time board debated options. It could do nothing and risk the shareholder vote on the Warner merger. It could take on debt and pay out a big dividend to the shareholders, enough to induce them to reject Paramount's bid. Or it could change the deal. Wasserstein told the board that by selling off 1.5 million cable subscribers (out of Time's 4.3 million) plus Scott Foresman, a Time textbook publishing subsidiary, and borrowing against the remaining assets, management could in theory raise enough cash to pay the stockholders $185 to $200 a share in a restructuring or leveraged buyout.

Only remotely did Time's board consider selling the company and delivering cash to the shareholders. The directors were convinced the Warner deal would pay off down the line. Only if the company lost Paramount's suit would they consider a sale. The lawyers assured the board there would be plenty of time to do that.

Having eliminated a sale, buying Paramount, or an LBO, the board focused on Warner. Says Finkelstein: "In looking at a variety of options that [the advisers] presented . . ., I came to the conclusion Time's a very valuable company, and it's my own judgment that the acquisition of Warner will magnify that value."

During the meeting on the 15th, advisers took the board through a variety of scenarios in which Time would buy Warner for $70 a share, either in cash or in combinations of cash and securities. The advisers favored a deal they had worked out with Warner: Time would tender for about 50% of Warner's stock in cash, with payment for the rest -- the so-called back end of the deal -- to be considered later.

Warner's stock was then selling for $55.63. Directors peppered the advisers with questions about why the back end was left so vague. The answer was straightforward: The back end was open because Warner negotiated it that way. Steve Ross was leaving himself some room to make a deal within a deal.

On the 16th the [Time] board voted unanimously to acquire about 50% of Warner for $70 a share in cash and to pick up the rest for cash or securities or some combination. The board then postponed the shareholders' meeting scheduled months earlier for June 23 to vote on the original merger.

The directors debated little whether to ask Time shareholders to approve the new proposal. Time executives later explained that it would take too long to mount the educational campaign to persuade them of the deal's long-term advantages. By that time Warner might have dropped out, and the overriding concern was getting the deal done. Even though most shareholders would have preferred to take Davis's cash, Time's board was persuaded that in the long run the Warner acquisition would be more valuable to them. Says Finkelstein: "Once you believe you are acting in the best interests of the shareholders, you can continue on until you have a better argument, and I don't think we were presented with a better argument."

When Munro explained the new deal to sometimes skeptical employee groups over the next couple of days, a number of them asked about the shareholder vote. He told them bluntly: "We are going by the law." Shareholder approval was not needed. It would not be asked for. . . .

After the [Warner board approved the revised deal], Ross told Time he was triggering the stock swap that the two companies negotiated as part of the original deal. The swap put 11% of Time's shares in Warner's hands and 9% of Warner's shares in Time's, an exchange that rendered a raid more costly and difficult to execute. Ross was playing defense: If Time did get taken over by Paramount, Warner would at least get a sweet going-away gift when Time's price rose.

On June 23 Davis turned up the pressure by increasing his bid to $200 a share, a maneuver the Time directors fully expected. They held firm.

DAVIS WOWS 'EM

Martin Davis won the media battle with startling ease. As a former movie publicist he understands how the press works. And as CEO of a once wide-ranging conglomerate he knows many industries and the reporters who cover them. Davis also happens to be a terrific source: knowledgeable, articulate, and unafraid to tackle tough questions.

On this issue Davis delivered a simple message: Here's the offer, it's cash, we don't plan to sell assets, and yes, we expect to have all the approvals we need just as quickly as we can get them. Clearly Paramount's deal was not that simple, but why complicate the issue?

Davis defused Munro's charge that Paramount would violate Time's editorial integrity. Why would he want to interfere with such great magazines? He told FORTUNE he would put in writing a pledge not to meddle with the magazines' editorial operations.

Munro told everyone who would listen that Paramount's offer was illusory, inadequate, and highly conditional, and that Davis was a lying so-and-so who would have to sell huge pieces of Time to finance his debt. His protestations did not get him far.

Some Time executives and Wall Street bankers had naively assumed the press would rally around a brother media company to repel such a raid. Instead, much of the press slammed Time. Davis framed the issue in black and white and left Munro to struggle with a dozen shades of gray. The media do not write much about gray.

[Time's directors] were disappointed by the cynicism shown their efforts to make an American institution into an international one. The cancellation of the shareholder vote, the rejection of a $200-a-share cash offer without negotiating, the high-paying, long-term contracts for top executives -- there were answers on all these issues, but explaining them took time and more willing ears, and Munro didn't find enough of either. Time could not even begin talking about Davis's bid until the board had fully considered all options -- and that took days. . . . [I]n a bizarre editorial the Wall Street Journal chastised Time for trampling shareholder rights -- bizarre because common shares of Dow Jones, the Journal's owner, have one vote, while the Class B shares, controlled mostly by insiders, have ten votes each. . . .

WAR IN DELAWARE

The day was July 11, and members of the Delaware bar said it was the damnedest thing they had ever seen. The 1989 Super Bowl of corporate litigation, Paramount Communications v. Time, was under way. A mob of photographers and TV cameramen, reporters tethered to them by microphone cables, waited on the steps of the Court of Chancery in Wilmington. At 9 A.M. men and women began wheeling huge cartons of documents up the steps. The gang with the cameras followed en masse, a media mummers' parade capturing for posterity what appeared to be an office move.

About 85 stultifying degrees of thermal energy and twice that many lawyers, arbitragers, and reporters crammed into the corridor when courtroom 301 opened. An ugly scramble for seats forced the bailiffs to call for order. This being Wilmington in July the heat would have shown up anyway, but the crowd might have been thinner had everyone known what Robert D. Joffe knew.

Cravath's Joffe, lead counsel for Time, was going to argue before Chancellor William T. Allen. Joffe knew that Paramount's lawyers had deposed 13 Time and Warner executives, directors, and advisers. He knew they had copies of the minutes of board meetings, handwritten notes of phone conversations, and presentations made by Time's and Warner's bankers. And he knew they didn't have the case they went looking for.

. . . Delaware law has always given directors wide latitude in determining corporate conduct. Only in recent years have the courts tightened the reins on them, and only in a few narrow cases. In Revlon v. MacAndrews & Forbes Holdings, a 1986 case now known as Revlon, the Delaware Supreme Court ruled that if the directors decide to sell a company, they must sell it to the highest bidder. No favorites. In a 1985 case, Unocal Corp. v. Mesa Petroleum Co., called Unocal, the court ruled that directors defending their company from a raider may respond only in a reasonable way. "Reasonable" did not necessarily mean "fair" to the raider. To prevail, Paramount would have to demonstrate clearly that Time had broken the Revlon or Unocal mode rules.

Paramount built its case on two foundations, the first being that Time put itself up for sale when it agreed to merge with Warner on March 3. The argument was largely technical: When Time acceded to a swap at a .465 ratio, 60% of its shares -- a majority -- would have gone to Warner stockholders, and Paramount said that's a sale. If it was, then Time was in the so-called Revlon mode and had to sell to the highest bidder. The second and more complex argument charged Time managers with entrenching themselves at shareholder expense and responding unreasonably to Paramount's bid, violating the Unocal rule. Time's plan to acquire Warner without shareholder approval was Exhibit A.

Paramount's attorney, Melvyn L. Cantor of Simpson Thacher, tried to string together a cohesive tale of entrenchment. In a calm though faintly sardonic voice he led Allen through the negotiation of the merger ratio, the management contracts, the governance provisions, the refusal to negotiate with Paramount, the cancellation of the shareholder vote, and the new plan to acquire Warner. He also suggested that Time didn't really believe that preserving the editorial culture is vital to the company. After all, he asked, "Who is going to preserve this culture, your honor? Nick Nicholas, a man who has worked 20 years in cable television."

The closest Paramount got to a smoking gun was a memo written by Time vice chairman Levin in August of 1987. Levin, Time's Big Thinker, outlined the logic for combining with Warner and Ted Turner's TBS. (Time then owned about 12% of TBS; Time Warner owns 18%.) He sketched what he believed would be the relative positions of Time's other businesses in the future. Levin also noted, "An overriding question would still be: Have we secured the company? Is sheer size sufficient protection, or will we still need a large block of stock in friendly hands?" To Paramount, the statement was direct evidence that Time's executives desired the company for themselves. But Levin closed the memo by saying, in effect, he was just thinking out loud, a postscript that may have been vital to Time's defense.

Cantor was terrific, but his argument didn't have much law behind it, and Joffe attacked it head on. Time's decision to merge with Warner was more than two years in the making, he pointed out. If that isn't thoughtful corporate planning, what is? Warner attorney Herbert Wachtell asked the court: Had Paramount not appeared on the scene, would any court have prevented the original Time-Warner combination? The answer, as Wachtell knew, was no -- the proposed merger was clearly legal. Just because Paramount decided to make a bid for Time a day late and 50 bucks short, he argued, that was no reason for the court to stop the Time-Warner deal. Besides, for all Time had done, it had in no way prevented any future bids for the company. If Davis wanted to buy the new Time Warner, Wachtell noted, nobody was stopping him.

Chancellor Allen agreed wholeheartedly.

On appeal the Delaware Supreme Court upheld the decision unanimously. Justice Randy Holland asked Cantor, "Do you agree that Time and Warner is a good deal?" "Yes," Cantor agreed, but before he could add that Time Paramount was a better one, Holland shot back: "Then don't you lose?" You do.

The raid on Time cost Paramount more than $80 million pretax. But it resulted in Time's having to borrow $12 billion, an enormous debt load. As a result Time Warner paid $451 million in interest and financing fees in this year's third quarter and took a $40 million earnings hit for amortization of goodwill, contributing to a loss for the quarter of $176 million. The question is inevitable: Is this the reason Davis pulled the raid? "Just look at the depositions," says Davis. "You'll see that there isn't a shred of truth" to the charge.

A better question might be: Assuming Paramount really wanted to own Time, did it choose the right tactics? A lawyer involved on the Time side says, "Morgan Stanley had to know that Time was worth at least $225 a share. Why give the board a reason to reject you by coming in so low?" Court documents show Morgan Stanley valued Time at a minimum of $217 a share. Some investment bankers wonder why Davis didn't play the last card: bid for the merged Time Warner after prearranging a deal with some third party to take Warner off his hands. After losing in court Davis said he was not interested in further pursuit of Time Warner. He did not say he was not interested forever.

IS BIGGER BETTER?

Dick Munro, Nick Nicholas, and Steve Ross have their dream come true: Time Warner is the largest media empire on earth. Now these three men have some substantial promises to keep in the face of considerable uncertainty. They must show that an important premise of the deal was valid -- that the companies can enhance the value of print, video, and music and create new profit opportunities together. They must pay off at least some of Time Warner's $12 billion debt without divesting the core businesses of magazines, pay TV, cable systems, and film and record production -- though a rise in interest rates could poleax their repayment forecasts.

Munro must show that he was right to spend $13.1 billion for a company that depends enormously on one man. For now he acknowledges that "If I'm wrong about Steve Ross, it will be the biggest mistake I've ever made." Nicholas will eventually have to show that he was worth signing up as CEO five years in advance. All three executives will have to demonstrate that they merit their extraordinary long-term contracts.

Perhaps most important, Munro and Nicholas will have to show that their fundamental act of stewardship in this deal -- repulsing a highly conditional offer for Time shares in favor of a highly leveraged acquisition -- was sound. Remember that at one point they discounted the value of Paramount's offer by assuming Time investors demanded a 12% annual return. They also argued that their deal might not look as good as Paramount's in the short term but would be far more valuable in the long term. Fair enough. The $200 a share Time stockholders didn't get, at 12% a year, will be worth $352 in five years, $621 in ten years. The stock was recently around $140. The managers of Time Warner must now demonstrate that bigger is better. And in a big way.

No transaction turns out precisely as expected, but the period following Time's acquisition of Warner had some special surprises. First, the line of succession at Time-Warner turned out differently than had been expected. The co-CEO structure by which Nick Nicholas and Steve Ross would jointly run the combined company did not work out. In 1992, Nicholas was fired and Ross took over the lead management role, elevating Gerald Levin to the lead Time role. Late that same year Ross died, leaving Levin as the sole CEO.

The second surprise -- at least for Time shareholders -- was in the post-transaction performance of Time-Warner stock. Recall that the Time directors thought the company was worth much more than Wasserstein Perella's estimate of $238 to $287. Recall too that the stock would have to be worth $352 a share after 5 years to equal a 12% return on the $200 a share that Paramount had offered. Figure 1-8 shows Time-Warner's actual stock price from 1988 through 1992 along with a line showing the value of Paramount's $200 per share offer if it had been received by Time's shareholders and invested at a more conservative 10% return.

Figure 1-8
TIME-WARNER STOCK PRICE, Jan. 4, 1988 - Sept. 10, 1992

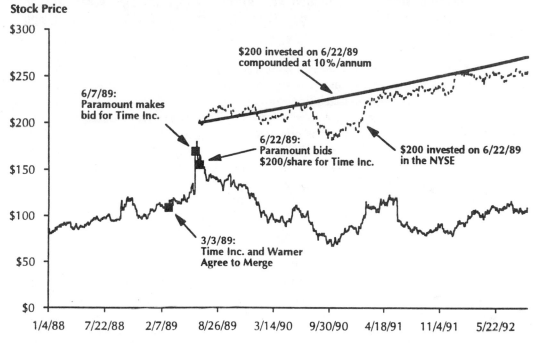

Source: Cornerstone Research

65

Modern financial theory is commonly treated as beginning in the late 1950's. Prior to that time, leading finance texts were rich in institutional detail, but offered little in the way of comprehensive theory.[1] Their normative statements on issues like the proper capital structure for a corporation were sometimes logically inconsistent and, in any event, could not be empirically tested. They were thus ad hoc both theoretically and empirically.

The late 1950's marked a shift in scholarly emphasis from description to theory, and finance began to change from a descriptive endeavor oriented in large measure to practitioners, to a specialized discipline with the theoretical rigor and mathematical complexity associated with academic economics. This shift was facilitated by the introduction in 1964 of computer tapes prepared by the Center for Research in Security Prices at the University of Chicago (CRSP). These tapes originally contained daily and monthly closing stock prices, dividends and changes in capital structure for all stocks listed on the New York and American Stock Exchanges. They have recently been extended to larger over-the-counter stocks. This database encouraged the development of statistical techniques that have made many of the theoretical statements of modern finance theory almost uniquely testable.[2]

This Part surveys the aspects of modern finance theory necessary to understand how business transactions are valued. It thus provides a foundation for later analysis of the motives for acquisitions and how business lawyers might increase transaction value. For example, it is commonly claimed that a company's publicly reported earnings are an important determinant of stock price, whether or not these earnings reflect actual cash flows. This assertion, in turn, has fueled a major controversy over the "right" way to account for acquisitions, with both sides taking seriously the idea that reported, as opposed to real earnings, influence share price. At bottom, this conflict is over what factors do or should determine the value of a capital asset -- in this case, do or should reported earnings influence the price of corporate stock, independent of the underlying cash flows? As a result, both finance theory and empirical tests of the theory are directly relevant.

Similarly, important elements of corporate law, such as when acquiring company and target company shareholders get to vote on an acquisition, depend on whether

---

[1] See, e.g., Arthur Dewing, *The Financial Policy of Corporations* (2d ed. 1953).

[2] For a more detailed history of modern financial theory, see Clifford Smith, *The Theory of Corporate Finance: An Historical Overview*, in *The Modern Theory of Corporate Finance* 3 (Clifford Smith ed. 2d ed. 1990).

different transaction *forms* are substantively similar. If similarity is taken to mean "of equal value," then understanding the factors that determine value is central to understanding when different forms of transactions should be subject to the same legal rules. Understanding the theory of asset valuation, and the techniques for testing the predictions of finance theory, is thus crucial to understanding and evaluating both the applicable law and the various motives for acquisitions.

A second point, less familiar but equally important, should also be stressed. Individuals often seek to maximize the value of their assets. As a result, understanding how assets are valued provides a useful way to predict, and to guide, private behavior. Suppose, for example, that you are negotiating the terms of a loan agreement on behalf of the lender. How do you anticipate what post-transaction behavior by the borrower the lender need to be protected against? Put differently, how might shareholders seek to increase their wealth at the creditors' expense? Finance theory, by specifying how the borrower's actions can shift value between shareholders and creditors, provides a coherent framework in which to address the problem. This will be particularly evident in our examination of option pricing in Chapter 7, and in our consideration of the private ordering aspects of corporate acquisitions in Part VI. Finance theory is thus important for both the public ordering and private ordering aspects of business transactions.

Chapters 2 and 3 lay the groundwork for the study of valuation. Chapter 2 examines valuation in a simple world where there is no risk -- the size and timely receipt of all future cash flows is certain. Chapters 3 and 4 introduce the concept of risk -- how should one value future cash flows when their size and eventual receipt are uncertain? We consider the uses and limits of the Capital Asset Pricing Model and alternative models of how assets should be priced under uncertainty. Chapter 5 examines the Efficient Capital Market Hypothesis, a central paradigm of modern finance theory. Here the issue is what mechanisms cause market prices to approach or depart from the "correct" values that asset pricing theory predicts. Chapter 5 then moves to a more practical perspective. How can we evaluate whether a transaction or other event has *changed* the value of a capital asset? Here the standard technique is regression analysis, especially cumulative abnormal returns analysis of stock price changes. Finally, Chapter 7 focuses on valuation of a different kind of asset -- an option -- and introduces a second paradigm of modern finance: option pricing theory. We will return to each of the concepts examined in this Part -- the time value of money, capital asset pricing, market efficiency, cumulative abnormal returns, and option pricing -- throughout our analysis of corporate acquisitions and the business lawyer's potential for creating value.

CHAPTER 2: VALUATION UNDER CERTAINTY

We begin learning how business transactions are valued by considering how assets would be valued in a world of complete certainty. In such a world, the only distinction between different assets is the quantity and timing of the future cash flows they generate. There is no risk (1) of not actually receiving the money, nor (2) of receiving a different amount than expected, nor (3) of receiving the money at a different time than expected.

This world of complete certainty, of course, is entirely artificial. Even so certain a cash flow as the interest payment on a short term Treasury bill is subject to the risk of change in the *inflation* rate -- the risk that the *real* amount received will purchase a different amount than expected, because inflation turns out to be higher or lower than expected over the investment period. A short-term Treasury bill is also subject to the risk of change in the *reinvestment* rate -- the risk that the rate of interest at which one can reinvest funds will change during the period of an investment.

In this simple world, value depends only on the *time value of money*. The concept of time value is equivalent to *opportunity cost*. A dollar now is worth more than one to be received in a year because a dollar received now can be swapped for goods that can be consumed now, rather than a year from now, or invested for a year at a positive rate of interest, so that it produces more than one dollar a year from now. Section A of this Chapter develops the mathematics of the time value of money. Section B applies the concept of time value to the task of valuing a stream of income across time.

A. The Time Value of Money

JAMES VAN HORNE [1]
FINANCIAL MANAGEMENT AND POLICY
13-24 (7th ed. 1986)

In any economy in which time preferences of individuals, firms, and governments result in positive rates of interest, the time value of money is an important concept. For example, stockholders will place a higher value on an investment that promises returns over the next five years than on an investment that promises identical returns for years six through ten. Consequently, the timing of expected future cash flows is extremely important in the investment of funds. In essence, the methods proposed allow us to isolate differences in the timing of cash flows for various investments by discounting these cash flows to their present value.

Compound Interest and Terminal Values

The notion of compound interest is central to understanding the mathematics of finance. The term itself merely implies that interest paid on a loan or an investment is added to the principal. As a result, interest is earned on interest. This concept can be used [for] a class of problems illustrated in the following examples. To begin with, consider a person who has $100 in a savings account. If the interest rate is 8% compounded annually, how much will he have at the end of a year? Setting up the problem, we solve for the terminal value of the account at the end of the year (TV_1)

$$TV_1 = \$100(1 + .08) = \$108$$

[If left for a second year, the $108 earns 8% interest again, and] becomes $116.64, as $8 in interest is earned on the initial $100 and $0.64 is earned on the $8 interest paid at the end of the first year. In other words, interest is earned on previously earned interest, hence the name compound interest. Therefore the terminal value at the end of the second year is $100 times 1.08 squared, or times 1.1664. Thus,

$$TV_{ii} = \$100(1.08)^2 = \$116.64$$

At the end of three years, the depositor would have

$$TV_3 = \$100(1 + .08)^3 = \$125.97$$

Looked at in a different way, $100 grows to $108 at the end of the first year if the interest rate is 8%, and when we multiply this amount by 1.08 we obtain $116.64 at the end of the second year. Multiplying $116.64 by 1.08, we obtain $125.97 at the end of the third year.

Similarly, at the end of n years, the terminal value of a deposit is

$$TV_n = X_{o\%i}(1 + r)^n \qquad (2\text{-}1)$$

where X_o = amount of savings at the beginning
r = interest rate

A calculator makes the equation very simple to use.

Table 2-1, showing the terminal values for our example problem at the end of years 1 through 10, illustrates the concept of interest being earned on interest. Equation 2-1 is our fundamental formula for calculating terminal values. Obviously, the greater the interest rate r, and the greater the number of periods n, the greater the terminal value.

Table 2-1
Illustration of Compound Interest with $100 Initial Deposit and 8% Interest

Period	Beginning Value	Interest Earned During Period (8% of Beginning Value)	Terminal Value
1	$100.00	$ 8.00	$108.00
2	108.00	8.64	116.64
3	116.64	9.33	125.97
4	125.97	10.08	136.05
5	136.05	10.88	146.93
6	146.93	11.76	158.69
7	158.69	12.69	171.38
8	171.38	13.71	185.09
9	185.09	14.81	199.90
10	199.90	15.99	215.89

Although our concern has been with interest rates, the concept involved applies to compound growth of any sort. Suppose that the earnings of a firm are $100,000, but we expect them to grow at a 10% compound rate. At the end of years 1 through 5 they will be as follows:

Year	Growth Factor	Expected Earnings
1	(1.10)	$110,000
2	$(1.10)^2$	121,000
3	$(1.10)^3$	133,100
4	$(1.10)^4$	146,410
5	$(1.10)^5$	161,051

Similarly, we can determine the level at the end of so many years for other problems involving compound growth. . . .

Tables of Terminal Values. Using Equation 2-1, one can derive tables of terminal values (also known as future values). An example is shown in Table 2-2 for interest rates of 1 to [10%]. In the 8% column, we note that the terminal values shown for $1 invested at this compound rate correspond to our calculations for $100 in Table 2-1. Notice, too, that in rows involving two or more years, the proportional increase in terminal value becomes greater as the interest rate rises. This heightened growth is particularly impressive when we look a century ahead. A dollar deposited today will be worth only $2.70 if the interest rate is 1%, but it will fatten to [$13,780.59] if the interest rate is [10%]. Behold (or let your heirs behold) the wonders of compound interest!

Table 2-2
Terminal Value of One Dollar at the End of n Years

Year	1%	2%	3%	4%	5%	6%	7%	8%	9%	10%
1	1.0100	1.0200	1.0300	1.0400	1.0500	1.0600	1.0700	1.0800	1.0900	1.1000
2	1.0201	1.0404	1.0609	1.0816	1.1025	1.1236	1.1449	1.1664	1.1881	1.2100
3	1.0303	1.0612	1.0927	1.1249	1.1576	1.1910	1.2250	1.2597	1.2950	1.3310
4	1.0406	1.0824	1.1255	1.1699	1.2155	1.2625	1.3108	1.3605	1.4116	1.4641
5	1.0510	1.1041	1.1593	1.2167	1.2763	1.3382	1.4026	1.4693	1.5386	1.6105
6	1.0615	1.1262	1.1941	1.2653	1.3401	1.4185	1.5077	1.5869	1.6771	1.7716
7	1.0721	1.1487	1.2299	1.3159	1.4071	1.5036	1.6058	1.7138	1.8280	1.9487
8	1.0829	1.1717	1.2668	1.3686	1.4775	1.5938	1.7182	1.8509	1.9926	2.1436
9	1.0937	1.1951	1.3048	1.4233	1.5513	1.6895	1.8385	1.9990	2.1719	2.3579
10	1.1046	1.2190	1.3439	1.4802	1.6289	1.7908	1.9672	2.1589	2.3674	2.5937
11	1.1157	1.2434	1.3842	1.5395	1.7103	1.8983	2.1049	2.3316	2.5804	2.8531
12	1.1268	1.2682	1.4258	1.6010	1.7959	2.0122	2.2522	2.5182	2.8127	3.1384
13	1.1381	1.2936	1.4685	1.6651	1.8856	2.1329	2.4098	2.7196	3.0658	3.4523
14	1.1495	1.3195	1.5126	1.7317	1.9799	2.2609	2.5785	2.9372	3.3417	3.7975
15	1.1610	1.3459	1.5580	1.8009	2.0789	2.3966	2.7590	3.1722	3.6425	4.1772
20	1.2202	1.4859	1.8061	2.1911	2.6533	3.2071	3.8697	4.6610	5.6044	6.7275
25	1.2824	1.6406	2.0938	2.6658	3.3864	4.2919	5.4274	6.8485	8.6231	10.835
50	1.6446	2.6916	4.3839	7.1067	11.467	18.420	29.457	46.902	74.358	117.39
100	2.7048	7.2446	19.219	50.505	131.50	339.30	867.71	2,199.8	5,529.0	13,780

Compounding More Than Once a Year

Up to now, we have assumed that interest was paid annually. Although this assumption is easiest to work with, we consider now the relationship between terminal value and interest rates for different periods of compounding. To begin, suppose that interest is paid semiannually, and $100 is deposited in a savings account at 8% [annual interest -- that is, 4% interest is paid every 6 months]. The terminal value at the end of six months will be

$$TV_{1/2} = \$100(1 + .08/2) = \$104.00$$

and at the end of a year it would be

$$TV_1 = \$100(1 + .08/2)^2 = \$108.16$$

This amount compares with $108.00 if interest were paid only once a year. The $0.16 difference is attributable to the fact that during the second 6 months, interest is earned on the $4.00 in interest paid at the end of the first 6 months. The more times during a year that interest is paid, the greater the terminal value at the end of a given year.

The general formula for solving for the terminal value at the end of year n where interest is paid m times a year [at an annual rate of r] is

$$TV_n = X_o(1 + r/m)^{mn} \tag{2-2}$$

To illustrate, suppose that in our previous example interest were paid quarterly and that we wished again to know the terminal value at the end of one year. It would be

$$TV_1 = \$100(1 + .08/4)^4 = \$108.24$$

which, of course, is higher than that which occurs either with semiannual or annual compounding.

The terminal value at the end of 3 years for the above example with quarterly interest payments is

$$TV_3 = \$100(1 + .08/4)^{12} = \$126.82$$

Compared to a terminal value with semiannual compounding of

$$TV_3 = \$100(1 + .08/2)^6 = \$126.53$$

and [a terminal value with] annual compounding of

$$TV_3 = \$100(1 + .08/1)^3 = \$125.97$$

The greater the number of years, the greater the difference in terminal values arrived at by two different methods of compounding.

As m approaches infinity, the term $(1 + r/m)^{mn}$ approaches e^{rn}, where e is approximately 2.71828 and is defined as

$$e \quad = \quad \lim_{m \to \infty} \quad (1 + 1/m)^m \qquad (2\text{-}3)$$

with ∞ being the sign for infinity . . . . [C]ontinuous compounding results in the maximum possible terminal value at the end of n periods for a given rate of interest. As m is increased in Eq. (2-2), the terminal value increases at a decreasing rate until ultimately it approaches the terminal value achieved with continuous compounding.

Present Values

Not all of us live by the credit card alone; some like to save now and buy later. For a $700 purchase one year from now, how much will you have to put aside in a bank paying 8% interest on one-year deposits? How much must you put aside in order to have $700 one year hence? If we let A_1 represent the amount of money you wish to have one year from now, PV the amount saved, and k the annual interest rate, we have

$$A_1 = PV(1 + k) \qquad (2\text{-}4)$$

For our example problem, this becomes

$$\$700 = PV(1.08)$$

Solving for PV, we obtain

$$PV = \$700/1.08 = \$648.15$$

Deposit $648.15 today and take home $700 one year hence. Stated another way, $648.15 is the *present value* of $700 to be received at the end of 1 year when the interest rate involved is 8%.

The present value of a sum to be received two years from now is

$$PV = A_2/(1 + k)^2 \qquad (2\text{-}5)$$

which for our example problem would be

$$PV = \$700/(1.08)^2 = \$700/1.1664 = \$600.14$$

Thus $700 two years from now has a lower present value than $700 one year from now. That is the whole idea of the time value of money.

In solving present-value problems, it is useful to express the interest factor separately from the amount to be received in the future. For example, our problem can be expressed as

$$PV = \$700 \times [1/(1.08)^2] = \$600.14$$

In this way we are able to isolate the interest factor, and this isolation facilitates present-value calculations. In such calculations, the interest rate is known as the *discount rate*, and henceforth we will refer to it as such.

So far we have considered present-value calculations for amounts of money to be received only 1 and 2 years in the future; however, the principles are the same for amounts to be received further in the future. The present value of $1 to be received at the end of n years is

$$PV = 1/(1 + k)^n \tag{2-6}$$

The present value of $1 to be received five years from now when the discount rate is 10%, is

$$\$1 \times [1/(1.10)^5] = \$.62092$$

The dollar we shall get 5 years from now is worth approximately 62 cents today if the discount rate is 10%.

Fortunately, present-value tables [and calculators] relieve us of having to make these calculations every time we have a problem to solve. Table 2-3 . . . shows present values of $1, known as discount factors, for discount rates from 1% to [10%] and for periods 1 through 25 [years] in the future. We see in the table that for a 10% discount rate, the discount factor for five years in the future is .62092, just as we calculated. For 1 year, 2 years, and 3 years in the future, we see that the discount factors are .90909, .82645, and .75131, respectively. These discount factors are merely the result of the following calculations: $1/(1.10)$; $1/(1.10)^2$; and $1/(1.10)^3$.

Table 2-3
Present Value of One Dollar Due at the End of *n* Years

n	1%	2%	3%	4%	5%	6%	7%	8%	9%	10%
1	.99010	.98039	.97007	.96154	.95238	.94340	.93458	.92593	.91743	.90909
2	.98030	.96117	.94260	.92456	.90703	.89000	.87344	.85734	.84168	.82645
3	.97059	.94232	.91514	.88900	.86384	.83962	.81630	.79383	.77218	.75131
4	.96098	.92385	.88849	.85480	.82270	.79209	.76290	.73503	.70843	.68301
5	.95147	.90573	.86261	.82193	.78353	.74726	.71299	.68058	.64993	.62092
6	.94204	.88797	.83748	.79031	.74622	.70496	.66634	.63017	.59627	.56447
7	.93272	.87056	.81309	.75992	.71068	.66506	.62275	.58349	.54703	.51316
8	.92348	.85349	.78941	.73069	.67684	.62741	.58201	.54027	.50187	.46651
9	.91434	.83675	.76642	.70259	.64461	.59190	.54393	.50025	.46043	.42410
10	.90529	.82035	.74409	.67556	.61391	.55839	.50835	.46319	.42241	.38554
11	.89632	.80426	.72242	.64958	.58468	.52679	.47509	.42888	.38753	.35049
12	.88745	.78849	.70138	.62460	.55684	.49697	.44401	.39711	.35553	.31863
13	.87866	.77303	.68095	.60057	.53032	.46884	.41496	.36770	.32618	.28966
14	.86996	.75787	.66112	.57747	.50507	.44230	.38782	.34046	.29925	.26333
15	.86135	.74301	.64186	.55526	.48102	.41726	.36245	.31524	.27454	.23939
16	.85282	.72845	.62317	.53391	.45811	.39365	.33873	.29189	.25187	.21763
17	.84438	.71416	.60502	.51337	.43630	.37136	.31657	.27027	.23107	.19784
18	.83602	.70016	.58739	.49363	.41552	.35034	.29586	.25025	.21199	.17986
19	.82774	.68643	.57029	.47464	.39573	.33051	.27651	.23171	.19449	.16351
20	.81954	.67297	.55367	.45639	.37689	.31180	.25842	.21455	.17843	.14864
21	.81143	.65978	.53755	.43883	.35894	.29415	.24151	.19866	.16370	.13513
22	.80340	.64684	.52189	.42195	.34185	.27750	.22571	.18394	.15018	.12285
23	.79544	.63416	.50669	.40573	.32557	.26180	.21095	.17031	.13778	.11168
24	.78757	.62172	.49193	.39012	.31007	.24698	.19715	.15770	.12640	.10153
25	.77977	.60958	.47760	.37512	.29530	.23300	.18425	.14602	.11597	.09230

If we had an uneven series of cash flows -- $1 one year hence, $3 two years hence, and $2 three years from now -- the present value of this series, using a 10% discount rate, would be

PV of $1 to be received at end of 1 year	= $1(0.90909)	=	0.90909
PV of $3 to be received at end of 2 years	= $3(0.82645)	=	2.47935
PV of $2 to be received at end of 3 years	= $2(0.75131)	=	1.50262
Present value of series		=	$4.89106

With a present-value table, we are able to calculate the present value for any series of future cash flows in this manner.

Present Value of an Annuity. The procedure can be simplified for a series of even cash flows. A series of this sort is known as an *annuity*. Suppose that $1 is to be received at the end of each of the next 3 years. The calculation of the present value of this stream, using a 10% discount rate, would be

PV of $1 to be received in 1 year	=	.90909
PV of $1 to be received in 2 years	=	.82645
PV of $1 to be received in 3 years	=	.75131
Present value of series	=	$2.48685

With an even series of future cash flows, it is unnecessary to go through these calculations. The discount factor, 2.48685, can be applied directly. Simply multiply $1 by 2.48685 to obtain $2.48685. Present-value tables for even series of cash flows [have been developed that] allow us to look up the appropriate [annuity] factor. . . .

If we trace across any of the rows in Table 2-3, we see that the higher the discount rate, the lower the discount factor. It is not a linear relationship because the discount factor decreases less and less as the discount rate increases. Therefore the present value of an amount of money to be received in the future decreases at a decreasing rate as the discount rate increases. The relationship is illustrated in Figure 2-1. At a zero rate of discount, the present value of $1 to be received in the future is $1. In other words, there is no time value of money. . . . As the discount rate approaches infinity, the present value of the future $1 approaches zero. . . .

Figure 2-1
Relationship Between Present Value and the Discount Rate

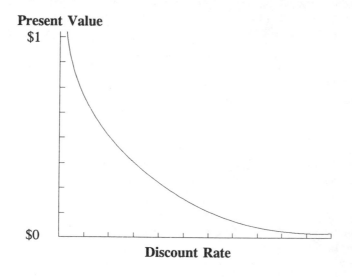

76

Present Value When Interest Is Compounded More Then Once a Year

When interest is compounded more than once a year, the formula for calculating present values must be revised along the same lines as for the calculation of terminal value. Instead of dividing the future cash flow by $(1 + k)^n$ as we do when annual compounding is involved, the present value is determined by

$$PV = A_n/(1 + k/m)^{mn} \qquad \text{(2-7)}$$

where, as before, A_n is the cash flow at the end of year n, m is the number of times a year interest is compounded, and k is the discount rate. The present value of $100 to be received at the end of year 3, the discount rate being 10% compounded quarterly, is

$$PV = \$100/(1 + .10/4)^{4 \times 3} = \$74.36$$

. . . [T]he fewer times a year the discount rate is compounded, the greater the present value. This relationship is just the opposite of that for terminal values. To illustrate the relationship between present value and the number of times a year the discount rate is compounded, consider again our example involving $100 to be received at the end of 3 years with a discount rate of 10%. The following present values result from various compounding intervals.

Compounding	Present Value
Annual	$75.13
Semiannual	74.62
Quarterly	74.36
Monthly	74.17
Continuously	74.08

We see that the present value decreases but at a decreasing rate as the compounding interval shortens, the limit being continuous compounding.

Internal Rate of Return or Yield

The internal rate of return or yield for an investment is the discount rate that equates the present value of the expected cash outflows with the present value of the expected inflows. Mathematically, it is represented by that rate, r, such that

$$\sum_{t=0}^{n} [A_t/(1 + r)^t] = 0 \qquad \text{(2-8)}$$

where A_t is the cash flow for period t, whether it be a net cash outflow or inflow, n is the last period in which a cash flow is expected, and the capital Greek sigma [Σ] denotes the sum of discounted cash flows at the end of periods 0 through n. If the initial cash outlay or cost occurs at time 0, Eq. (2-11) can be expressed as

$$A_0 = [A_1/(1+r) + (A_2/(1+r)^{2)} + \ldots + (A_n/(1+r)^n \qquad (2\text{-}9)$$

Thus r is the rate that discounts the stream of future cash flows (A_1 through A_n) to equal the initial outlay at time 0 -- A_0. [The higher the internal rate of return, the better the investment, other things equal.] We implicitly assume that the cash inflows received from the investment are reinvested to realize the same rate of return as r. . . .

To illustrate the use of Equation 2-9, suppose that we have an investment opportunity that calls for a cash outlay at time 0 of $18,000 and is expected to provide cash inflows of $5,600 at the end of each of the next five years. The problem can be expressed as

$$18{,}000 \;=\; \frac{5{,}600}{(1+r)} \;+\; \frac{5{,}600}{(1+r)^2} \;+\; \frac{5{,}600}{(1+r)^3} \;+\; \frac{5{,}600}{(1+r)^4} \;+\; \frac{5{,}600}{(1+r)^5}$$

Solving for the internal rate of return, r, involves an iterative procedure [commonly done using calculators or computer programs]. . . .

B. Time Value in a Transactional Context: Discounting in Project Choice

The discounting techniques developed in Section A reflect the impact of the time value of money on the value of a stream of income. In our assumed world of certainty, this offers a simple way to value an asset. The asset's value is the *present value* of the income it generates over its life. Present value is a summary statistic for the size of that income stream that takes into account when income will be received.

The *net present value* of an investment opportunity is the present value of the cash inflows that it generates, minus the present value of the cash outlays that it requires. Putting money in a bank at the market rate of interest has a net present value of zero -- the present value of the cash to be received just equals the present value of the cash deposited. Thus, net present value is a summary statistic for the desirability of an investment, compared to the alternative of putting money in a bank.

The next step in understanding how transactions are valued is to apply the discounting techniques to the choice among different investments -- typically called "capital budgeting." Put simply, capital budgeting is the analysis by which a firm or an individual decides how to invest resources. A number of different techniques are commonly used in capital budgeting, but all share the same three stages. First, the amount and timing of the income stream that an investment will generate is estimated. Second, net present value, internal rate of return, or another summary statistic for the income stream is calculated. Third, the summary statistic is compared to an acceptance criterion that represents the least favorable investment the firm will accept. Investments that meet or exceed the acceptance criterion are made, those that do not are rejected.

Because we are still working in a world of certainty, the first step in capital budgeting -- estimating the amount and timing of an investment's income stream -- can be passed over. We can assume that the amounts and timing of these cash flows are known. It is at the second stage -- computing a summary statistic for the income stream from an investment -- that different capital budgeting techniques diverge. Most important, the techniques differ fundamentally in the extent to which the summary statistic takes into account the time value of money.

1. Average Rate of Return and Payback Methods

Two frequently used techniques, the average rate of return method and the payback method, do not adequately account for the time value of money. The average rate of return technique involves dividing the average annual accounting net profit from a project by the project's average book value. The result is a measure of the average return on the amount invested in the project. Suppose that Project X requires a $9,000 investment in a machine with a useful life of 3 years. The project will result in a cash flow of $4,500 in each of three years. If the up-front cost of the machine is taken into account prorata over the three years, through a $3,000 per year charge for *depreciation*, the annual net profit will be $1,500:

Project X	Year 1	Year 2	Year 3
Cash Flow	$4,500	$4,500	$4,500
Depreciation	3,000	3,000	3,000
Net Profit	$1,500	$1,500	$1,500

Average net profit = [$1,500 + $1,500 + $1,500]/3 = $1,500/year

The project's average book value is calculated as follows:

Project X	Year 1	Year 2	Year 3
Initial Investment	$9,000	$9,000	$9,000
Cumulative Depreciation	3,000	6,000	9,000
Net Book Value	$6,000	$3,000	$ 0

Average book value = [($6,000 + $3,000 + $0)/3] = $4,500

And average rate of return is:

[average net profit/average book value] = [$1,500/$4,500] = 33.3%

The project will be accepted if this average rate of return exceeds the minimum acceptance rate that the firm sets as part of its capital budgeting process.

The problem with the average rate of return technique is that it ignores the time value of money: all cash flows are treated equally whether they are received in the first year or in the last. This can be seen by comparing Project X with Project Y, which has the same cash flow, initial investment and depreciation schedule, and thus has the same average rate of return as Project X, but has a different cash flow pattern.

Net Profit from Projects With Different Cash Flow Patterns

	Project X	Project Y
Year 1	$1,500	$3,000
Year 2	1,500	0
Year 3	$1,500	$1,500

The average rate of return technique treats both cash flows as equivalent. If the time value of money is taken into account, even visual inspection of the cash flows shows that Project Y is preferable to Project X.

The payback period approach is somewhat of an improvement in this regard. Here the idea is to calculate the number of periods necessary for the cash flows from a project to repay its initial investment. For example, the payback period for Project X -- the time necessary to recover the initial investment -- is two years. The cash flow, *before* depreciation, is $4,500 per year, so it takes two years to recover the initial $9,000

80

investment. The project will be accepted if this period is shorter than the maximum payback period that the firm sets as part of its capital budgeting process.

Other things equal, a project whose cash flows come sooner is preferable to one whose cash flows come later. Nonetheless, the method still fails to adequately account for the time value of money. It gives no value to cash flows that are received after the project's initial investment is repaid. As a result, projects with identical payback periods and identical returns *within* the payback period are deemed equivalent even if one has a large return in the year after the payback period ended while the other does not. In this sense, the payback period technique *over*-discounts payments outside the payback period.

The payback period technique also takes no account of differences in the timing of receipts during the payback period. For example, the payback period for Projects *X* and *Y* is the same -- two years -- so the payback technique, like the average rate of return technique, would treat the two projects as equivalent, despite the faster receipt of income from Project *Y*. In this sense, the payback period *under*-discounts payments within the payback period.

The average rate of return and the payback period techniques fail to provide appropriate guidance for capital budgeting decisions because they don't fully take into account the time value of money. We now turn to two techniques for evaluating potential investments that do fully consider time value.

2. Internal Rate of Return and Net Present Value Methods

The mathematics of the internal rate of return and net present value techniques are described in the Van Horne excerpt in Section A of this Chapter. Both are discounted cash flow techniques that reduce future cash receipts to present value in determining the value of the asset giving rise to the payments. The internal rate of return technique solves for the discount rate -- the internal rate of return -- at which the net present value of the investment is zero: the present value of the cash invested equals in a project to the present value of the cash flows from the project. If the internal rate of return exceeds the minimum rate set by the firm as part of its capital budgeting process, the project is undertaken.

The net present value rule discounts to present value each cash outflow (including the original investment) and each cash inflow, using the rate of return available in the market for comparable investments as the discount rate. If net present value is positive, the project is undertaken.

Both techniques have substantial support in the financial community. Under most circumstances, the internal rate of return technique, with a minimum acceptable rate set equal to the rate of return available in the market for comparable investments, will yield the same results as the net present value technique. One important difference, however, is the discount rate each technique uses to reduce intermediate cash flows from a project to present value.[3] The internal rate of return technique assumes that all intermediate cash flows can be reinvested during the life of the project at the internal rate of return earned from the project. Thus, the actual rate of return achieved by a project will equal the internal rate of return calculated in the capital budgeting decision *only* if the intermediate cash flows generated by the project can be reinvested in an equally profitable investment. A similar problem exists with the net present value technique. Here the assumption is that all intermediate cash flows can be reinvested at the chosen discount rate. Again, the actual return will match the initial calculation *only* if opportunities for reinvestment at the discount rate exist when the cash flows are received.

It is often argued that the net present value technique is preferable because the discount rate chosen is presumably the external cost of capital, a market rate, while the discount rate implicit in the internal rate of return technique is the return associated with a particular project, which is less likely to be duplicable on reinvestment. However, both reinvestment rate assumptions highlight the artificiality of our assumed zero-risk world, and the difficulty associated with using these techniques in a world with uncertainty.

An example helps clarify the point. Suppose you are the Chief Financial Officer of an insurance company with $100,000 to invest. Your actuaries tell you that five years from now you will need $190,000 to pay anticipated life insurance claims. You have an opportunity to lend $100,000 for five years, with annual interest payments at 14% which is, we will assume, the current market rate of interest. The future value of $100,000 in five years at this rate of interest is:

$$TV_5 = \$100,000 \times (1.14)^5 = \$192,541$$

What keeps you in the office, and away from the beach, is the knowledge that, even if there is no *credit* risk -- no risk that the borrower won't make all payments in full and on time -- there is still a substantial risk that you won't earn enough over five years to meet the anticipated claims. The future value calculation assumes that the 14% annual interest payments can be reinvested at the same 14% rate. You still face *reinvestment*

---

[3] Among the difficulties with the use of the internal rate of return in contrast to net present value is the potential for a project to have multiple internal rates of return when cash flows change signs more than once over the life of the project. This can happen for a project that requires an initial investment, generates some cash, and then requires an additional mid-stream investment of capital. Problems also exist in taking into account the different scale of alternative projects. Because internal rate of return is a relative measure of return, while net present value is an absolute measure, project rankings will differ when the projects are of different size. A small project with a high internal rate of return may generate fewer dollars, and therefore have a lower net present value, than a large project. See Richard Brealey & Stewart Myers, *Principles of Corporate Finance* 79-88 (4th ed. 1991).

risk--the risk that this assumption will prove wrong. If interest rates drop during the five years, your actual reinvestment rate will be lower than 14% and your company may not have $190,000 on hand when the anticipated claims are presented for payment in five years. Present value and future value calculations ignore that risk.

Thus, if there is no credit risk, valuation techniques that are designed for a world without risk fail when reinvestment risk (or inflation risk) is introduced. This is not to say that the discounting techniques examined in this Chapter are not helpful. Rather, they are designed to deal with one aspect of valuation -- the time value of money. More complete valuation requires adding additional factors to take into account various kinds of risk.

Problems to Accompany Chapter 2

1. Assume that the market rate of interest is 6%. How much must you invest today to have $1 at the end of one year?

2. Assume that the market rate of interest is 6%. How much will you have in one year if you invest $1 today?

3. Assume that the market rate of interest is 12% and that:

    a. you have $162.53 in your bank account today
    b. you opened the account exactly one year ago
    c. your initial deposit was the only deposit you've made
    d. you've made no withdrawals
    e. the market rate of interest has not changed in the last year

How much was your initial deposit?

4. If you have $756,213 in your bank account today, and you opened the account one year ago with only $734,011, what rate of interest (to the nearest hundredth of a percentage point) did the bank pay you over the previous year?

5. You have two investment alternatives, investment 1 and investment 2. Both investments require the expenditure of $250,000, and both require that you wait one year to receive your return. Investment 1 will pay back $300,000 at the end of one year and investment 2 will pay back 400,000 at the end of one year. Which investment has a higher net present value?

6. (a) You have the opportunity to invest $75,000 today, for a payback of $100,000 in one year. What is the rate of return on this investment?

b) What is the net present value of this investment opportunity, if the discount rate is 10%?

7. You are advising Mortimer Bucks, who has a lot of money. He wants to put his money in the bank, but he cannot choose which bank to use. Banks A & B are both insured by the Federal Deposit Insurance Corporation, so a deposit in either has zero credit risk. Both offer attractive gifts to large depositors. In fact the two banks are as similar as two banks can be except for one thing. Bank A pays 6% interest compounded annually, and Bank B pays 5.8% interest compounded quarterly (1.45% interest every 3 months). Which bank would you advise Mortimer to use and why?

8. Why would you expect the nominal rate of interest to be greater than zero?

CHAPTER 3: VALUE UNDER UNCERTAINTY: RISK AND DIVERSIFICATION

Our next step is to relax the assumption of certainty. What happens to the net present value technique if we are not certain about the amount and timing of the cash flows that will flow from an asset? Suppose, for example, that the profit we expect from a proposed project depends on whether a particular technological problem can be solved. How do we express this uncertainty about future returns? How does that uncertainty affect the discount rate that one uses to account for the time value of money? This chapter and the next address these questions.

Different projects will involve both different *kinds* of risks, and different *degrees* of risk, about future returns. For example, a 30-year Treasury bond is usually assumed to have zero risk that payments will not be made in the amounts and at the times promised. After all, the government can simply print more money. But Treasury bonds still carry a substantial degree of *inflation risk* -- the risk that dollars to be received in the future will be worth more or less in *real* terms than investors now expect. A 10-year corporate bond carries some *default risk* -- the risk that the promised payments won't be made, or won't be made on time. But it carries less inflation risk than a 30-year Treasury bond because of its shorter duration. For common stocks, there isn't even a set of promised payments written down. Investors have to guess about future dividends and other cash payments. They might be right in their estimates, or they might be too high or too low. How does the value of risky assets reflect different kinds and degrees of risk, in a world in which investors are risk-averse, and insist on being paid for bearing risk through higher expected return?

It will turn out that all of these risks affect the *expected cash flows* from a risky investment. *Some* risks -- nondiversifiable risks -- also affect the expected *rate of return* that that investors demand in order to make a risky investment. That is, *all* risks affect the numerator in a net present value calculation. Nondiversifiable risks also affect the discount rate that appears in the denominator. Which risks are diversifiable, and exactly how nondiversifiable risks affect the discount rate, though, are subject to active controversy in the finance literature.

Section A of this Chapter considers how to take uncertainty into account in expressing the expected cash flows from an asset. Section B considers how one can measure the extent of uncertainty associated with an asset's returns -- what financial economists mean when they use the term *risk*. Section C develops the value of diversifying one's investment portfolio, which can reduce risk without reducing expected cash flows. Finally, Section D consider the relationship between nondiversifiable risk and expected rate of return, and develops the Capital Asset Pricing Model as an example of how nondiversifiable risk might affect the expected rate of return demanded by risk-averse investors.

A. Expected Return Under Uncertainty

Elementary probability theory, familiar to many of you, offers guidance in expressing *expected return* when actual return is uncertain. Let's try an example:

Suppose that your good-natured grandmother makes you the following offer: You can flip a coin once, and she'll pay you $1000 if it lands on heads and nothing if it lands on tails. Or you can flip the coin twice, and she'll pay you $500 for each head, or three times, and you'll get $333 for each head, and so on. Your maximum gain is $1000 if you get all heads. You choose how many times to flip the coin.

If you flip the coin once, your expected return is $500. There is a 50% chance that you'll earn $1,000 and a 50% chance that you'll end up unhappy with your grandmother. In mathematical terms, the only possible outcomes are heads and tails. The *expected return* is:

expected return = (return to heads $\times$ probability of heads) +
(return to tails $\times$ probability of tails)

In symbols, we can write this as:

$$ER_{1\ \text{flip}} = (ret_h \times p_h) + (ret_t \times p_t)$$

Where:

ER = expected return
ret_h = return if you get heads
ret_t = return if you get tails
p_h = probability of getting heads
p_t = probability of getting tails

For the coin flip example, we have:

$ret_h = \$1000$ $\qquad\qquad$ $ret_t = \$0$ $\qquad\qquad$ $p_h = p_t = 0.5$

Thus, your expected return is:

$$ER = (\$1,000 \times 0.5) + (\$0 \times 0.5) = \$500 + \$0 = \$500$$

Suppose that you instead choose to flip the coin twice, so that you will earn $500 for each head. The expected return is still $500, but getting there is a little more complicated. There are three possible outcomes: 2 heads (which we will denote **hh**); one head and one tail (which we will denote **ht**); and two tails (which we will denote **tt**). To compute expected return, we again multiply the return in each possible state of the world by the probability that the state will occur. The formula for expected return now becomes:

$$ER_{2 \text{ flips}} = (ret_{hh} \times p_{hh}) + (ret_{ht} \times p_{ht}) + (ret_{tt} \times p_{tt})$$

The possible returns and associated probabilities are:

$$ret_{hh} = \$1000 \qquad\qquad ret_{ht} = \$500 \qquad\qquad ret_{tt} = \$0$$
$$p_{hh} = p_{tt} = 0.25^1 \qquad\qquad p_{ht} = 0.5$$

Thus, expected return is:

$$ER_{2 \text{ flips}} = (\$1000 \times .25) + (\$500 \times .5) + (\$0 \times .25)$$
$$= \quad \$250 \qquad + \quad \$250 \qquad + \quad \$0$$
$$= \quad \$500$$

For three flips, each head is worth $333.33. The possible outcomes and associated probabilities are:

Expected Return for Three Coin Flips

Outcome	Conditional Return	Probability	Value × Probability
hhh	$1000	.125	$125
hht	$666.67	.375	$250
htt	$333.33	.375	$125
ttt	$0	.125	$0
		Expected Return =	**$500**

The last column shows the calculation of expected return. The return for each possible outcome (called a *conditional return*) is computed, and multiplied by the probability of that outcome. These dollar amounts are then added together to get the

---

[1] The probability of getting two heads equals the .5 probability of getting a head on the first toss, multiplied by the .5 probability of getting a head on the second toss, for a total *compound* probability of .25. The probability of getting two tails is computed in similar fashion.

expected return. For the coin flip example, the expected return is still $500. Indeed, expected return will continue to be $500 no matter how many coins you flip.

More formally, for any set of possible outcomes, expected return is defined as the sum over all outcomes of: (the conditional return if a particular outcome occurs) $\times$ (the probability of that outcome occurring). If we use the letter i to label the possible outcomes:

$$ER \quad = \quad \sum_i (ret_i \times p_i) \tag{3-1}$$

So far, we have considered only the situation where all returns are received at the same time. If an investment has expected returns at several different times, we must compute the expected return for each time t at which a non-zero return is expected. We can write this formally by using a subscript t to label both expected return at time t and the conditional returns and associated probabilities at time t:

$$ER_t \quad = \quad \sum_i (ret_{i,t} \times p_{i,t})$$

This section has discussed how we can compute expected return at particular points in time. But we don't yet know how to discount those expected returns to the present to determine the *present value* of a stream of expected income. To do that, we must first learn how to express risk.

B. Expressing Risk: Variance and Standard Deviation

For the coin flip example, the expected return is $500 no matter how many times you flip the coin. If so, one might ask, why bother to flip the coin more than once? The answer is risk. Flipping the coin once can be thought of as investing your entire *expected* wealth of $500 in a double or nothing gamble -- a single coin flip that will return either $1000 or $0. If you instead flip the coin ten times, that's like investing $50 in each of ten coin flips, each of which returns $100 or $0. On average, you'll get 5 heads. You're reasonably likely to get somewhere between 3 and 7 heads, and thus to end up with between $300 and $700. You could get 8, 9 or even 10 heads, or 0,1 or 2 heads, but that's less likely. With ten flips, you'll *probably* end up with between $300 and $700.[2]

---

[2] The chance of ending up with between 3 and 7 heads is about 89%.

Now suppose you flip the coin a hundred times. That's like investing $5 of your expected wealth in each of 100 coin flips, each of which returns $10 or 0. Once again, your expected return is $500, but now the possibility of an extreme return like zero becomes vanishingly small. You might throw ten tails in a row, but the chance of throwing a hundred in a row is almost zero. In fact, the probability of ending up with somewhere between 45 and 55 heads is pretty good (about 2 in 3) and the probability of ending up with between 40 and 60 heads is excellent, about 95%. If we repeat the experiment, and throw a hundred coins over and over again, the percentage of heads will fall along the familiar bell curve distribution, shown in Figure 3-1.

The more times you flip the coin, the narrower the bell curve distribution; the more tightly the actual outcomes will cluster around the expected or *mean* outcome of $500. So the difference between throwing a coin once and throwing it a hundred times is **risk**. The more throws, the more likely you are to come close to the expected return, and the less likely you are to be high or low by very much.

Figure 3-1
Bell Curve Distribution of Returns to 100 Coin Flips

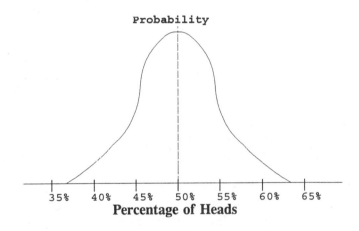

If you are like most investors, you are *risk-averse* where your investments are concerned. Given a choice between two investments with the same expected return and different levels of risk, you are likely to prefer the one with less risk. In the coin flip example, that means that you will probably flip the coin a substantial number of times, to reduce your risk. You will keep flipping up to the point where the nuisance value of flipping the coin more times exceeds the gains from further reduction in risk.

Put differently, suppose you were asked: How much would you *pay* for the opportunity to flip a coin *n* times for $1000/*n* per head? What is the *value* of the coin flip "investment" to you? Risk-aversion means that you will pay *less* than $500 for a chance to flip the coin once. It also means that you will pay more for two flips for $500 each than for a single $1000 flip; more for three flips than for two; and so on.

How much you will pay for a single flip, and how much extra you will pay for more flips, depends on your individual level of risk-aversion. The proposition that most investors are risk-averse is well-supported by empirical studies. But there is no theory to tell us *how* risk-averse investors ought to be, nor any reason to think that all investors have the same level of distaste for risk. Some may even be risk-preferring gamblers.

For symmetrical gambles like the coin flip, statisticians have developed a measure of risk, called *variance*, that treats risk as the extent to which possible outcomes depart from the expected return. Variance has some nice mathematical properties, which we develop below. But first two caveats. Just because variance, and its close relative, *standard deviation*, have useful mathematical properties doesn't mean that they correspond to the risks to which investors are averse, and thus must be paid to bear. Indeed, variance and standard deviation are somewhat counterintuitive measures of risk. They treat better-than-expected outcomes as adding as much to risk as worse-than-expected outcomes. Risk, in common parlance, means risk of *loss*. One would not commonly speak of the "risk" of getting heads and winning $1,000. Moreover, psychological experiments show that most people are *loss-averse* -- they are troubled more by a loss, relative to the status quo, than attracted by an equal dollar gain.[3]

Variance is thus an imperfect measure of the risks to which investors are averse. But we lack a better measure. Also, for important classes of investments, the risk of gain and loss are distributed, as in the coin flip example, more or less symmetrically. That is, an increase (decrease) in the likelihood of a better-than-expected outcome is accompanied by an equivalent increase (decrease) in the likelihood of a worse-than-expected outcome. This is especially true when one makes not one but a number of investments -- when one owns an investment *portfolio*. When risk of gain and risk of loss are symmetrically distributed, it doesn't matter whether we treat both good and bad deviations from expected return as adding to risk, or only count bad deviations as adding to risk.

A second caveat: Some of the desirable mathematical properties of variance and standard deviation hold in a strict sense only for certain types of distributions of returns,

---

[3] See, e.g., Daniel Kahneman, Jack Knetsch & Richard Thaler, *Anomalies: The Endowment Effect, Loss Aversion, and Status Quo Bias*, 5 J.Econ.Persp. 193 (1991). We discuss loss aversion and other common cognitive biases in Chapter 5.

of which the *normal* distribution -- illustrated by the bell curve of returns to a large number of coin flips -- is the best known example. For other return distributions, variance is an incomplete measure of risk. To make matters worse, returns on actual investments often depart from normality. Fortunately, returns on investment *portfolios* come closer to normality than returns on individual investments. Moreover, many of the empirical tests of theories about finance, accounting, and related subjects rely on returns on publicly traded securities over relatively short time periods, for which portfolio returns come reasonably close to matching the "normal" distribution.

With these caveats in mind, we turn to how one calculates variance -- how one measures how far the possible outcomes depart from the expected return. First, one computes expected return. Each difference between a conditional return and the expected return is then *squared*, which gives heavier weight to large departures from the expected return. This is broadly consistent with intuitions about risk -- many people fear large losses much more than small ones. Squaring also results in counting positive and negative departures equally. Each squared departure is then weighted by the probability of that outcome, and the squared, weighted departures are summed:

$$Var = \sum_i p_i \times (ret_i - ER)^2 \qquad (3\text{-}2)$$

If there is only one possible return, with probability one, variance is zero, as it should be because whatever measure of risk we choose should go to zero when uncertainty is zero.

We can illustrate the concept of variance using the coin flip example. Consider a single flip, with a head worth $1,000 and a tail worth $0. The expected return is $500, so the variance is:

$$
\begin{aligned}
Var_{1\ flip} \quad &= \quad p_h \times (ret_h - ER)^2 \quad &+ p_t \times (ret_t - ER)^2 \\
&= \quad .5 \times (\$1000 - \$500)^2 \quad &+ .5 \times (\$0 - \$500)^2 \\
&= \quad .5 \times (\$500)^2 \quad &+ .5 \times (-\$500)^2 \\
&= \quad .5 \times 250{,}000(\$^2) \quad &+ .5 \times 250{,}000(\$^2) \\
&= \quad 250{,}000(\$^2)
\end{aligned}
$$

Notice that the good result adds as much to the variance as the bad result.

One problem with squaring the difference between each conditional return and the expected return is that it is hard to offer an intuitive interpretation of variance. What, after all, are dollars *squared*? The statistician's response is to introduce a third term, *standard deviation*, which is simply the square root of variance (variance raised to the ½ power):

$$Std\ Dev\ =\ Var^{1/2}$$

For the coin flip example, we have:

$$Std\ Dev_{1\ flip}\ =\ [250{,}000(\$^2)]^{1/2}\ =\ \$500$$

Standard deviation, unlike variance, has an intuitive explanation. It is a rough measure of how far away from the expected outcome you will end up in a typical actual trial. If you flip the coin once, you will end up with either $1,000 or $0. In either case, that's $500 away from the expected return of $500. In a more complicated case, the correspondence is only rough because the procedure for computing variance gives heavy weight to outliers. Nonetheless, this qualitative explanation of standard deviation holds up reasonably well for a variety of return distributions.

If the conditional returns are normally distributed, then, as shown in Table 3-1, the odds are about 2 out of 3 that the actual return will be within one standard deviation of the expected return. The actual return will be within two standard deviations of the expected return about 95% of the time, and will be within three standard deviations of the expected return 99.7% of the time.

Table 3-1
The Normal Distribution

Departure from Expected Return (in standard deviations)	Probability that Actual Departure is Less than This
0	0%
0.5	38.3%
1.0	68.3%
1.5	86.6%
2.0	95.4%
2.5	98.8%
3.0	99.7%

Let's now flip a coin twice for $500 per head, to get a feel for how reduction in risk is reflected in variance and standard deviation. At the same time, we will introduce conventional notation for variance and standard deviation: standard deviation is denoted by the small Greek letter sigma [σ], and variance by σ^2. For two coin flips:

$$
\begin{aligned}
\sigma^2_{2 \text{ flips}} \quad &= \quad p_{hh} \times (ret_{hh} - ER)^2 \quad + p_{ht} \times (ret_{ht} - ER)^2 \quad + p_{tt} \times (ret_{tt} - ER)^2 \\
&= \quad (.25 \times 250,000(\$^2)) \quad + (.5 \quad \times \quad 0) \quad + \quad (.25 \times 250,000(\$^2)) \\
&= \quad 62,500(\$^2) \quad + \quad 0 \quad + \quad 62,500(\$^2) \\
&= \quad 125,000(\$^2)
\end{aligned}
$$

Variance is smaller, as we expected. In fact, it is half as big as for one coin flip.

For three coin flips, we have:

$$
\begin{aligned}
\sigma^2_{3 \text{ flips}} \quad &= p_{hhh} \times (ret_{hhh} - ER)^2 \quad + p_{hht} \times (ret_{hht} - ER)^2 \quad + p_{htt} \times (ret_{htt} - ER)^2 \quad + p_{ttt} \times (ret_{ttt} - ER)^2 \\
&= .125 \times (\$1000\text{-}\$500)^2 \quad + .375 \times (\$667\text{-}\$500)^2 \quad + .375 \times (\$333\text{-}\$500)^2 \quad + .125 \times (\$0\text{-}\$500)^2 \\
&= 31,250(\$^2) \quad + 10,416.67(\$^2) \quad + 10,416.67(\$^2) \quad + 31,250(\$^2) \\
&= 83,333(\$^2)
\end{aligned}
$$

A pattern is emerging, where the variance of n coin flips equals the variance of one coin flip, 250,000, divided by the number of flips:

$$
\sigma^2_{n \text{ flips}} = \sigma^2_{1 \text{ flip}}/n
$$

Standard deviation also declines with the number of coin flips. But since standard deviation equals the *square root* of variance, standard deviation declines more slowly as the number of flips increases -- it declines as the *square root of n*:

$$
\sigma_{n \text{ flips}} = \sigma_{1 \text{ flip}}/n^{1/2}
$$

This is illustrated in Table 3-2 and Figure 3-2 below:

Table 3-2
Expected Return, Variance, and Standard Deviation for Multiple Coin Flips

Number of Flips	Expected Return	Variance	Standard Deviation
1	$500	250,000(^{2})	$500
2	$500	125,000(^{2})	$353.55
3	$500	83,333(^{2})	$288.67
4	$500	62,500(^{2})	$250
. . .			
9	$500	27,778(^{2})	$166.67
16	$500	15,625(^{2})	$125
25	$500	10,000(^{2})	$100
. . .			
n	$500	250,000(^{2})/n	$500/n^{1/2}$

Figure 3-2
Reducing Risk Through Diversification: The Coin Flip Example

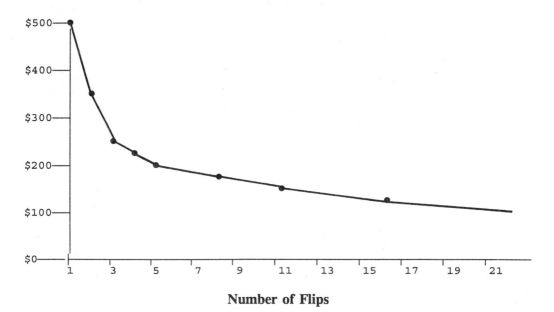

Standard Deviation

Number of Flips

C. The Value of Diversification

We have now quantified the reduction in risk from flipping a coin more times. You can see multiple coin flips as a form of diversification. You've decided to invest in coin flips. By flipping once, you earn $1000 for a head. If you flip twice, you earn $500 for each head. That's as if you invested $250 of your expected return in each of two coin flips, instead of investing $500 in a single flip. By flipping three times, you invest one-third of your expected return in each of three flips, and so on.

Diversification, investing fewer dollars per flip in more flips, reduces the chance that you will earn less or more than $500. The statistical measures of risk -- variance and standard deviation -- reflect this. In a nutshell, this is why investors should diversify their investment portfolios. Investors can reduce risk, *without reducing expected return*, by splitting their investment dollars among a number of different investments. If investors are risk-averse, that makes the expected return *more valuable* -- investors will pay more for an investment with the same expected return but less risk.

For publicly traded investments, such as stocks and bonds, diversification is easy, so that others will diversify even if you do not. Having diversified, they are willing to pay a higher price for publicly traded stocks and bonds. If most investors are diversified, the market price will reflect the value that *diversified investors* place on risky securities. Undiversified investors will bear extra risk, *and will not be compensated for bearing that risk*.

There is, though, one critical difference between publicly traded investments such as stocks and our coin flip example. In the coin flip example, risk could be reduced *virtually to zero* by additional diversification. Flipping the coin 100 times instead of once will reduce variance by a factor of 100, and will reduce standard deviation by a factor of 10, from $500 to $50. Flipping the coin 1,000,000 times instead of once will reduce standard deviation by a factor of 1,000, to only $0.50.

In contrast, for stocks, diversifying by buying a large number of different stocks will reduce risk only to some irreducible minimum risk. Suppose that we run the following experiment: Take $1,000, divide it into n pieces of $1000/n$ each, and purchase n randomly selected stocks traded on the New York Stock Exchange. Then measure the percentage change in the value of the portfolio over a one-year period. The stock price database compiled by the Center for Research in Security Prices (CRSP) allows one to run this experiment for different time periods, and different stock portfolios. This experiment, run over and over, produces the results shown in Figure 3-3:

Figure 3-3
Reducing Risk Through Diversification: Stock Portfolios

Standard Deviation

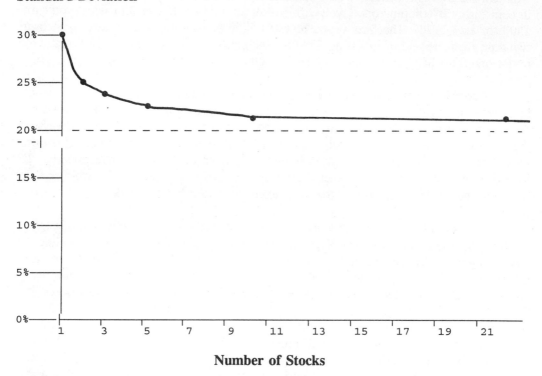

Number of Stocks

Why can diversification eliminate all risk in the the coin flip example, but only *reduce* risk for common stocks? To answer these questions, we need to consider the types of risks that a particular firm faces.

Any firm is subject to two qualitatively different types of risk. Some risks are common to many firms across the stock market, though perhaps to differing degrees. The economy as a whole may do better or worse than expected, inflation may be higher or lower than expected, real interest rates may be higher or lower than expected, and so on. These risks affect the profits of all firms, so one cannot eliminate them by buying a portfolio of different stocks. We call the base level of stock market risk, which remains after full diversification, *systematic risk* or *market risk*. The systematic risk of a U.S. stock portfolio for a one-year holding period is a gain or loss of about 20%, relative to the average or expected return.

Each firm is also subject to various risks that are peculiar to it or to its industry. Maybe a plant burns down, or a competitor comes out with a great new product, or a competitor cuts prices and the firm must cut its own prices in response, or there's a strike, or the firm's managers do an unexpectedly good or bad job of running the business, or the firm makes a particular investment that turns out good or bad. These kinds of risks *can* be reduced by diversifying across firms and across industries. If one firm has a plant fire, another will not. If one firm is unexpectedly badly run, another will be unexpectedly well run. We call these company-specific or industry-specific risks *unsystematic risk* or *unique risk*. These risks fall above the dotted line in Figure 3-3; they decrease as the number of stocks in an investment portfolio increases.

The total percentage gain or loss from holding an average stock is about 30% per year. Thus, diversification reduces the overall risk of holding a stock portfolio, measured by standard deviation, by about one-third, from 30% per year to 20% per year. Diversification also greatly reduces the extreme outliers -- a diversified investor is far less likely to become rich or to go broke.

More formally, holding a portfolio of *n* properly chosen stocks reduces unsystematic variance by a factor of roughly $1/n$ compared to holding one stock. Holding 20 properly chosen stocks reduces unsystematic variance by roughly 95% and thus achieves most of the value of diversification. Holding 100 stocks reduces unsystematic variance by roughly 99%. This is shown in Table 3-3, which corresponds to Figure 3-3. In Table 3-3, we have assumed that each firm in the portfolio has a systematic standard deviation of 20% per year, and a total standard deviation of 30% per year. The pattern in Table 3-3 is the same as that shown for coin flips in Table 3-2, except that *total* variance and standard deviation decline toward the base established by systematic risk, rather than toward zero. *Only total variance and total standard deviation are directly measurable.*

The first central lesson of modern portfolio theory is: **Investors should hold a diversified portfolio to reduce unsystematic risk**. An immediate corollary: if diversification is easy, the market price -- the *value* -- of a stock, bond, or other capital asset **should depend only on systematic risk**. *How far* investors should diversify depends on comparing the risk reduction benefits to the transaction costs of additional diversification, and to any other costs of greater diversification, such as reduced ability of shareholders to monitor the actions of corporate managers.

Table 3-3
Reducing Unsystematic Risk By Holding a Diversified Portfolio

Number of Stocks	Total Variance $(\%^2)$	Total Standard Deviation (%)	Unsystematic Variance $(\%^2)$
1	900	30	500
2	650	25.5	250
3	567	23.8	167
4	525	22.9	125
. . .			
10	450	21.2	50
20	425	20.6	25
50	410	20.2	10
100	405	20.1	5
500	401	20.02	1
. . .			
n	$[400 + 500/n]$	$[400 + 500/n]^{1/2}$	$[500/n](\%^2)$

Example: Diversification in Law Firms[4]

Diversification can be important in contexts having nothing to do with stocks and bonds. Suppose that a lawyer is considering making the investment in human capital necessary to become either a securities lawyer, specializing in public offerings of securities, or a bankruptcy lawyer, specializing in reorganization of financially distressed companies. Further assume that the training for each of these specialties take the same amount of time, and are mutually exclusive. The lawyer believes that the expected return on an investment in becoming a securities or bankruptcy lawyer will depend on the performance of the economy. The expected return and its relationship to the strength of the economy are as follows:

---

[4] This example is adapted from Gilson & Mnookin, *Sharing Among the Human Capitalists: An Economic Inquiry into the Corporate Law Firm and How Partners Split Profits*, 37 Stan.L.Rev. 313, 327-28 (1985).

Strength of Economy	Probability	Earnings as Securities Lawyer	Earnings as Bankruptcy Lawyer
Strong	1/3	$200,000	$0
So-so	1/3	$100,000	$100,000
Poor	1/3	$0	$200,000

Suppose, however, that two lawyers face this choice. They can go into partnership with each other, with profits evenly split. One will become a securities lawyer; the other a bankruptcy lawyer. The combined profits will now be $200,000 in all states of the world. The partnership lets both lawyers diversify the risk of a specialized investment in human capital.

In the real world, diversification will never be perfect. Sometimes, both bankruptcy and securities work will be booming; other times both specialties will be slow. Nonetheless, partial diversification is possible. Some scholars believe that diversification is an important (though not the only) reason for formation of professional partnerships.

As the stylized example of the lawyer's investment in specialization illustrates, the risk of a portfolio depends on the *covariance* of the returns on the investments in the portfolio -- the extent to which the returns vary together, rather than independently. If the returns move in exactly opposite directions in exactly the same amounts (*perfect negative covariance*, as in the example, all risk is eliminated; the portfolio return is always $200,000.

The value of diversification is not limited, though, to settings of perfect negative covariance. Two coin flips are independent of each other -- they have *zero covariance*. That is enough for diversification through multiple coin flips to eliminate risk. We must, however, flip often enough so that the independent risks can average out. Two flips won't do. Stocks generally have *positive* covariance -- they move up together in bull markets and down together in bear markets. Nonetheless, *partial* reduction of the risk of investing in stocks is possible. Diversification will reduce risk as long as the returns from two investments are not perfectly positively correlated.

D. Measuring Systematic Risk: Beta

We have learned that diversification can reduce unsystematic risk, but not systematic risk. We don't yet know, though, how to measure these two separate components of risk. We loosely called the portion of the risk on an individual stock that is due to marketwide factors its systematic risk and the remainder of the risk its unsystematic risk. But it isn't obvious how one draws that distinction. A change in interest rates affects all stocks to some extent, but will have special significance for banks. A change in the price of oil affects all companies, but will have special significance for oil companies and airlines. And so on.

In the real world, all we can observe is *total* risk. How do we determine what part of a company's total risk is systematic and what part is unsystematic? The best available way is to run a regression analysis where we treat the return on each company's stock as a dependent variable, to be partially explained by one or more independent variables that are believed to contribute to systematic risk. Part of the return on a particular stock will correlate with the chosen risk factor(s), and part will not. The part that correlates with the risk factor(s) is treated as systematic risk; the remainder is treated as unsystematic risk.

Below, we explore how one measures systematic risk for a simple, commonly used model of stock price returns called the *market model*. In the market model, the only systematic risk factor is the return on the entire stock market. The market return is assumed to act as a proxy for the underlying economic factors that cause the market to rise or fall. We will return in the next chapter to the question of which risk factor(s) are best able to separate systematic from unsystematic risk, and how the market model might be improved on.

Graphically, the market model involves developing a scatter plot in which the daily or monthly returns on a firm's stock are plotted against the returns on a broad market index, such as the Standard & Poor's 500 Composite Stock Index (the S&P 500 Index). We then use least-squares statistical analysis to construct a "best fit" straight line that tells us how much the firm's stock will rise or fall, *on average*, when the market rises or falls 1%. Such a scatter plot is shown in Figure 3-3 for Host International, using monthly returns between 1975 and 1979.

The *slope* of the best-fit straight line is conventionally labelled by the Greek letter beta [β]. For Host International, the slope of the best-fit line is $\beta = 1.4$. This means that *on average*, when the market rises in price by 10%, Host International gains 14%. Similarly, on average, when the market drops in price by 10%, Host International drops 14%.

Figure 3-3
Scatter Plot of Returns on Particular Stock Versus Market Returns

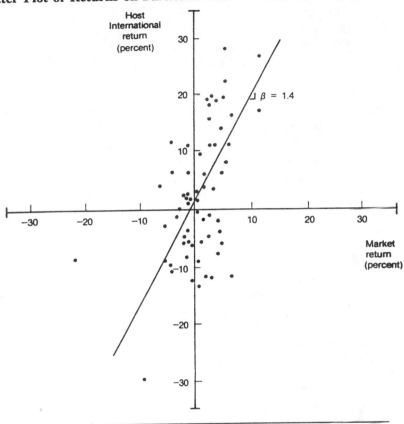

Source: James Lorie, Peter Dodd & Mary Kimpton, *The Stock Market: Theories & Evidence* 37 (2d ed. 1985).

Beta is a measure of the *systematic risk* of a particular firm's stock, *relative* to the risk of the market as a whole. The market as a whole has only systematic risk; all unsystematic risk has been diversified away. If we know a stock's β, and we know the riskiness of the market as a whole, then we know how much of the variance of an individual stock is systematic, and can't be diversified away. The remaining risk is unsystematic, and can be diversified away.

An average firm's stock cannot rise or fall faster or slower than the value of a well-constructed market index, since the purpose of the index is to reflect what is happening to the market as a whole. Thus, an average firm will have $\beta = 1$. Host International, with $\beta = 1.4$, has above-average sensitivity to market risk.

The next reading provides a more formal introduction to β as a measure of systematic risk, and extends the β measure to stock *portfolios*.

FRANCO MODIGLIANI & GERALD POGUE, AN INTRODUCTION TO RISK AND RETURN: CONCEPTS AND EVIDENCE (Part I)
Fin. Analysts J. 68, 76-79 (Mar.-Apr. 1974)

[T]he systematic risk of an individual security is that portion of its total risk (standard deviation of return) which cannot be eliminated by combining it with other securities in a well diversified portfolio. We now need a way of quantifying the systematic risk of a security and relating the systematic risk of a portfolio to that of its component securities. This can be accomplished by dividing security return into two parts: one dependent (*i.e.*, perfectly correlated), and a second independent (*i.e.*, uncorrelated) of market return. The first component of return is usually referred to as "systematic," the second as "unsystematic" return. Thus we have

$$\text{Security Return} = \text{Systematic Return} + \text{Unsystematic Return} \qquad \text{(3-3)}$$

Since the systematic return is perfectly correlated with the market return, it can be expressed as a factor, designated beta (β), times the market return, R_m. The beta factor is a market sensitivity index, indicating how sensitive the security return is to changes in the market level. The unsystematic return, which is independent of market returns, is usually represented by a factor epsilon (ϵ'). Thus the security return, R, may be expressed

$$R = \beta\,R_m + \epsilon' \qquad \text{(3-4)}$$

For example, if a security had a β factor of 2.0 (e.g., an airline stock), then a 10% market return would generate a systematic return for the stock of 20%. The [total] security return for the period would be the 20% plus the unsystematic component. The unsystematic component depends on factors unique to the company, such as labor difficulties, higher than expected sales, etc.

The security returns model given by Equation 3-4 is usually written in a way such that the average value of the residual term, ϵ, is zero. This is accomplished by adding a factor, alpha (α), to the model to represent the average value of the unsystematic returns over time. That is, we set $\epsilon' = \alpha + \epsilon$ so that

$$R = \alpha + \beta\,R_m + \epsilon \qquad \text{(3-5)}$$

where the average [of] ϵ over time is equal to zero.

The model for security returns given by Equation 3-5 is usually referred to as the "market model." Graphically, the model can be depicted as a line fitted to a plot of security returns against rates of return on the market index [as in Figure 3-3]. . . . The beta factor can be thought of as the slope of the line. It gives the expected increase in security return for a one per cent increase in market return. . . .

The alpha factor is represented by the intercept of the line on the vertical security return axis. It is equal to the average value over time of the unsystematic returns (ϵ) on the stock. For most stocks, the alpha factor tends to be small and unstable. . .

The systematic risk of a security is equal to β times the standard deviation of the market return:

$$\text{Systematic Risk} = \beta \; \sigma_m \qquad \qquad \text{(3-6)}$$

. . . Given measures of individual security systematic risk, we can now compute the systematic risk of [a] portfolio. It is equal to the beta factor for the portfolio, β_p, times the risk of the market index, σ_m:

$$\text{Portfolio Systematic Risk} = \beta_p \; \sigma_m \qquad \qquad \text{(3-7)}$$

The portfolio beta factor in turn can be shown to be simply an average of the individual security betas, weighted by the proportion of each security in the portfolio, or

$$\beta_p = \sum_{j=1}^{n} X_j \; \beta_j \qquad \qquad \text{(3-8)}$$

where

$X_j \quad = \quad$ the proportion of portfolio market value represented by security j

$n \quad = \quad$ the number of securities.

Thus the systematic risk of the portfolio is simply a weighted average of the systematic risk of the individual securities. If the portfolio is composed of an equal dollar investment in each stock. . . , the β_p is simply an unweighted average of the component security betas. . . .

The implications of these results are substantial. First, we would expect realized rates of return over substantial periods of time to be related to the systematic as opposed to total risk of securities. Since the unsystematic risk is relatively easily eliminated, we should not expect the market to offer a risk premium for bearing it. Second, since security systematic risk is equal to the security beta times σ_m (which is common to all securities), beta is useful as a *relative* risk measure. The β gives the systematic risk of a security (or portfolio) relative to the risk of the market index. Thus it is often convenient to speak of systematic risk in relative terms (*i.e.*, in terms of beta rather than beta times σ_m).

Problems to Accompany Chapter 3

1. You are the chief asset manager at Monolithic Multinational Corp. One day, while you have your feet up on your desk in your spacious office, you get a call from your old schoolmate, Barney Straightarrow. Barney was the most honest person in your sixth-grade class, so you are surprised that he is now an institutional salesperson at the firm of Fast, Buck and Run. Barney's got some bonds to sell, and he'd love to tell you about them. The bonds are issued by the Irregular Company, and they come in two varieties, coupon bonds paying 10% annual interest and zero-coupon bonds. Both varieties have a face value of $1,000 and mature in 10 years. The zero coupon bonds sell for $370 (to yield 10.45% to maturity) and the coupon bonds sell for $1000 (and thus yield 10% to maturity). Why might the yields differ?

2. You're still with Monolithic-Multinational, and, on a fine Tuesday morning, one of your underlings bursts into your office claiming that she has found the fixed-income investment opportunity of the century. There's a new bond in town called an increasing rate note, being underwritten by Drexel Hutton Inc., and issued by Watcher Wallet Industries. The bond has a time to maturity of seven years, a face value of $1,000, and it makes a series of annual interest payments that grow (or compound) at a constant rate of 12%. The first interest payment will be made one year from today. The bond sells for $485.27 and its yield to maturity is 15.91%.

After citing these statistics, your underling gushes that a 12% growth opportunity is hard to find in the current economy. This must be a good bond. What's wrong with her reasoning? Explain briefly how she should analyze whether to buy this bond.

3. Jimmy Jumpshot, prized power forward of the Newark Vultures, has just signed a $20,000,000 contract with his team. He boasts to you that managing his new wealth is as easy as making layups. He simply chooses the stocks with the highest betas since these stocks offer the highest returns. Over the past year, during which the economy expanded rapidly, Jimmy achieved a return of 43%. What's wrong with Jimmy's reasoning?

4. An investment in Alpha Corp. has the following expected returns over a one-year period:

return (%)	probability (%)
-15	10
0	20
10	20
20	20
25	20
35	10

a) What is the expected return on this investment?

b) What is the variance of this investment?

c) What is the standard deviation of this investment?

5. An investment in Gamma Inc. has the following expected returns compared to the expected returns on Alpha Corp. over a one-year period:

Gamma return (%)	Alpha return (%)	probability(%)
-10	-15	10
-5	0	20
0	10	20
5	20	20
10	25	20
5	35	10

a) What is the variance of the expected returns for Gamma Inc.?

b) What is the expected return on a portfolio in which half of your money is invested in Alpha and half in Gamma?

c) What is the variance of the expected return on a portfolio in which half of your money is invested in Alpha and half in Gamma?

CHAPTER 4: THE RELATIONSHIP BETWEEN RISK AND RETURN: THE CAPITAL ASSET PRICING MODEL AND ALTERNATIVES

Most investors are risk-averse. In return for bearing more risk, they must be compensated with a higher expected return. In Chapter 3, we learned that the risk of an investment can be divided into systematic and unsystematic components, and that unsystematic risk can be diversified away. Since unsystematic risk can be shed through diversification, investors should hold diversified portfolios and should *not* require a higher expected return because an investment has unsystematic risk. Risk-averse investors *should* require a higher expected return for bearing systematic risk.

We do not yet know, though, the relationship between risk and expected return. How much extra expected return should investors receive for bearing various amounts of systematic risk? What kinds of systematic risk should investors be paid for bearing?

All asset pricing models share two common goals: (i) developing a framework for understanding how systematic risk affects security prices; and (ii) measuring the market price of various types of systematic risk. Our interest in this book is mostly in the first goal. Understanding what factors affect asset prices provides a necessary base for understanding how the purchase of a particular asset -- an ongoing business -- can affect the value of that asset. It also provides a base for understanding how the lawyer's efforts -- in structuring the transaction, drafting the contracts of sale and financing, and conducting a due diligence investigation of the target -- can enhance the value of the transaction to the buyer, the seller, or both.

In this Chapter, we develop a simple two-factor model of the relationship between risk and expected return, known as the *Capital Asset Pricing Model (CAPM)*. This model is related to the market model of systematic risk presented in Chapter 3. We then discuss the uses and limits of CAPM, including the equivocal empirical evidence supporting the model and theoretical questions about whether CAPM can properly be tested at all. We then introduce multifactor asset pricing models, such as Arbitrage Pricing Theory, that have been developed in response to the limitations of CAPM.

For a long time, CAPM was a central paradigm of modern finance theory. New doubts about how well it predicts stock price returns have weakened that status, but the model retains predictive value for the differences in the returns on broad asset classes, such as stocks, corporate bonds, and Treasury bills. CAPM also offers a theoretically attractive way to begin thinking about how risk and expected return *might* be related. And, despite CAPM's weaknesses, we lack, as yet, a better asset pricing model.

A. The Capital Asset Pricing Model

The readings below describe the Capital Asset Pricing Model, with some assumptions explicitly stated and others left implicit. The Van Horne excerpt provides a qualitative introduction to CAPM. It is followed by a more formal development of the model by Modigliani and Pogue. Section B then explicitly states the assumptions underlying the model, and discusses some implications of relaxing various assumptions.

1. A Qualitative Approach to CAPM

JAMES VAN HORNE, FINANCIAL MANAGEMENT AND POLICY
60-65 (7th ed. 1986)[*]

The best combination of expected value of return and standard deviation depends upon the investor's utility function. This function is derived [by asking the investor to rank order different combinations of expected return and risk]. If you are a risk-averse investor who [requires higher expected return to compensate you for an increase in the risk that actual return will diverge from expected return], your utility function might be that depicted graphically by Figure 4-1. The expected value of return is plotted on the vertical axis, while the standard deviation is along the horizontal. The curves are known as *indifference curves*; the investor is indifferent between any combination of expected value of return and standard deviation on a particular curve. In other words, [each indifference] curve is defined by those combinations of expected return and standard deviation that result in a fixed level of expected utility.[4] . . . [A]ll points on a specific indifference curve have the same certainty equivalent.

The greater the slope of the indifference curves, the more averse the investor is to risk. As we move to the left in Figure 4-1, each successive curve represents a higher level of expected utility. It is important to note that the exact shape of the indifference curves will not be the same for different investors. While the curves for all risk-averse investors will be upward-sloping, a variety of shapes are possible, depending on the risk preferences of the individual.

---

[*] © 1986. Reprinted by permission of Prentice-Hall, Inc., Englewood Cliffs, N.J.

[4] For further discussion and proof that indifference curves for a risk-averse investor are concave [curve upward], see Eugene Fama & Merton Miller, *The Theory of Finance* 226-28 (1972).

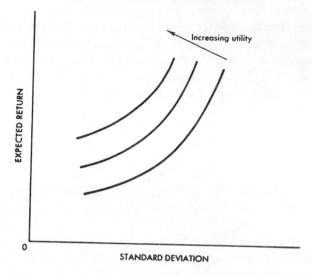

Figure 4-1
Hypothetical Indifference Curves

As an investor, you want to hold that portfolio of securities that places you on the highest indifference curve . . . . An example of an opportunity set, based upon the subjective probability beliefs of an individual investor, is shown in Figure 4-2. This opportunity set reflects all possible portfolios of securities as envisioned by the investor, every point in the shaded area representing a portfolio that is attainable. The dark line at the top of the set is the line of efficient combinations, or the efficient frontier. It depicts the tradeoff between risk and expected value of return. . . .

Figure 4-2
Hypothetical Opportunity Set

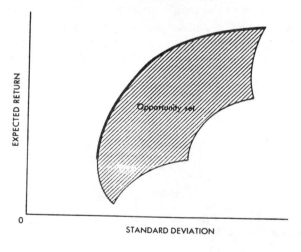

According to the Markowitz mean-variance maxim, an investor should seek a portfolio of securities that lies on the efficient frontier.[5] A portfolio is not efficient if there is another portfolio with a higher expected value of return and a lower standard deviation, a higher expected value and the same standard deviation, or the same expected value but a lower standard deviation. If your portfolio is not efficient, you can increase the expected value of return without increasing the risk, decrease the risk without decreasing the expected value of return, or obtain some combination of increased expected value and decreased risk by switching to a portfolio on the efficient frontier. . . . Portfolios of securities tend to dominate individual securities because of the reduction in risk obtainable through diversification. . . .

[Suppose that your personal tradeoff between risk and expected return is shown by the indifference curves in Figure 4-3. You should choose, from the efficient set of investment portfolios, shown by the heavy line in Figure 4-3, the particular portfolio *x* that will put you on the highest (furthest to the left) indifference curve. It can be shown mathematically that you should choose a portfolio where the efficient frontier is *tangent* to -- just barely touches at one point -- the highest reachable indifference curve.]

Figure 4-3
Choosing an Optimal Portfolio

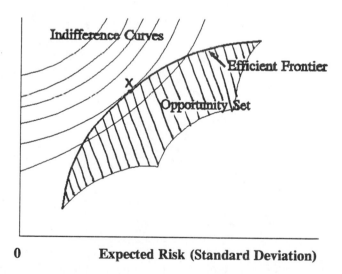

Expected Return

0   **Expected Risk (Standard Deviation)**

---

[5] Harry Markowitz, *Portfolio Selection: Efficient Diversification of Investments* chs. 7-8 (1959).

Presence of Risk-Free Security

Your objective is to choose the best portfolio from those that lie on the efficient frontier. In addition to the risky securities that fall in the opportunity set, you will usually be able to invest in a risk-free security that yields a certain future return. This security might be a U.S. Treasury security that is held to maturity. Although the expected return may be low, relative to other securities, there is complete certainty as to return. Suppose for now that you can not only lend at the risk-free rate but borrow at it as well. . . . To determine the optimal portfolio under these conditions, we first draw a line from the risk-free rate, r_f, through its point of tangency with the opportunity set of portfolio returns, as illustrated in Figure 4-4. This line then becomes the new efficient frontier. Note that only one portfolio of risky securities -- namely, m -- would be considered; it now dominates all others, including those on the efficient frontier of the opportunity set [of risky investments].

Figure 4-4
Selection of Optimal Portfolio When Risk-Free Asset Exists

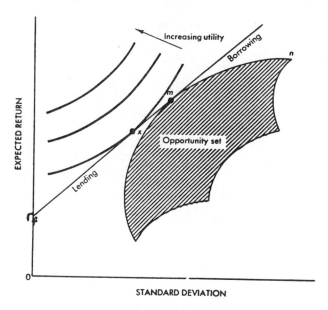

Any point on the straight line tells us the proportion [in your overall portfolio] of the risky portfolio, m, and the proportion of loans or borrowings at the risk-free rate. To the left of point m, you would [put a fraction of your total funds in] the risk-free security and [the remainder in] portfolio m. To the right, you would hold only portfolio m and would borrow funds, in addition to your initial investment funds, in order to invest further in it. The farther to the right in the figure, the greater borrowings will be. The

110

overall investment return = [w × (expected return on risky portfolio)] + [(1 - w) × (risk-free rate)], where w is the proportion of wealth invested in portfolio m, and 1 - w is the proportion invested in the risk-free asset. If lending were involved, w would be less than 1.0; if borrowing occurred, it would be greater than 1.0. The overall standard deviation is simply w times the standard deviation of the risky portfolio. No account is taken of the risk-free asset because its standard deviation is zero.

The optimal investment policy is determined by the point of tangency between the straight line in Figure 4-4 and the highest indifference curve. As shown in the figure, this point is portfolio x, and it consists of lending at the risk-free rate [which is the same thing as investing in the risk-free security] and investing in the risky security portfolio, m. If borrowing were prohibited, the efficient frontier would no longer be a straight line throughout but would consist of line r_f-m-n. . . .

If market participants have homogeneous expectations, in market equilibrium point m represents a portfolio of all securities available in the market, weighted by their respective total market values. By definition, this weighted average portfolio is the *market portfolio*.

Capital Market Line

If both borrowing and lending are at the risk-free rate, the *capital market line* will be a straight line passing through the risk-free rate on the vertical axis and the expected return-standard deviation point for the market portfolio. The line is shown in Figure 4-4, but we illustrate it separately in Figure 4-5. This line describes the tradeoff between expected return and risk for various holdings of the risk-free security and the market portfolio. Thus two things are involved: the price of time and the price of risk. The former is depicted by the intercept of the capital market line and the vertical axis. The risk-free rate, then, can be thought of as the reward for waiting. The slope of the capital market line represents the market price of risk. It tells us the amount of additional expected return that is required for an increment in standard deviation. Thus the capital market line depicts the *ex ante* equilibrium relationship between return and risk.

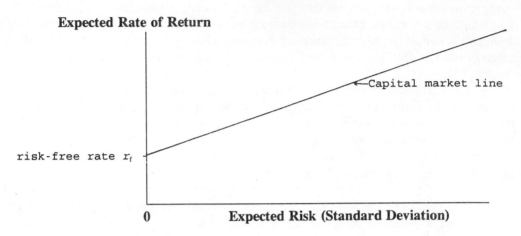

Figure 4-5
The Capital Market Line

Separation Theorem

In the context of the capital market line, the utility preferences of the individual affect only the amount that is borrowed or loaned. They do not affect the optimal portfolio of risky assets. Turning back to Figure 4-4, we would select portfolio *m* of risky assets no matter what the nature of our indifference curves. The reason is that when a risk-free security exists, and borrowing and lending are possible at that rate, the market portfolio dominates all others. As long as they can freely borrow and lend at the risk-free rate, two investors with very different preferences will both choose portfolio *m*.

Thus the individual's utility preferences are independent or separate from the optimal portfolio of risky assets. This condition is known as the *separation theorem*. Put another way, it states that the determination of an optimal portfolio of risky assets is independent of the individual's risk preferences. Such a determination depends only on the expected returns and standard deviations for the various possible portfolios of risky assets. In essence, the individual's approach to investing is two phased; first determine an optimal portfolio of risky assets; then determine the most desirable combination of the risk-free security and this portfolio. Only the second phase depends on utility preferences. The separation theorem . . . allows the management of a corporation to make decisions without reference to the utility preferences of individual owners.

2. Relaxation to Equilibrium

The Van Horne excerpt above is misleading in one important respect. The opportunity set of risky portfolios depicted in Figures 4-2 to 4-4 cannot exist in equilibrium. All investors will want to hold the same portfolio *m*, because this lets them reach the highest possible indifference curve. No one will want to hold portfolios that lie below and to the right of the capital market line. The demand for portfolio *m* will cause its price to rise, which will reduce its expected rate of return. Similarly, the prices of portfolios that lie below and to the right of the capital market line will fall, which will increase their expected rates of return. This process will continue until, in equilibrium, all diversified portfolios lie along the capital market line.

Technically, any portfolio *except* the market portfolio is not fully diversified, and must lie at least infinitesimally to the right of the capital market line. But many diversified portfolios will, for all practical purposes, lie on the capital market line. Indeed, if one plots expected return not against *total risk*, as in Figures 4-2 to 4-5, but against *systematic risk*, then *all assets* should lie on the capital market line. This is shown in Figure 4-6.

If many diversified portfolios with different degrees of risk lie on the same capital market line, then investors can, over a broad range of risk, obtain their desired level of risk, and a commensurate expected return, by directly buying a portfolio with that level of risk. They don't need to invest only in the market portfolio and the risk-free asset.

Figure 4-6
Asset Pricing in Equilibrium

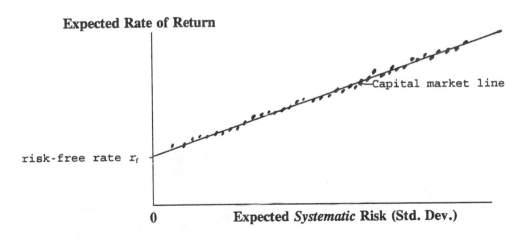

113

3. A More Formal Development of CAPM

FRANCO MODIGLIANI & GERALD POGUE, AN INTRODUCTION TO RISK AND RETURN: CONCEPTS AND EVIDENCE (Part II)
Fin. Analysts J. 69, 69-70 (May-June 1974)

[We have] developed two measures of risk: one is a measure of total risk (standard deviation), the other a relative index of systematic or nondiversifiable risk (beta). The beta measure would appear to be the more relevant for the pricing of securities. Returns expected by investors should logically be related to systematic as opposed to total risk. Securities with higher systematic risk should have higher expected returns.

The question to be considered now is the form of the relationship between risk and return. In this section we describe a relationship called the "Capital Asset Pricing Model" (CAPM), which is based on elementary logic and simple economic principles. The basic postulate underlying finance theory is that assets with the same risk should have the same expected rate of return. That is, the prices of assets in the capital markets should adjust until equivalent risk assets have identical expected returns.

To see the implications of this postulate, let us consider an investor who holds a risky portfolio with the same risk as the market portfolio (beta equal to 1.0). What return should he expect? Logically, he should expect the same return as that of the market portfolio.

Let us consider another investor who holds a riskless portfolio (beta equal to zero). The investor in this case should expect to earn the rate of return on riskless assets such as treasury bills. By taking no risk, he earns the riskless rate of return.

Now let us consider the case of an investor who holds a mixture of these two portfolios. Assuming he invests a proportion X of his money in the risky portfolio and $(1 - X)$ in the riskless portfolio, what risk does he bear and what return should he expect? The risk of the composite portfolio is easily computed when we recall that the beta of a portfolio is simply a weighted average of the component security betas, where the weights are the portfolio proportions. Thus the portfolio beta, β_p, is a weighted average of the beta of the market portfolio and the beta of the risk-free rate. However, the market beta is 1.0, and that of the risk-free rate is zero. Therefore

$$\beta_p = (1 - X) \cdot 0 + X \cdot 1 = X \qquad \text{(4-1)}$$

Thus, β_p is equal to the fraction of his money invested in the risky portfolio. If 100% or less of the investor's funds is invested in the risky portfolio, his portfolio beta will be between zero and 1.0. If he borrows at the risk-free rate and invests the proceeds in the risky portfolio, his portfolio beta will be greater than 1.0.

The expected return of the composite portfolio is also a weighted average of the expected returns on the two component portfolios; that is,

$$E(R_p) = (1 - X) \cdot R_f + X \cdot E(R_m) \tag{4-2}$$

where $E(R_p)$, $E(R_m)$, and R_f are the expected returns on the portfolio, the market index, and the risk-free rate. Now, from Equation 4-1 we know that X is equal to β_p. Substituting into Equation 4-2, we have

$$E(R_p) = (1 - \beta_p) \cdot R_f + \beta_p \cdot E(R_m)$$

or

$$E(R_p) = R_f + \beta_p \cdot [E(R_m) - R_f] \tag{4-3}$$

Equation 4-3 is the Capital Asset Pricing Model (CAPM), an extremely important theoretical result. It says that the expected return on a portfolio should exceed the riskless rate of return by an amount which is proportional to the portfolio beta. That is, the relationship between return and risk should be linear. . . .[*]

We can illustrate the model by assuming that [the] short-term (risk-free) interest rate is 6% and the expected return on the market is 10%. The expected risk premium for holding the market portfolio is just the difference between the 10% and the short-term interest rate of 6%, or 4%. Investors who hold the market portfolio expect to earn 10%, which is 4% greater than they could earn on a short-term market instrument for certain. In order to satisfy Equation 4-3, the expected return on securities or portfolios with different levels of risk must be:

---

[*] Equation 4-3 is the equation for the capital market line shown in Figures 4-5 and 4-6. Ed.

Expected Return for Different Levels of Portfolio Beta

Beta	Expected Return
0.0	6%
0.5	8%
1.0	10%
1.5	12%
2.0	14%

The predictions of the model are inherently sensible. For safe investments ($\beta =$ 0), the model predicts that investors would expect to earn the risk-free rate of interest. For a risky investment ($\beta > 0$) investors would expect a rate of return proportional to the market sensitivity (β) of the investment. Thus, stocks with lower than average market sensitivities (such as most utilities) would offer expected returns less than the expected market return. Stocks with above average values of beta (such as most airline securities) would offer expected returns in excess of the market.

B. The Assumptions Underlying CAPM

CAPM offers a simple and elegant model of how security prices ought to reflect different degrees of systematic risk. The model, though, depends on a series of strong assumptions. A set of assumptions that allow the model to be derived is listed below. Some of the assumptions can be relaxed without doing great damage to the model; others cannot be relaxed without making the model so complex that it becomes intractable. The assumptions are worth exploring in some detail, because many of the motives for corporate acquisitions, and many of the opportunities for lawyers to add value to an acquisition, involve departures from the simplifying assumptions underlying CAPM and other asset pricing models.

1. *Zero transaction costs*: Investors incur zero transaction costs to buy and sell assets. This assumption is reasonable for large institutions when they buy and sell publicly traded securities such as stocks and bonds. It fails for smaller investors, and for investments other than publicly traded securities. For example, the acquisition of a

116

business, an investment of special concern in this book, is a complex and costly proposition.

The more important transaction costs are, the more asset prices will not fall exactly on the capital market line. Instead, some assets may be on one side of the line or the other because transaction costs outweigh the advantages of swapping a security that is slightly below the line for another security that is slightly above the line. The capital market line then becomes not a single line, but a band within which asset prices should lie. The greater transaction costs are, the wider the band.

When transaction costs are positive, it also no longer makes sense for investors to hold the entire market portfolio. At some point, the diversification gains from holding smaller and smaller pieces of more and more assets will be outweighed by the transaction costs of further diversification.

2. *Perfectly divisible assets*: All assets are infinitely divisible, so that an investor can buy a tiny fraction of each asset. This assumption is necessary if investors are to be able to purchase fully diversified portfolios. This assumption is reasonable for some assets, such as stocks and bonds; it is less reasonable for other assets, such as real estate and private businesses. Nondivisible assets also commonly involve higher transaction costs upon sale. Generally speaking, the less divisible an asset is, the more likely it is to lie outside the capital market band established by the transaction costs of trading highly divisible assets.

3. *Zero taxes*: The model assumes that no taxes are charged either on the sale of assets, or on the cash generated by an investment. In fact, taxes affect asset prices in a number of complex ways that can only be sketched here. First, taxes affect the expected return to a taxable investor, and thus affect the prices that taxable investors will pay. Second, capital gains taxes charged on the sale of a capital asset have much the same effect as transaction costs in allowing minor mispricing of assets, and thus spreading out the band within which asset prices will fall.

Third, if different assets are taxed differently (*e.g.*, if dividends are taxed at a higher effective rate than capital gains), then investors should hold higher proportions of those assets which are most tax-favorable *to them*. In theory, this *clientele effect* could lead to complete separation, with only tax-exempt investors holding assets of type *A*, and only taxable investors holding assets of type *B*. In practice, only partial separation occurs. The question of why firms pay tax-disfavored dividends, instead of the lower-tax alternative of occasionally repurchasing some of their shares, remains one of the unsolved mysteries of finance.[1]

4. *Homogeneous expectations*: Investors have the same beliefs about the expected returns and risks of all available investments. Thus, once a market price for risk is established, investors agree on the value of each investment. This is obviously a rough approximation. If all investors agreed on value, they would do far less swapping of stocks and bonds, and probably less buying and selling of businesses as well.

With heterogeneous expectations, asset prices depend on a complex mix of investor expectations and risk preferences. In essence, each investor has his own capital market line, and buys those assets which appear most favorably priced. Market prices reflect a blend of the expectations of different investors. Overall, the capital market line becomes fuzzy. If expectations are only moderately heterogeneous, rough estimates of the tradeoff between expected return and systematic risk can still be developed.

5. *Two-period world*: All available investments involve an investment at time $t = 0$, and a cash return at a known later time $t = 1$. This is a gross oversimplification of the complex returns on actual investments. It is possible to derive CAPM without this assumption, but only at the cost of making other equally strong assumptions. For example, one can relax the two-period assumption if the risk-free interest rate and the market price of risk: (i) are the same for all investment periods; and (ii) will not change over time, so that there is certainty about future reinvestment opportunities.

In a multi-period world, with different interest rates and risk premia for different time periods, we end up with a separate capital market line for each investment time horizon, plus some loose limits, established by the possibility of arbitrage between shorter and longer time periods, on interest rates and risk premia for different time periods.

6. *Known inflation rate*: CAPM can accommodate a nonzero inflation rate, but the inflation rate must be known at $t = 0$, when an investment is made. This assumption is reasonable for short periods of time, but becomes increasingly unrealistic as the investment horizon lengthens.

---

[1] See, e.g., Fischer Black, *The Dividend Puzzle*, J. Portfolio Mgmt. 5 (Winter 1976); Frank Easterbrook, *Two Agency-Cost Explanations of Dividends*, 74 Am.Econ.Rev. 650 (1984), both reprinted in *The Modern Theory of Corporate Finance* (Clifford Smith ed. 2d ed. 1990).

7. *Existence of a zero-risk security*: A zero-risk security must exist, in quantities large enough to satisfy the demand of all those who want to own it. In empirical tests of the model, short-term Treasury bills are commonly assumed to be zero-risk. If fact, even Treasury bills have reinvestment risk if one's investment time horizon extends beyond the T-bill maturity date, some inflation risk, and currency risk (the risk that changes in the purchasing power of different currencies will not track differences in inflation rates, which will affect one's ability to use funds received at $t = 1$ to purchase goods priced in other currencies). In the real world, it is not be possible to construct a completely risk-free security.

One can relax this assumption by positing unlimited ability to sell assets *short* -- to sell an asset one doesn't own today, and buy it back at a later time, thus profiting if the price goes down and losing money if the price goes up. Unlimited short selling allows investors to construct a *zero-beta* portfolio, which can substitute for the zero-risk security. If a zero-beta portfolio cannot be constructed, then security prices will still fall along a straight line, but only some portions of the line will be reachable through actual investment strategies.

8. *Purely passive investment*: Investors are purely passive. They purchase fractional interests in investments with known expected returns and risks. They cannot, by their actions, change an investment's expected return or risk. This assumption is reasonable for modestly sized investments in publicly traded stocks and bonds. It becomes less true as an investment becomes large enough to confer influence over future decisions by business managers. Indeed, the value of control, which carries with it the opportunity to affect future business decisions, is central to understanding many corporate acquisitions.

9. *Ability to borrow at risk-free rate*: Investors can lend money at the risk-free rate of interest by investing in the zero-risk security, assuming it exists. CAPM assumes that they can also *borrow* at the risk-free rate. This assumption is approximately true for large institutional investors who want to borrow an amount that is a modest fraction of their total assets. It is increasingly violated as investor size becomes smaller and as an investor's borrowing increases as a fraction of the investor's assets, thus increasing the risk of default.

If investors can borrow at the risk-free rate r_f plus an increment x which is the same for all investors, the capital market line becomes kinked, with one slope for $\beta <$ 1, where investors are lending at the risk-free rate, and a lower slope for $\beta > 1$, where investors are borrowing. The lower slope reflects the higher cost of borrowed funds. If different investors have different borrowing rates, they each have their own kinked capital market line, and it becomes harder to generalize about asset prices for $\beta > 1$.

10. *Beta is a complete measure of risk*: The standard deviation of an investment's systematic risk, measured relative to the standard deviation on the market as a whole, is assumed to be a complete measure of the risk for which investors must be compensated. In fact, while β is a plausible measure of a particular kind of risk, it does not fully capture some risks, such as inflation risk or liquidity risk (the risk of not being able to sell an asset quickly at the current market price, if your risk preferences change or you need funds).

In addition, as we discussed in Chapter 3, standard deviation is a complete measure of risk only when the distribution of returns perfectly matches the normal, or bell-curve, distribution. Fluctuations in asset prices don't perfectly follow the normal distribution, especially over long periods of time. In particular, long-term returns show a long positive tail, reflecting the occasional firm -- like Microsoft or Walmart -- that becomes a spectacular success, and the many more firms that increase fivefold or tenfold in value. In contrast, no firm's stock can lose more than 100% of its starting value. Thus, standard deviation can't fully describe the systematic risks that investors face, and presumably must be compensated for.

C. Empirical Tests of CAPM

In light of the strong assumptions underlying CAPM, a key question is how well the model fit the facts. Is it valuable in explaining how security prices actually behave? Or is it only a theoretical construct that suggests how security prices ought to behave under highly artificial circumstances?

Unfortunately, testing CAPM (or any other asset pricing model) is surprisingly difficult. One problem is that asset pricing theories predict a relationship between *expected risk* and *expected return*. All we can actually measure is *actual risk* and *actual return*. To test the connection between risk and return, we must hope that, on average and over time, actual returns will correlate with expected returns, and actual price fluctuations will correlate with expected risk.

Given actual patterns of asset price fluctuation, the time period needed to estimate the relationship between risk and return is very long. Over limited time periods, high-risk assets may -- and sometimes will -- produce *lower* returns than low-risk assets. That possibility is inherent in the concept of risk.

Estimating expected risk is also hard. A beta estimate depends on regression analysis of the returns on a particular stock versus the returns on the stock market as a whole. The regression is noisy, as you can see from the Host International example in

Figure 3-3. Thus, even the historical β estimate isn't very accurate. Moreover, the riskiness of the market as a whole, and the riskiness of particular stocks relative to the market, change over time, especially over the long time periods needed to test the model. In practice, β estimates for particular companies are not very stable over time. CAPM tests are typically conducted on portfolios of 20 or more stocks, for which beta estimates are more stable, though with some tendency for *regression to the mean* -- high β values tend to decline over time, and low β values tend to increase.

A further problem for CAPM (but not some other asset pricing models) is that CAPM defines the market portfolio as a *complete* portfolio of risky assets, both liquid and illiquid. The complete market portfolio includes not only publicly traded common stocks but also bonds, real estate, oil wells, private companies, etc., on a *worldwide* basis. CAPM posits a relationship between expected risk and the expected return on this complete market portfolio. All one can measure, though, is the relationship between risk and return for publicly traded securities. Empirical tests typically use a proxy for the complete market portfolio, such as the S&P 500 Index or the New York Stock Exchange index. This makes the tests ambiguous. Observed returns may differ from those that CAPM predicts because we have used an incomplete market portfolio. Conversely, if observed returns match CAPM's predictions, that too may be an artifact resulting from use of an incomplete market portfolio.[2]

In practice, tests of CAPM are generally not sensitive to small changes in the proxy for the market portfolio, such as switching from the S&P 500 Index to the New York Stock Exchange index. But efforts to conduct asset pricing tests using a worldwide index of publicly traded stocks are still in their infancy.[3] And we are far from being able to construct a good proxy for the worldwide market portfolio.

Finally, all asset pricing models offer a *normative* theory of how assets *should* be priced. If assets are not priced as the theory predicts, that could mean that the theory is wrong. But it could also mean that assets are mispriced. In effect, every test of an asset pricing theory is a joint test of (i) the theory; and (ii) the efficiency of market pricing. To test the asset pricing theory, we must assume that assets are efficiently priced. Conversely, to test pricing efficiency, we must assume that a particular asset pricing theory, such as CAPM, describes how assets should be priced.

---

[2] See Richard Roll, *A Critique of Asset Pricing Theory's Tests, Part 1: On Past and Potential Testability of the Theory*, 4 J.Fin. 129 (1977).

[3] See, e.g., Campbell Harvey, *The World Price of Covariance Risk*, 46 J.Fin. 111 (1991); K.C. Chan, G. Andrew Karolyi & Rene Stulz, *Global Financial Markets and the Risk Premium on U.S. Equity* (Nat'l Bureau Econ. Res. Working Paper No. 4074, May 1992).

These practical problems aside, what do the tests show? Broad asset classes -- short-term Treasury bills, government bonds, corporate bonds, and common stocks -- show *roughly* the relationship that CAPM predicts. Over the period from 1926-1991 (1926 is as far back as we have good data), asset classes with higher levels of risk have produced higher returns. Table 4-1 shows the nominal and real (inflation adjusted) returns, assuming annual compounding, on different asset classes:

Table 4-1
Annual Returns on Asset Classes: 1926-1991

Asset Class	Nominal Return	Real Return	Standard Deviation of Annual Returns	Risk Premium Over Treasury Bills
Short-Term Treasury Bills	3.7%	0.5%	3.4%	0%
Intermediate-Term Treasury Bonds	5.1	1.9	5.6	1.4
Long-Term Treasury Bonds	5.4	2.2	8.6	1.7
Corporate Bonds	5.4	2.2	8.5	1.7
Large-Company Stocks	10.4	7.1	20.8	6.6
Small-Company Stocks	12.1	8.7	35.3	8.2

Source: Ibbotson Associates, *Stocks, Bonds, Bills and Inflation* (1992 Yearbook)

The   risk premia shown in Table 4-1 are historical averages.   The average estimated risk premium on large-company stocks (proxied by the S&P 500) *has been* 6-7%. The risk premium *today* may be lower or higher than this. In 1993, when this is written, many analysts believe that the risk premium on common stocks is lower than its historical mean, perhaps only 3-4%. Moreover, 6.6% is merely our best *estimate* of the average risk premium. The standard deviation of that estimate is about 2.5%. This means that there is about a 2/3 chance that the actual risk premium averaged between 4% and 9%, about a 1/6 chance that the actual risk premium was less than 4%, and a 1/6 chance that the actual premium was more than 9%.

Even over long time periods, greater risk does not ensure greater return. For example, short-term Treasury bills produced a *higher* total return from 1926-1981 than long-term Treasury bonds, because long-term bond prices are sensitive to inflation, which increased over much of the period. Long-term Treasuries performed much better than T-bills over the last decade, as interest rates generally fell. Only in the last couple of years did the cumulative return since 1926 on long-term Treasury bonds overtake the cumulative return on intermediate-term Treasuries, even though intermediate-term Treasuries have significantly lower risk.

While CAPM has predictive power for the long-run relationship between risk and return for broad asset classes, its prediction that high-β stocks should produce higher returns than low-β stocks is not as well supported. At the least, β seems not to be a complete measure of the risks that are priced in securities markets. The next reading is from a recent, critical evaluation of CAPM's ability to predict stock returns.

EUGENE FAMA & KENNETH FRENCH, THE CROSS-SECTION OF EXPECTED STOCK RETURNS
47 J.Fin. 427 (1992)

The [Capital Asset Pricing Model] has long shaped the way academics and practitioners think about average returns and risk. The central prediction of the model is that . . . (a) expected returns on securities are a positive linear function of their market βs (the slope in the regression of a security's return on the market's return), and (b) market βs suffice to describe the cross-section of expected returns.

There are several empirical contradictions of [CAPM]. The most prominent is the size effect of Banz (1981).[a] He finds that market equity, ME (a stock's price times shares outstanding), adds to the explanation of the cross-section of average returns provided by market βs. Average returns on small (low ME) stocks are too high given their β estimates, and average returns on large stocks are too low.

Another contradiction . . . is the positive relation between leverage and average return documented by Bhandari (1988).[b] It is plausible that leverage is associated with risk and expected return, but in [CAPM], leverage risk should be captured by market β.

---

[a] Rolf Banz, *The Relationship Between Return and Market Value of Common Stocks*, 9 J.Fin.Econ. 3 (1981).

[b] Laxmi Bhandari, *Debt/Equity Ratio and Expected Common Stock Returns: Empirical Evidence*, 43 J.Fin. 507 (1988).

Bhandari finds, however, that leverage helps explain the cross-section of average stock returns in tests that include size (ME) as well as β.

Stattman (1980) and Rosenberg, Reid & Lanstein (1985) find that average returns on U.S stocks are positively related to the ratio of a firm's book value of common equity, BE, to its market value, ME.[c] Chan, Hamao & Lakonishok (1991) find that book-to-market equity, BE/ME, also has a strong role in explaining the cross-section of average returns on Japanese stocks.[d]

Finally, Basu (1983) shows that earnings-price ratios (E/P) help explain the cross-section of average returns on U.S stocks in tests that also include size and market β. Ball (1978) argues that E/P is a catch-all proxy for unnamed factors in expected returns; E/P is likely to be higher (prices are lower relative to earnings) for stocks with higher risks and expected returns, whatever the unnamed sources of risk.[e]

Ball's proxy argument for E/P might also apply to size (ME), leverage, and book-to-market equity. All these variables can be regarded as different ways to scale stock prices, to extract the information in prices about risk and expected returns. Moreover, since E/P, ME, leverage, and BE/ME are all scaled versions of price, it is reasonable to expect that some of them are redundant for describing average returns. Our goal is to evaluate the joint roles of market β, size, E/P, leverage, and book-to-market equity in the cross-section of average returns on NYSE, AMEX, and NASDAQ stocks.

Black, Jensen & Scholes (1972) and Fama & MacBeth (1973) find that, as predicted by [CAPM], there is a positive simple relation between average stock returns and β during the pre-1969 period.[f] Like Reinganum (1981) and Lakonishok & Shapiro (1986), we find that the relation between β and average return disappears during the

---

[c] Dennis Stattman, *Book Values and Stock Returns*, 4 Chi. MBA: J. Selected Papers 25 (1980); Barr Rosenberg, Kenneth Reid & Ronald Lanstein, *Persuasive Evidence of Market Inefficiency*, J. Portfolio Mgmt. 9 (Spr.1985).

[d] Louis Chan, Yasushi Hamao & Josef Lakonishok, *Fundamentals and Stock Returns in Japan*, 46 J.Fin. 1739 (1991).

[e] Sanjoy Basu, *The Relationship Between Earnings Yield, Market Value, and Return for NYSE Common Stocks: Further Evidence*, 12 J.Fin. Econ. 129 (1983); Ray Ball, *Anomalies in Relationships Between Securities' Yields and Yield-Surrogates*, 6 J.Fin.Econ. 103 (1978).

[f] Fischer Black, Michael Jensen & Myron Scholes, *The Capital Asset Pricing Model: Some Empirical Tests*, in *Studies in the Theory of Capital Markets* (Michael Jensen ed.1972); Eugene Fama & James MacBeth, *Risk, Return and Equilibrium: Empirical Tests*, 81 J.Pol.Econ. 607 (1973). These studies were key early studies that provided empirical support for CAPM, and led to its widespread acceptance. Ed.

more recent 1963-1990 period, even when β is used alone to explain average returns.[g] The . . . simple relation between β and average return is also weak in the 50-year 1941-1990 period. In short, our tests do not support the most basic prediction of [CAPM], that average stock returns are positively related to market βs.

Unlike the simple relation between β and average return, the univariate relations between average return and size, leverage, E/P and book-to-market equity are strong.[h] In multivariate tests, the negative relation between size and average return is robust to the inclusion of other variables.[i] The positive relation between book-to-market equity and average return also persists in competition with other variables. Moreover, although the size effect has attracted more attention, book-to-market equity has a consistently stronger role in average returns. Our bottom-line results are: (a) β does not seem to help explain the cross-section of average stock returns, and (b) the combination of size and book-to-market equity seems to absorb the roles of leverage and E/P in average stock returns, at least during our 1963-1990 sample period.

If assets are priced rationally, our results suggest that stock risks are multidimensional. One dimension of risk is proxied by size, ME. Another dimension of risk is proxied by BE/ME, the ratio of the book value of common equity to its market value.

It is possible that the risk captured by BE/ME is the relative distress factor of Chan & Chen (1991).[j] They postulate that the earning prospects of firms are associated

---

[g] Marc Reinganum, *A New Empirical Perspective on the CAPM*, 16 J.Fin. & Quantitative Analysis 439 (1981); Josef Lakonishok & Alan Shapiro, *Systematic Risk, Total Risk, and Size as Determinants of Stock Market Returns*, 10 J. Banking & Fin. 115 (1986).

[h] *Univariate* regression analysis involves asking whether one variable, called the *dependent* variable, correlates with a second variable, called the *independent* variable. For example, in the market model, $R = \alpha + \beta \cdot R_m + \epsilon$, we measure whether the daily returns R on a particular firm's stock correlate with the daily returns R_m on the stock market as a whole. Here R is the dependent variable, R_m is the independent variable, and β is a measure of how the two variables are related. In the market model, there is *one* independent variable (R_m) on the right hand side of the regression equation, hence the term *univariate* analysis.

[i] *Multivariate* regression analysis involves asking whether a dependent variable, such as the daily returns R on a firm's stock, is simultaneously correlated with *two or more* independent variables. Sometimes, the dependent variable will correlate with a particular independent variable in a univariate analysis, but the correlation will disappear when more independent variables are added to the regression. This suggests that the variation in the dependent variable is better explained by the variables which remain statistically significant in the multivariate analysis than by the variable whose significance disappears when other variables are added. We discuss the concept of statistical significance in Chapter 6.

[j] K.C. Chan & Nai-fu Chen, *Structural and Return Characteristics of Small and Large Firms*, 46

with a risk factor in returns. Firms that the market judges to have poor prospects, signalled here by low stock prices and high ratios of book-to-market equity, have higher expected stock returns (they are penalized with higher costs of capital) than firms with strong prospects. It is also possible, however, that BE/ME just captures the unraveling (regression toward the mean) of irrational market whims about the prospects of firms.

Whatever the underlying economic causes, our main result is straightforward. Two easily measured variables, size (ME) and book-to-market equity (BE/ME), provide a simple and powerful characterization of the cross-section of average stock returns for the 1963-1990 period. . .

[W]hen common stock portfolios are formed on size alone . . ., average return is positively related to β. The βs of size portfolios are, however, almost perfectly correlated with size, so tests on size portfolios are unable to disentangle β and size effects in average returns. Allowing for variation in β that is unrelated to size breaks the logjam, but at the expense of β. Thus, when we subdivide size portfolios on the basis of preranking βs, we find a strong relation between average return and size, but no relation between average return and β. . .

Can β Be Saved?

What explains the poor results for β? One possibility is that other explanatory variables are correlated with true βs, and this obscures the relation between average returns and measured βs. But this line of attack cannot explain why β has no power when used alone to explain average returns. Moreover, leverage, book-to-market equity, and E/P do not seem to be good proxies for β. The averages of the monthly cross-sectional correlations between β and the values of these variables for individual stocks are all within 0.15 of 0.

Another hypothesis is that . . . there is a positive relation between β and average return, but the relation is obscured by noise in the β estimates. However, our full-period post-ranking βs do not seem to be imprecise. Most of the standard errors of the βs are 0.05 or less, only 1 is greater than 0.1, and the standard errors are small relative to the range of the βs (0.53 to 1.79). . . [k]

Our evidence on the robustness of the size effect and the absence of a relation between β and average return is so contrary to [CAPM] that it behooves us to examine whether the results are special to 1963-1990 . . . NYSE returns for 1941-1990 behave like the NYSE, AMEX, and NASDAQ returns for 1963-1990; there is a reliable size

---

J.Fin. 1467 (1991).

[k] "Standard error" is another term for standard deviation.

effect over the full 50-year period, but little relation between β and average return. Interestingly, there is a reliable simple relation between β and average return during the 1941-1965 period. These 25 years are a major part of the samples in the early studies of [CAPM]. Even for the 1941-1965 period, however, the relation between β and average return disappears when we control for size. . .

β and the Market Factor: Caveats

Some caveats about the negative evidence on the role of β in average returns are in order. The average premiums for β, size, and book-to-market equity depend on the definitions of the variables used in the regressions. For example, suppose we replace [the logarithm of the ratio of book-to-market equity] (ln(BE/ME)) with [the logarithm of] book equity (ln(BE))[1]. As long as [the logarithm of] size (ln(ME)) is also in the regression, this change will not affect the intercept, the fitted values or the R^2.[m] But the change in variables increases the average slope (and the t-statistic) on ln(ME). In other words, it increases the risk premium associated with size. Other redefinitions of the β, size, and book-to-market variables will produce different regression slopes and perhaps different inferences about average premiums, including possible resuscitation of a role for β. And, of course, at the moment, we have no theoretical basis for choosing among different versions of the variables.

Moreover, the tests here are restricted to stocks. It is possible that including other assets will change the inferences about the average premiums for β, size, and book-to-market equity. . . Extending the tests to bills and other bonds may well change our inferences about average risk premiums, including the revival of a role for market β.

We emphasize, however, that different approaches to the tests are not likely to revive [CAPM]. Resuscitation of [CAPM] requires that a better proxy for the market portfolio (a) overturns our evidence that the simple relation between β and average stock returns is flat and (b) leaves β as the *only* variable relevant for explaining average returns. Such results seem unlikely, given Stambaugh's (1982) evidence that tests of

---

[1] "Ln" is a commonly used abbreviation for natural logarithm. Fama and French work with the logarithms of variables like book equity and market equity because this improves the statistical properties of these variables.

[m] R^2 is a measure of how much of the variation in a dependent variable (here, stock price) is explained, in a regression analysis, by variation in the independent variables (here β, size, and book-to-market equity). A high R^2 (close to 1) indicates that the independent variables explain most of the variation in the dependent variable; a low R^2 (close to 0) indicates that the independent variables explain only a small fraction of the variation in the dependent variable. Most asset-pricing theories produce only modest values of R^2. See Richard Roll, R^2, 43 J.Fin. 541 (1988).

[CAPM] do not seem to be sensitive to the choice of a market proxy.[n] Thus, if there is a role for β in average returns, it is likely to be found in a multi-factor model that transforms the flat simple relation between average return and β into a positively sloped conditional relation.

Rational Asset-Pricing Stories

. . . [Our results] are not economically satisfying. What is the economic explanation for the roles of size and book-to-market equity in average returns? We suggest several paths of inquiry.

. . . Examining the relations between the returns on [portfolios formed based on size and book-to-market equity] and economic variables that measure variation in business conditions might help expose the nature of the economic risks captured by size and book-to-market equity.

Chan, Chen & Hsieh (1985) argue that the relation between size and average return proxies for a more fundamental relation between expected returns and economic risk factors. Their most powerful factor in explaining the size effect is the difference between the monthly returns on low- and high-grade corporate bonds, which in principle captures a kind of default risk in returns that is priced.[o] It would be interesting to test whether loadings on this or other economic factors . . . can explain the roles of size and book-to-market equity in our tests. . . .

[I]f stock prices are rational, BE/ME, the ratio of the book value of a stock to the market's assessment of its value, should be a direct indicator of the relative prospects of firms. For example, we expect that high BE/ME firms have low earnings on assets relative to low BE/ME firms. Our work (in progress) suggests that there is indeed a clean separation between high and low BE/ME firms on various measures of economic fundamentals. Low BE/ME firms are persistently strong performers, while the economic performance of high BE/ME firms is persistently weak.

Irrational Asset-Pricing Stories

The discussion above assumes that the asset-pricing effects captured by size and book-to-market equity are rational. For BE/ME, our most powerful expected-return variable, there is an obvious alternative. The cross-section of book-to-market ratios

---

[n] Robert Stambaugh, *On the Exclusion of Assets from Tests of the Two-Parameter Model: A Sensitivity Analysis*, 10 J.Fin.Econ. 237 (1982).

[o] K.C. Chan, Nai-fu Chen & David Hsieh, *An Exploratory Investigation of the Firm Size Effect*, 14 J.Fin.Econ. 451 (1985).

might result from market overreaction to the relative prospects of firms. If overreaction tends to be corrected, BE/ME will predict the cross-section of stock returns. Simple tests do not confirm that the size and book-to-market effects in average returns are due to market overreaction, at least of the type posited by DeBondt & Thaler (1985).[p] . . .

If our results are more than chance, they have practical implications for portfolio formation and performance evaluation by investors whose primary concern is long-term average returns. If asset-pricing is rational, size and BE/ME must proxy for risk. Our results then imply that the performance of managed portfolios (e.g., pension funds and mutual funds) can be evaluated by comparing their average returns with the average returns of benchmark portfolios with similar size and BE/ME characteristics. Likewise, the expected returns for different portfolio strategies can be estimated from the historical average returns of portfolios with matching size and BE/ME properties.

If asset-pricing is irrational and size and BE/ME do not proxy for risk, our results might still be used to evaluate portfolio performance and measure the expected returns from alternative investment strategies. If stock prices are irrational, however, the likely persistence of the results is more suspect. . .

D. Multi-Factor Asset Pricing Models

Beta, as a measure of the risk that is priced in securities markets, has been weakened by recent studies such as Fama & French. At the least, we need a multi-factor asset pricing model that accounts for different types of risk. We also need a better understanding of how measurable quantities, like size or book-to-market equity, which don't directly measure risk, proxy for risk. There is nothing intrinsic about size or BE/ME that makes them obvious surrogates for systematic risk, which is why Fama & French comment that their results are "not economically satisfying." For size, one possibility is that liquidity, which is correlated with size, is an important underlying risk factor. The premium that investors are willing to pay for higher liquidity can potentially explain much of the size effect that Fama & French discuss.

The leading alternative to CAPM is Arbitrage Pricing Theory (APT). APT posits that, rather than a single factor determining returns as in the CAPM, a number of risk factors interact to determine expected returns. An asset's expected return is determined by its sensitivity to each risk factor. Expected return is assumed to be linearly related to each risk factor. In effect, each risk factor has its own "beta." Empirical evidence that return is determined by factors in addition to β, so troublesome for CAPM, is

---

[p] Werner Debondt & Richard Thaler, *Does the Stock Market Overreact?*, 40 J.Fin. 557 (1985).

expressly contemplated by APT. Indeed, CAPM can be seen as a special case of the APT where one particular factor -- systematic risk -- determines returns.

Suppose that the expected return on a portfolio p depends on two factors -- say systematic risk (proxied by $\beta_p r_m$) and liquidity. APT predicts that the capital market line will become a *plane*, as shown in Figure 4-7. If expected return depends on three or more factors, the capital market plane will become a multidimensional hyperplane, which can't be shown visually.

Mathematically, APT predicts that the expected return on portfolio p is related to the various risk factors by:

$$ER_p = a + (b_1 \cdot RF_1) + (b_2 \cdot RF_2) + (b_3 \cdot RF_3) + \ldots \qquad \textbf{(4-4)}$$

For our example of two risk factors -- systematic risk and liquidity -- this becomes:

$$ER_p = a + (b_1 \cdot \beta_p r_m) + (b_2 \cdot L_p) \qquad \textbf{(4-5)}$$

where:

L_p = a measure of the liquidity of portfolio p
b_1 = the weighting factor for systematic risk
b_2 = the weighting factor for liquidity

Equation 4-5 is the equation of the plane shown in Figure 4-7. Since investors like more liquidity, the plane slopes *down* in the liquidity dimension.

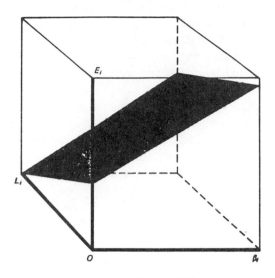

Figure 4-7
A Possible Capital Market Plane

Source: William Sharpe, *Investments* 178 (3d ed.1985)

APT, like CAPM, requires a set of strong assumptions, similar but not identical to the CAPM assumptions. If these assumptions hold, then if an asset's price departs from the capital market hyperplane, investors will be able to engage in arbitrage transactions that will tend to push the security's price back towards the hyperplane.

The generality of APT comes at a price. CAPM makes the *normative* prediction that a particular risk factor -- beta -- *should* affect asset prices. APT is agnostic on which risk factors count. Its usefulness will depend on whether future research allows us to determine which risk factors influence expected returns, and measure the sensitivity of expected returns to each factor. Empirical efforts to resolve these questions are still in a preliminary stage. There is evidence to support at least five risk factors: the level of industrial activity; the rate of inflation; the spread between short and long-term interest rates; the spread between the yields of low and high-risk corporate bonds (which is a measure of default risk); and liquidity (proxied by bid-asked spread).[4]

Given the uncertainties of asset-pricing theory, perhaps the most we can say is that systematic risks affect the expected returns demanded by risk-averse investors. But we lack, as yet, a solid understanding of *which systematic risks matter*, or *how much* they

---

[4] See Nai-fu Chen, Richard Roll & Stephen Ross, *Economic Forces and the Stock Market*, 59 J.Bus. 383 (1986); Yakov Amihud & Haim Mendelson, *Liquidity, Asset Prices and Financial Policy*, Fin. Analysts J. 56 (Nov.-Dec. 1991).

matter. An investment in a venture capital startup is clearly riskier than an investment in a large, profitable firm, and venture capital investors should (and presumably do) demand a higher expected rate of return for to compensate for that risk. But we can only crudely estimate the extra risks that the venture capital investor is taking, or how much the investor should be paid for taking those risks. We must also keep in mind the possibility that *unsystematic risk* may affect prices, in a complex world where diversification is costly and no one is sure which risks are systematic and which aren't.

These uncertainties are less troublesome for our purposes than for stock traders. The potential for business combinations to affect risk will still be central in understanding how business combinations can increase the combined value of the merging firms. And the potential for the actions of lawyers and other professionals to reduce various risks will still be central in understanding their role in adding value. If lawyers can influence *any* factor bearing on asset value, the potential for value creation is present. Thus, the inability of financial theory to fully specify which risk factors affect asset values does not interfere with our project. (Though, to be sure, the more we know about the factors that determine value, the greater the potential for value creation.)

E. Value Additivity and Capital Budgeting under Uncertainty

In Chapter 2, we discussed capital budgeting in a world without risk. There we stressed the need to take the time value of money into account in evaluating the returns from a prospective investment. In this Chapter and in Chapter 3, we introduced the concept of risk. In a risky world, the required return for a project is composed of two elements: a payment that reflects the time value of money; and a payment for bearing the risks associated with the project. It is now time to return to capital budgeting and ask how a firm should take risk into account in determining the appropriate discount rate for a project. The accepted approach to this question is developed in the excerpt below:

RICHARD BREALEY & STEWART MYERS, PRINCIPLES OF CORPORATE FINANCE
181-83 (4th ed.1991)[*]

Long before the development of modern theories linking risk and expected return, smart financial managers adjusted for risk in capital budgeting. They realized intuitively that, other things being equal, risky projects are less desirable than safe ones. Therefore they demanded a higher rate of return from risky projects or they based their decisions on conservative estimates of the cash flows.

Various rules of thumb are often used to make these risk adjustments. For example, many companies estimate the rate of return required by investors in its securities and use the **company cost of capital** to discount the cash flows on all new projects. Since investors require a higher rate of return from a very risky company, such a firm will have a higher company cost of capital and will set a higher discount rate for its new investment opportunitites. . .

This is a step in the right direction. Even though we can't measure risk or the expected return on risky securities with absolute precision, it is still reasonable to assert that [a computer company such as Digital Equipment Corp. (DEC) faces] more risk than the average firm and, therefore, should have demanded a higher rate of return from its capital investments.

But the company cost of capital rule can also get a firm into trouble if the new projects are more or less risky than its existing business. Each project should be evaluated at its *own* opportunity cost of capital. This is a clear implication of the value-additivity principle. For a firm composed of assets A and B, firm value is

$$\text{Firm value} \ = \ PV(AB) \ = \ PV(A) + PV(B)$$

. . . Here $PV(A)$ and $PV(B)$ are valued just as if they were mini-firms in which stockholders could invest directly. *Note:* Investors would value A by discounting its forecasted cash flows at a rate reflecting the risk of A. They would value B by discounting at a rate reflecting the risk of B. The two discount rates will, in general, be different.

If the firm considers investing in a third project C, it should also value C as if it were a mini-firm. That is, the firm should discount the cash flows of C at the expected rate of return investors would demand to make a separate investment in C. *The true cost of capital depends on the use to which the capital is put.*

[If a] project has a high risk, DEC needs a higher prospective return than if the project has a low risk. Now contrast this with the company cost of capital rule, which is to accept any project *regardless of its risk* as long as it offers a higher return than the *company's* cost of capital.

It is clearly silly to suggest that DEC should demand the same rate of return from a very safe project as from a very risky one. If DEC used the company cost of capital rule, it would reject many good low-risk projects and accept many poor high-risk projects. It is also silly to suggest that just because AT&T has a low company cost of capital, it is justified in accepting projects that DEC would reject. If you followed such a rule to its seemingly logical conclusion, you would think it possible to enlarge the company's investment opportunities by investing a large sum in Treasury bills. That would make the common stock safe and create a low company cost of capital.

The notion that each company has some individual discount rate or cost of capital is widespread, but far from universal. Many firms require different returns from different categories of investment. The following discount rates might be set . . .:

Category	Discount Rate(%)
Speculative ventures	30
New products	20
Expansion of existing business	15 (company cost of capital)
Cost improvement, known technology	10

Problems to Accompany Chapter 4

1. Using the information in Table 4-1, use CAPM to estimate the expected rate of return on an investment with $\beta = 1.3$. Assume that the S&P 500 Index has $\beta = 1$.

2. How would your answer to question 1 change if you were told that the current return on short-term Treasury bills was 6%, and that the estimated risk premium on a portfolio with $\beta = 1$ was equal to 4%?

3. Assume that the S&P 500 Index has $\beta = 1$, and that the return on the S&P 500 over the past five years has averaged 14% annually. In contrast, the return on a portfolio of stocks with an estimated beta of .8 has been 11.5% annually over the same period. Based on the information given, use CAPM to estimate the return on a portfolio of 90-day Treasury bills over the five year period. Explain how you arrived at your estimate.

4. What are the principal sources of error in your estimate in problem 3?

5. Assume that over the last 10 years, large-company stocks have produced an average return of 15% per year, while small-company stocks have produced an average return of only 12% per year. Your stockbroker claims that this proves that the size effect is no longer valid, and large-company stocks are a better buy. Do you agree or disagree, and why?

6. You are the CEO of Widget Corp. Your friendly (and fee-hungry) local investment banker, having read the Fama & French study, comes to visit you one day, and explains that this study proves that bigger is better. If a company is bigger, he explains, investors will demand a smaller expected rate of return. Thus, all you need to do to reduce the expected rate of return on Widget Corp. stock, and thus raise the stock price, is issue $5 billion in new stock, and use the proceeds to buy other companies. He has a few companies in mind. What's wrong with the investment banker's reasoning?

CHAPTER 5: THE EFFICIENT CAPITAL MARKETS HYPOTHESIS

Chapters 2 through 4 surveyed the theory of how capital assets *should* be valued. In this chapter, we introduce a central paradigm of modern finance theory -- the *Efficient Capital Markets Hypothesis* -- the hypothesis that the prices of publicly traded assets, such as stocks and bonds, match the value that asset pricing theory says these assets should have. We will be interested principally in the *semistrong* form of the Efficient Capital Market Hypothesis (ECMH), which states that, at any point in time, market prices *are an unbiased forecast of future cash flows that fully reflects all publicly available information*. The semistrong form has considerable empirical support, at least for the common stock of large public companies.

In contrast, the *strong* form of ECMH states that market prices are an unbiased estimate of future cash flows that fully reflects *all* information, both public and private. The strong form of ECMH is an extreme hypothesis that is not satisfied in the real world. If it were, inside trading would not be a profitable activity. The *weak* form of ECMH states that investors can't earn an above-market return by relying on the past history of stock prices and stock trading. The weak form is subsumed in the semistrong form, since past prices and trading history are particular types of publicly available information.

Unfortunately, common usage of the phrase "market efficiency" often does not distinguish between different types of efficiency. For example, a statement that "the stock market is inefficient" might be a claim that the prices of publicly traded common stocks do not correctly reflect all information available to investors (semistrong inefficiency), or a claim that market prices differ from the price that a fully informed investor would pay (strong-form inefficiency). References in this book to "ECMH" or "market efficiency" mean semistrong efficiency, unless we explicitly state otherwise.

Semistrong market efficiency has far-reaching ramifications. At a practical level, semistrong efficiency implies that *new* information that bears on the expected risk or return of an asset is quickly reflected in the asset's price -- so quickly that no one can profit by being the first to trade on the new information. An immediate corollary: If you don't have better information than other investors, you can't consistently beat the market by picking particular stocks that *you think* are undervalued. All you can do is incur trading costs by trying. This has led to a popular strategy known as *indexing*. An index fund seeks to closely mirror the return on a stock market index such as the S&P 500. The index investor hopes that the buy-sell decisions of other, more active investors will keep prices efficient.

Understanding when assets are likely to be fairly valued in the market, and when they might be misvalued, is central to evaluating the motives for corporate acquisitions and the social value of an active takeover market. Consider takeover motives first. Profit opportunities can arise if assets aren't correctly priced. For example, an acquirer could gain by paying $75 per share for a target that is worth $100 per share, but is valued at $50 per share in the market.

Conversely, if market prices are semistrong efficient, buying a public company, at a premium to the target's market price, makes sense *only* if: (i) the acquisition will increase the combined cash flows to the sharcholders of the bidder and target, or reduce the systematic risks associated with those cash flows; or (ii) the acquirer has private information about the target's expected cash flows or risks that the market lacks. To be sure, in any one case, the acquirer's forecast of future cash flows could be right and the consensus forecast of other investors, reflected in the market price, could be wrong. But on average and over time, the market price is more likely to be right than the value estimate, based on the same information set, of any one market participant. This is what it means for the market price to be an *unbiased* forecast of future cash flows.

With regard to the social value of takeovers, if markets are semistrong efficient, we can infer that the premium paid to the target's shareholders, unless offset by losses to other parties, reflects a real increase in social wealth. On the other hand, a takeover that reflects a smart bidder finding a bargain permits no such inference. The new owner, instead of the old shareholders, will receive the target's cash flows, but total social wealth hasn't increased.

Semistrong market efficiency has important implications for takeover policy. If shareholders are good at valuing public companies, that strengthens the case for a relatively free market in corporate control -- for letting shareholders decide whether a target should be sold. Conversely, if shareholders are prone to irrational fads, that strengthens the case for giving the target's board of directors some discretion to resist a takeover proposal that the shareholders would endorse.

Efficient market theory is also important outside the takeover context. For example, much regulation of public capital markets is intended to provide information to investors. The Securities Act of 1933 (the "Securities Act") requires an issuer of securities to distribute a prospectus -- a lengthy document filled with detailed information about the issuer -- before the issuer can sell its securities. Similarly, the Securities Exchange Act of 1934 (the "Exchange Act") requires public companies to issue periodic reports containing a wide range of information about their activities. Both acts assume that this disclosure is necessary if public investors are to pay a fair price for publicly traded securities.

Disclosure of *new* information can close the gap that might otherwise arise between the public price and the price that a fully informed investor would pay. In contrast, disclosure of information that investors already have is valuable only if capital markets are *not* semistrong efficient. This insight led the Securities and Exchange Commission, in the 1980s, to adopt an "integrated disclosure" system under which public companies, which already issue periodic financial reports under the Exchange Act, can omit most of this information from their Securities Act prospectuses. The theory is that investors already have the information contained in the financial reports. In contrast, new issuers must continue to prepare long-form prospectuses. For firms that qualify to use a short-form prospectus, integrated disclosure has greatly reduced the cost and increased the speed of issuing new securities to the public.

ECMH has also affected judicial doctrine on liability and damages in securities fraud cases. The "fraud on the market" doctrine, which presumes semistrong market efficiency, was endorsed by the Supreme Court in *Basic, Inc. v. Levinson*, 485 U.S. 224 (1988). The Court concluded that investors need not show that they actually read or relied on a statement by Basic, that falsely denied that Basic was engaged in merger negotiations. Instead, investors were entitled to assume that Basic's market price reflected the reaction of other investors to the misleading statement. This all but eliminates the reliance requirement from a securities fraud class action. The difference between the price under correct information and the actual market price becomes a measure of the damages suffered by an investor who buys at an artificially inflated price, or (as in *Basic*) sells at an artificially low price.

Section A of this Chapter reviews the history and empirical support for the different flavors of ECMH. Section B explores the factors that tend to lead asset prices to obey, or depart from, theoretically correct pricing. Section C examine recent research that chips away at the edges of efficient market theory, as well as recent "noise trading" theories, which combine theoretical claims about why prices might depart from true value with statistical claims that some departures from correct pricing can't be detected by the available tests. Finally, section D reviews the evidence on systematic biases in human cognition, which may underlie inefficient pricing.

A. The Empirical Evidence Supporting ECMH

Development of the empirical evidence on ECMH must begin with a number of caveats. First, we don't know what the "right" price for an asset is. Thus, we can't test ECMH directly, by comparing the actual price to a theoretically correct price. This means that we can never prove that a market *is* efficient. All we can do is speculate about particular ways that prices might be *inefficient*, and test for evidence of those departures from efficiency. A study that fails to find evidence of a particular departure from efficient pricing is *consistent* with ECMH. Many such studies can give us confidence that ECMH is a useful theory. But no study can ever *prove* ECMH.

Second, even in its semistrong form, ECMH is an extreme null hypothesis that can't be strictly true. Prices can become and remain "right" only if investors, in a constant search for bargains, work at getting them that way. Investors will engage in this effort only if there is profit in it. The profit, though, must come from inefficiencies of one sort or another. Thus, there must be enough inefficiency to induce investors to search for and trade on mispricing -- an equilibrium level of inefficiency.[1] The interesting empirical question is how close public securities markets come to being semistrong efficient, not whether they are perfectly efficient.

Third, our ability to test ECMH is limited by the noisiness of stock prices. It is relatively easy to test whether today's stock price is an unbiased estimate of stock price tomorrow or next week. It is far harder to test whether today's stock price is an unbiased estimate of stock price in five years, or of the long-term future stream of dividends that a firm will pay. The few long-term tests that are available show some interesting departures from efficient market predictions. Unfortunately, these departures aren't statistically significant, so we don't know whether they are real or not.

Fourth, almost all tests of semistrong market efficiency involve asking whether particular investors, or particular investment strategies, can *beat the stock market as a whole*. They test whether Mobil is correctly priced *relative* to Exxon, or Ford is correctly priced *relative* to General Motors. It is very difficult to test whether the stock market as a whole is correctly priced in an *absolute* sense -- that is, would an all-knowing observer agree that the market value of all stocks equals the discounted present value of all expected corporate cash flows. It is also very hard to test whether stocks as a whole are correctly priced compared to other broad asset categories such as bonds or real estate.[2]

---

[1] See Sanford Grossman & Joseph Stiglitz, *On the Impossibility of Informationally Efficient Markets*, 70 Am.Econ.Rev. 393, 393 (1980).

[2] Absolute and relative efficiency should be understood as rough endpoints along a continuum. The more that a test of pricing efficiency compares apples to apples (Mobil to Exxon, or Ford to GM), the stronger the statistical tests tend to be, and the stronger the qualitative reasons for believing that investors will do a reasonable job of comparing the value of *A* to the value of *B*. Conversely, the more a test of pricing efficiency compares apples to ice cream (stocks to bonds, or stocks to real estate), the weaker the statistical tests tend to be, and the more difficult the investor's task of valuation, because more variables are involved. An assessment of whether auto manufacturers are correctly priced relative to biotechnology firms would fall somewhere in between a relative test and an absolute test, both in terms of the analytical difficulty of the task, and in terms of our confidence in the statistical tests.

The terms *absolute* and *relative* efficiency are our own. Samuelson uses the terms *macro*-efficiency and *micro*-efficiency; Brealey & Myers use the terms *intrinsic* and *relative* efficiency. Paul Samuelson, *Foreword* to Marshall Blume & Jeremy Siegel, *The Theory of Security Pricing and Market Structure*, 1 Fin.Markets, Institutions & Instruments 1 (1992); Richard Brealey & Stewart Myers, *Principles of Corporate Finance* 299-300 (4th ed. 19921). For discussion of the similar but not identical

The stock market crash of 1987, when the Dow Jones Industrial Average fell 23% in a single day and 36% in two weeks, casts doubt on the absolute efficiency of stock market prices. Even in hindsight, scholars can't find any economic news that can explain the unprecedented one-day drop. This suggests that prices were too high before the crash, too low afterward, or perhaps some of both. But it is as hard to disprove absolute pricing efficiency as to prove it. The price decline *could* be explained by a sudden change in investor expectations about future growth rates (a 1% change in expected growth rates would suffice). Perhaps there was some economic reason for such a change in expectations that we're not yet smart enough to understand.[3]

Still, after the 1987 market crash, many finance scholars are skeptical about absolute pricing efficiency. Some are also readier to believe that *relative* prices can be inefficient as well, though the market crash does not directly contradict the studies of relative pricing efficiency discussed below. Even skeptics about market efficiency, though, are generally also skeptical about whether investors, except perhaps a very few exceptional individuals, can regularly outperform the market as a whole. We will return in later chapters to the implications of absolute mispricing for takeover motives, and for regulatory policy toward takeovers.

A final difficulty with empirical tests of CAPM is the joint hypothesis problem. Recall from Chapter 4 that *every* test of market efficiency is also a test of the asset pricing model used to generate the prices against which market prices are compared. If observed prices differ from the prices predicted by the asset pricing model, that could mean that the market is inefficient, the asset pricing model is incorrect, or both. For example, Fama & French find a correlation between firm size and realized return. They interpret this as evidence against CAPM. But it could equally well be evidence against market efficiency.

Only by running many different tests for different types of inefficiency, using different asset pricing models, can we develop some sense for which is more robust -- ECMH or asset pricing theory. While definitive proof is (and will continue to be) unavailable, most financial economists believe that the evidence for relative pricing

---

concepts of *allocative* and *speculative* efficiency, see Jeffrey Gordon & Lewis Kornhauser, *Efficient Markets, Costly Information and Securities Research*, 60 NYU L. Rev. 761 (1985).

[3] For a sampling of the literature on the implications of the market crash for ECMH, see Merton Miller, *Financial Innovations and Market Volatility* ch. 6 (1991); Richard Roll, *The International Crash of October 1987*, and Eugene Fama, *Perspectives on October 1987, or What Did We Learn from the Crash?*, both in Robert Barro, Eugene Fama, Daniel Fischel, Allan Meltzer, Richard Roll & Lester Telser, *Black Monday and the Future of Financial Markets* (1989), and Fischer Black, *An Equilibrium Model of the Crash*, Kenneth French, *Crash Testing the Efficient Market Hypothesis*, and Robert Shiller, *Portfolio Insurance and Other Investor Fashions as Factors in the 1987 Stock Market Crash*, all in *NBER Macroeconomics Annual 1988*.

efficiency is stronger than the evidence for any particular asset pricing model. Thus, they interpret anomalies such as the size effect as indicating a need to rethink asset pricing theory, rather than a need to rethink efficient market theory.

With these caveats in mind, the next reading reviews the empirical tests supporting the semistrong efficiency of public securities markets. Section C will review evidence on various *departures* from efficient pricing. Consider, as you read, the extent to which the studies provide evidence for relative pricing efficiency of one stock relative to another, and the extent to which they provide evidence for absolute pricing efficiency. How might one test for absolute pricing inefficiency?

JAMES LORIE, PETER DODD & MARY KIMPTON, THE STOCK MARKET: THEORIES & EVIDENCE 55-75 (2d ed. 1985)[*]

During the 1960s, there was a curious and extremely important controversy about the process which determines common stock prices. Initially, the controversy focused on the extent to which successive changes in common stock prices were independent of each other. In more technical terms, the issue was whether or not common stock prices follow a random walk. If they do, knowledge of the past sequence of prices cannot be used to secure abnormally high rates of return. . . .

[Evidence that the walk is random] led to the theory of efficient markets. . . . [A useful definition of market efficiency] is from Jensen:

> A market is efficient with respect to a given information set if it is impossible to make profits by trading on the basis of that information set. By economic profits is meant the risk-adjusted returns net of all costs.[2]

. . . As the controversy and related work have progressed through the years, three forms of the efficient-market hypothesis have been distinguished: (1) the weak form; (2) the semistrong form; and (3) the strong form. The weak form asserts that current prices fully reflect the information implied by the historical sequence of prices. In other words, an investor cannot enhance his/her ability to select stocks by knowing the history of successive prices and the results of analyzing them in all possible ways. The semistrong form asserts that current prices fully reflect public knowledge about the underlying companies, and that efforts to acquire and analyze this knowledge cannot be expected to produce superior investment results. For example, one cannot expect to earn

---

[2] Michael Jensen, *Some Anomalous Evidence Regarding Market Efficiency*, 6 J.Fin.Econ. 95 (1978).

superior rates of return by analyzing annual reports, announcements of dividend changes, or stock splits. The strong form asserts that not even those with privileged information can make use of it to secure superior investment results. . . .

Early Beginnings

The term *random walk*, [first used in 1905, provides] the proper answer to a common, vexing problem: If one leaves a drunk in a vacant field and wishes to find him at some later time, what is the most efficient search pattern? It has been demonstrated that the best place to start is the point where the drunk was left. That position is an unbiased estimate of his future position, since the drunk will presumably wander without purpose or design in a random fashion.

Even before [1905], Louis Bachelier . . . presented convincing evidence that commodity speculation in France was a "fair game."[6] This meant that neither buyers nor sellers could expect to make profits. In other terms, the current price of a commodity was an unbiased estimate of its future price. . . .

Bachelier's earlier work was pregnant with meaning for investors, but the gestation period was one of the longest on record. . . . [In 1959], Roberts indicated that a series of numbers created by cumulating random numbers had the same appearance as a time series of stock prices. An observer with a predisposition to see familiar patterns in these wavy lines could detect the well-known head-and-shoulders formations and other patterns both in the stock price series and in the random series. . . . [Roberts' pictures are shown in Figures 5-1 and 5-2]:

---

[6] Louis Bachelier, *Théorie de la Spéculation* (1900).

142

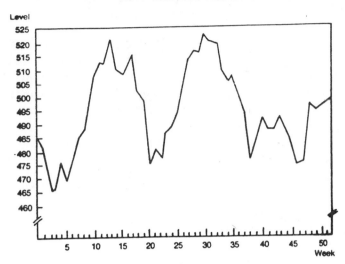

Figure 5-1
Actual Stock Market Prices for 1956

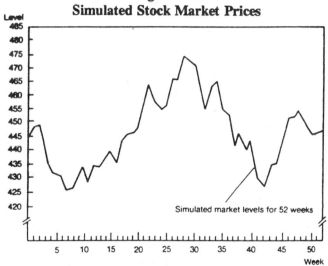

Figure 5-2
Simulated Stock Market Prices

Simulated market levels for 52 weeks

Source: Harry Roberts, *Stock Market "Patterns" and Financial Analysis: Methodological Suggestions*, 14 J.Fin. 1 (1959).

Early Tests of the Weak Form

[Random walk theory] was taken seriously only by a small group of academics at first. . . . Based on measurements of serial correlations between price changes, through investigation of successive changes of a given sign, and in other ways, these

workers tested the statistical independence or the randomness of successive changes in stock prices. They uniformly found only insignificant departures from randomness. . .
.

[Scholars also tested a trading rule with] the following form: Wait until stock prices have advanced by *x* percent from some trough and then buy stocks; next, hold those stocks until they have declined *y* percent from some subsequent peak, and then sell them or sell them short. Continue this process until bankrupt or satisfied. . . . Fama & Blume[17] demonstrated that filter schemes cannot, in general, provide returns larger than a naive policy of buying and holding stocks. Very small filters can generate larger profits before commissions, suggesting some persistence in short-term price movements. . . . However, the trends are so short that the profits are wiped out by commissions. The only ones to be enriched by using filter techniques to buy and sell stocks would be the brokers; the investors would be bankrupt.

All of these early investigations were tests of the so-called "weak form" of the random-walk hypothesis. That is, they tested the statistical properties of price changes themselves without reference to the relationship of these changes to other kinds of financial information. The evidence strongly supports the view that successive price changes are virtually independent. . . .

Tests of the Semistrong Hypothesis

. . . Investigations of the semistrong form of the [efficient market] hypothesis are concerned with market efficiency and to what extent prices reflect public knowledge without bias. The focus of the empirical tests is the speed of adjustment to new information. Fama, Fisher, Jensen, & Roll[23] looked at the effect of stock splits on stock prices. The folklore about stock splits was that the total value of an issue of common stock was increased by increasing the number of shares. Efforts to explain this apparent irrationality were numerous and untested. . . .

[Fama, Fisher, Jensen & Roll's] hypothesis was that splits, which are usually accompanied by dividend increases, were interpreted by the market as a predictor of a dividend change. A dividend change can convey information about management's confidence about future earnings. In an efficient market, the only price effects of a split would be those associated with the information implied by a possible dividend change. . . . [They found that, *prior to the split*], the stocks earn higher returns than predicted

---

[17] Eugene Fama & Marshall Blume, *Filter Rules and Stock Market Trading*, 39 J.Bus. 226 (1966 Supp.).

[23] Eugene Fama, Lawrence Fisher, Michael Jensen & Richard Roll, *The Adjustment of Stock Prices to New Information*, 10 Int'l Econ.Rev. 1 (1969).

by their historical relationship with the market. *After the split*, however, there is no evidence of abnormal returns . . . .[a]

After the split, stocks that did *not* have a subsequent dividend increase had relatively declining rates of return. The authors interpret these findings as an indication that the announcement of a stock split implies the strong likelihood of a subsequent increase in dividends. In fact, [71% of the stock splits] are followed by dividend increases. When it is disclosed, after the split, that the expected dividend increase will *not* eventuate, the stock price falls to reflect this unexpected bad news. For stocks that increase dividends as expected, the confirmation is reflected in higher prices. The fact that there is normal post-split stock price behavior for the sample of splits as a whole shows that the market makes an unbiased expectation of the dividend increase at the time of the split. . . .

Perhaps the transactions that best illustrate both the speed and unbiased nature of the efficient capital market are corporate takeovers . . . [Figure 5-3 shows the stock price reaction to tender offer announcements]. The striking results include the magnitude of the stock price effect and the speed with which the market reacts. . . .

It is important to note that at the time of the first public announcement of the acquisition, the transaction's outcome is unknown. In many cases, the first offer is followed by higher competing offers from other bidders and higher revised offers by the same bidder. In other cases, the transaction fails, and the stock price falls dramatically when the failure is announced. [The large returns to guessing the outcome have] attracted an industry of arbitrageurs who effectively bet on the outcomes of acquisition transactions. If the stock market is efficient, the returns from this arbitrage game should [equal the arbitrageur's cost of capital], on the average.

---

[a] The term *abnormal return* refers to the return on a particular company's stock, *relative* to the stock market as a whole, after adjusting for risk. We discuss techniques for measuring abnormal returns in Chapter 6.

Figure 5-3
Abnormal Returns to Stockholders of Target Firms in Tender Offers

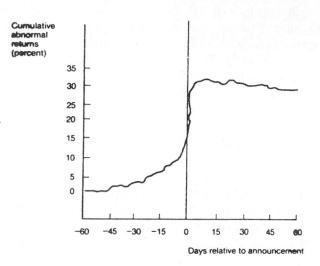

[Other studies examine] the performance of professionally managed portfolios. The argument is that the performance of professionally managed portfolios, [if] consistently superior to market performance as a whole or to relevant subsets of stocks in that market, would indicate an element of inefficiency in the price-setting process. . . .

[Michael Jensen[35]] compared the performance of [115] mutual funds [from 1955 to 1964] with the expected performance from randomly selected portfolios of equal riskiness [measured by β]. . . . [*Before expenses*], about half performed better and half performed worse than the control portfolios. [*After expenses*], only 43 of 115 mutual funds had superior performance. For the 10-year period, the average terminal value of mutual funds would have been about 9% less than the terminal value of the randomly selected portfolios . . . .[b]

---

[35] Michael Jensen, *The Performance of Mutual Funds in the Period 1945-64*, 23 J.Fin. 389 (1968).

[b] When first conducted, the tests of mutual fund performance were interpreted as providing support for the *strong form* of ECMH. The investigators assumed that professional money managers had access to information that was not available to the general public. They sought to test whether these managers could beat the market by trading on this "nonpublic" information. Today, in light of evidence that corporate insiders *can* outperform the market, the inability of professional money managers to beat the market is generally interpreted as evidence that (i) securities markets are semistrong efficient; and (ii)

[Jensen also studied whether] some mutual funds *consistently* outperform randomly selected portfolios. . . . [A] mutual fund that was superior to a randomly selected portfolio in one period was superior to a randomly selected portfolio in a subsequent period about half the time. Jensen also sought to determine whether any fund was more often superior to randomly selected portfolios during the 10-year period than would be expected on the basis of chance alone. He found no evidence of such superiority. . . . One can readily imagine that [these findings] did not create strong euphoria in the mutual funds industry.

B. How Markets Get to Be Efficient

The empirical evidence consistent with semistrong market efficiency begs the question of how markets get to be efficient. Semistrong efficiency can be explained under perfect market assumptions -- for example, that capital markets are complete, information is immediately and costlessly available to all investors, and all investors have homogeneous expectations and time horizons.[4] But this explanation is, in the words of a joke commonly directed at both lawyers and economists, "absolutely accurate and totally useless."[5] What makes ECMH non-trivial is its prediction that market prices will act *as if* information is immediately and costlessly available to all participants, and *as if* all investors have the same expectations about the future, even though these assumptions are obviously false. The next article explores the market processes that lead toward -- and limit -- market efficiency.

---

money managers *do not* have valuable private information.

[4] See Paul Samuelson, *Proof that Properly Anticipated Prices Fluctuate Randomly*, 6 Indus.Mgmt.Rev. 41 (1965).

[5] The story usually begins with two people in a hot air balloon who have lost their way. They notice someone on the ground and call out, "Where are we?"

Unhesitatingly the ground observer responds, "You're in a balloon."

At this point one balloonist turns to the other and says, "He must be a lawyer (economist)."

"How can you tell?" the second passenger asks.

"It's easy," the first responds. "What he said was absolutely accurate and totally useless."

RONALD GILSON & REINIER KRAAKMAN,
THE MECHANISMS OF MARKET EFFICIENCY
70 Va.L.Rev. 549, 554-610 (1984)

The language of efficient capital market theory reveals its origins as a vocabulary of empirical description. The common definition of market efficiency, that "prices at any time 'fully reflect' all available information,"[22] is really a shorthand for the empirical claim that "available information" does not support profitable trading strategies or arbitrage opportunities. Similarly, . . . the now-familiar division of the ECMH into "weak," "semi-strong," and "strong" forms [began] as a device for classifying empirical *tests* of price behavior. . . .

Over time, however, scholars have pressed the weak, semi-strong, and strong form categories beyond their original service as a classification of empirical tests into more general duty as a classification of market responses to *particular kinds of information*. For example, prices might be said to incorporate efficiently one genre of information that is semi-strong or public, but fail to reflect another that is strong form, or non-public. Indeed, taken a step further, scholars sometimes describe markets themselves as weak, semi-strong, or strong form efficient. Without ever being quite explicit, this powerful shorthand implies that different market dynamics are involved in the reflection of different kinds of information into price, and that varying degrees of market efficiency might well be the consequence.

The recognition that different market mechanisms operate on different types of information is central to our analysis of market efficiency. But before we explore this conclusion in greater detail, it is first necessary that we define the key terms of the ECMH, and that we do so conceptually rather than operationally. . . . We need a concept of "relative efficiency" that distinguishes among and ranks the different market dynamics according to how closely they approximate the ideal of ensuring that prices *always* fully reflect all available information.

. . . Following Beaver's analysis, the requirement that prices "fully reflect" information means that prices must behave "*as if* everyone knows" the relevant information. . . .[32] By contrast, the second basic concept embodied in the operational definition of market efficiency, that prices mirror *all available information*, is less in need of reformulation than of expansion. The availability of information is a function of its distribution among traders in a given market. Different "bits" of information are more or less "available" depending on how many traders are aware of them. . . .

---

[22] Eugene Fama, *Efficient Capital Markets: A Review of Theory and Empirical Work*, 24 J.Fin. 383, 383 (1970).

[32] William Beaver, *Market Efficiency*, 56 Acct.Rev. 23, 28 (1981).

[D]ifferent market mechanisms may be responsible for the reflection in price of differentially available categories of information. Differences among market mechanisms will matter, however, only if these mechanisms operate with unequal results. We still require a measure of success -- a yardstick of "relative efficiency" -- in order to assess the importance of differences in the mechanisms of price formation. . . .

The operational definition of market efficiency tightly restricts the speed of the market's response to new information by requiring prices to reflect such information "always" -- i.e., very promptly. It is a short step from this emphasis on the rapidity of price response to a definition of "relative efficiency." The market, and the mechanisms that operate to reflect new information in price, are more or less efficient depending on how quickly they yield efficient equilibrium prices; relative efficiency is a measure of the *speed* with which new information is reflected in price. Similarly, the relative efficiency of market mechanisms determines the magnitude of arbitrage opportunities that new information creates for the fortunate traders who "know" it first. . . .

Mechanisms of Market Efficiency

Review of the basic vocabulary of efficient market theory reveals a missing link: an account of the mechanisms of market efficiency that its terms foreshadow but do not explicitly detail. . . . [These mechanisms] must be trading processes that, with more or less promptness (or "relative efficiency"), force prices to a new, fully informed equilibrium. Moreover, clarifying the meaning of informational "availability" also reveals the chief obstacle to any mechanism that serves to push prices toward a fully informed equilibrium. New information is "available" to the capital market under an extraordinary variety of circumstances, ranging from the extreme of near-universal initial distribution of information -- when everyone really does know the information -- to the opposite extreme of initial distribution to only a very few traders. A satisfactory account of the mechanisms of market efficiency must describe their operation over this entire continuum of availability, including those circumstances in which the initial distribution is extremely limited or incomplete. . . .

Over the past dozen years, financial economists have proposed four general forms of mechanisms, which may be termed "universally informed trading," "professionally informed trading," "derivatively informed trading," and "uninformed trading." . . . [We can] array the four market mechanisms on a continuum based on the initial distribution of information among traders, that is, on *how many* traders learn of the new information. Although all four mechanisms can ultimately lead to efficient equilibrium prices, the dynamics of equilibration will take longer as one moves from wide to narrow distribution . . . .

Universally Informed Trading

The simplest efficiency mechanism that causes prices to behave "as if" all traders knew of information is a market in which all traders are, in fact, costlessly and simultaneously informed. . . . [S]everal varieties of price-relevant information at least approximate the ideal of universal dissemination. "Old" information, embedded in securities prices, is one example. Ongoing market activity assures its distribution to all interested traders, and precisely because all know it, we do not expect it to reveal arbitrage opportunities in the form of lucrative screens or trading rules that all alike could exploit. Another example is important news items -- from presidential election results, which most citizens learn almost instantaneously, to changes in Federal Reserve Board policy, which are announced after trading hours precisely in order to ensure widespread dissemination. Thus, the universally informed trading mechanism ranges over all "old" price information and much that is new. It lumps together traditional "weak-form" information about price histories with information about current events into a single information set that prices reflect rapidly and with near perfect dynamic efficiency.

Professionally Informed Trading

In contrast to news about price and current events, however, much so-called "public" information is not universally disseminated among traders. Many traders are too unsophisticated to make full use of the technical accounting information contained in mandated disclosure reports; much disclosure data is accessible in the first instance only through documents on file with government agencies; and much information about a firm's prospects may be announced initially only to small groups of securities analysts and other market professionals. How, then, do prices come to reflect this semi-public information? The answer . . . is that rapid price equilibration does not require widespread dissemination of information, but only a minority of knowledgeable traders who control a critical volume of trading activity. From this perspective, the universally informed trading mechanism is actually only a special case of price formation through the activity of traders who are direct recipients of information. . . .

The rapidity of such price adjustments depends on the volume of informed trading. And although a precise account of that process has yet to be offered, it seems plausible that the relative efficiency of price adjustment to new information that proceeds through professionally informed trading declines only gradually as initial access to the information narrows to a threshold minority of traders, after which it declines rapidly.[67]

---

[67] This account still begs the question of exactly *how* informed minority trading can lead to the rapid price reflection of new information even when the minority is too small to dominate trading volume. If *un*informed traders held widely divergent beliefs about the value of a security, a short answer would be "price pressure": trading by informed investors that alters the demand or supply for particular securities,

In today's securities markets, the dominant minority of informed traders is the community of market professionals, such as arbitrageurs, researchers, brokers and portfolio managers, who devote their careers to acquiring information and honing evaluative skills. The trading volume in most securities that these professionals control, directly or indirectly, seems sufficient to assure the market's rapid assimilation into price of most routine information. Of course, the relative efficiency of the assimilation is never perfect. Since informed trading is costly, market professionals must enjoy some informational advantage that permits them to earn a commensurate return. But given competitive arbitrage and the market for analyst services, we would not expect the long-run returns of individual professionals to exceed the market average by very much, especially in exchange markets where professionals dominate trading. This expectation is largely confirmed by empirical studies of mutual fund returns.

In sum, the professionally informed trading mechanism explains why any information that is accessible to significant portions of the analyst community is properly called "public," even though it manifestly is not. Such information is rapidly assimilated into price, with only minimal abnormal returns to its professional recipients. And it is these characteristics, we submit, that largely convey the meaning of a "semi-strong form" market response.

Derivatively Informed Trading

Yet not all information is public, even within the narrow confines of the professional analyst community. Corporate insiders and exchange specialists, for example, enjoy easy access to information that would be prohibitively costly for anyone else to obtain,[73] while professional analysts conduct in-depth research that generates occasional informational monopolies. In these and similar instances of monopolistic access, information first enters the market through a very small number of traders whose

---

the depiction of securities as fungible commodities with large numbers of near-perfect risk-return substitutes. A far more plausible answer is that suggested by Myron Scholes, who demonstrated that secondary offerings affect securities prices primarily through the release of information rather than through price pressure. Myron Scholes, *The Market for Securities: Substitution versus Price Pressure and the Effects of Information on Share Prices*, 45 J.Bus. 179 (1972). Similarly, intense trading by an informed minority will trigger temporary fluctuations in price and volume that may, in turn, alert an uninformed majority to the existence of new information. The ways in which uninformed traders may "learn" from price changes are discussed [below].

[73] The strong form efficiency tests amply document the systematic informational advantage enjoyed by corporate insiders and other "insider" groups. Indeed, if anything, these tests radically underestimate the magnitude of this advantage by relying on data about trades that are registered or otherwise public. Because trading on inside information is both unlawful and easily hidden, data limited only to publicly disclosed trading by insiders systematically excludes the trades most likely to reflect important informational advantages. See Keown & Pinkerton, *Merger Announcements and Insider Trading Activity: An Empirical Investigation*, 36 J.Fin. 855, 856-57 (1981).

151

own resources are not large enough to induce speedy price equilibration. But reflection of this information in price does not depend exclusively on the trading efforts of these insiders. Derivatively informed trading enhances relative efficiency and erodes the insider's advantage by capitalizing on the "informational leakage" associated with trading itself.

Informational leakage can assume many forms. Pure leakage -- inadvertent, direct communication of trading information to outsiders -- doubtlessly plays a significant role in rendering markets more efficient,[76] even if its effects remain erratic. But beyond such direct disclosure by accident or "theft," two forms of *indirect* leakage also contribute to market efficiency. These are trade decoding and price decoding.

Trade decoding occurs whenever uninformed traders glean trading information by directly observing the transactions of informed traders. Myron Scholes' classic study of secondary distributions documents a common example of this phenomenon by demonstrating that only *some* large block sales of stock lead to substantial, permanent declines in share price. The declines are especially pronounced when sellers are officers or other insiders of the issuer; moderate when sellers are investment companies and mutual funds (which act on the advice of research staffs); and barely noticeable when sellers are individuals, bank trust departments, and other traders who may liquidate their holding for reasons other than investment gain. The clear implication is that uninformed traders use the identities of large sellers to deduce whether the latter are likely to possess valuable information, and then proceed to trade accordingly. . . .[80]

[T]rade decoding remains limited by a significant constraint: uninformed traders must be able to identify informed traders individually and observe their trading activities directly. By contrast, the second form of indirect leakage, price decoding, does not require uninformed traders to discover the identity of their informed cohorts. It merely requires uninformed traders to observe and interpret anonymous data on price and trading

---

[76] A professional in a major tender solicitation firm explains the "pure" informational leakage that precedes public announcement of tender offers as follows:

> You start with a handful of people, but when you get close to doing something the circle expands pretty quickly . . . . You have to bring in directors, two or three firms of lawyers, investment bankers, public-relations people, and financial printers, and everybody's got a secretary. If the deal is a big one, you might need a syndicate of banks to finance it. Every time you let in another person, the chance of a leak increases geometrically.

Klein, *Merger Leaks Abound, Causing Many Stocks To Rise Before the Fact*, Wall St.J., July 12, 1978, at 1, 31.

[80] Scholes (1972), supra note 67, at 202.

volume against the backdrop of other information or expectations that these traders possess.

In theory, at least the logic of price decoding is simple. When trading on inside information is of sufficient volume to cause a change in price, this otherwise inexplicable change may itself signal the presence of new information to the uninformed. . . . But beyond the "weak" learning involved in identifying the presence of new information, uninformed traders may also succeed in decoding the actual content of the information. The trick here, and admittedly it is no mean feat, is the uninformed trader's ability to employ knowledge of the informational constituents of the old price to deduce which possible accretion of new infomration would successfully explain observed price changes. Yet, probabilistically, such "strong" learning may be less difficult than it at first appears; consider, for example, how frequently increases in price signal the presence of inside information about impending tender offers. . . .[86]

Thus, the reflection of non-public information into price is a two-stage process; it is first triggered by initially informed "inside" trading, but, at a critical threshold, it rapidly accelerates as a result of reactive trades. This much ensures that price reflects each "bit" of decoded information with a moderate degree of relative efficiency -- less, to be sure, than a wider initial distribution might provide, but far more than the trades of initially informed investors alone could produce. . . . Derivatively informed trading thus explains how prices can come to reflect much information that is truly "non-public," even while suggesting the inevitable limits to the process.

Uninformed Trading

. . . [I]nformation is not limited to hard facts; it also includes soft information, the stuff of forecasts and predictions . . . . [In making forecasts, traders rely on] a wide variety of secondary facts, differing beliefs, and diverse levels of predictive skills. . . .

---

[86] See Keown & Pinkerton (1981), supra note 73, who report not only accelerating price increases during the three weeks that precede tender offers, but also

> that 79, 60, and 64 *percent* of the acquired firms exhibited higher volume one, two and three weeks prior to the announcement date than they had three months earlier with the weekly average volume over this three week period 247, 112, and 102 percent higher than it was three months earlier.

Id. at 863.

It is impossible to determine how much such crescendos of trading activity owe to pure leakage, trade decoding, or price decoding, respectively. The very strength of the incipient price and volume changes, however, suggests that "strong" price decoding plays a major role, especially as the other forms of informational leakage amplify the strength of the price signals.

What is the mechanism by which the market comes to reflect the diverse and imperfect forecasts of individual traders into the aggregate forecast of price, and how well does this mechanism function as measured against the yardstick of optimal forecast data?

The final market efficiency mechanism, uninformed trading, permits prices, in some circumstances, to reflect aggregate -- or consensus -- forecasts that are more nearly optimal over the long run than those of any individual trader. In this sense, prices can reflect information about which *all* traders are uninformed. . . .[100]

If each trader's forecast about the likelihood of a future event is informed in part by secondary facts and evaluations to which only he has access, then an aggregation of all forecasts draws on an information pool much larger than that possessed by any individual trader. Although each trader's own forecasts are skewed by the unique constraints on his or her judgment, other traders will have offsetting constraints. As trading proceeds, the random biases of individual forecasts will cancel one another out, leaving price to reflect a single, best-informed aggregate forecast. . . . In this respect, unsystematic bias "washes out" over trading in the same way that unsystematic risk "washes out" in a diversified portfolio. . . .

[Robert Verrecchia has modeled the conditions under which [the market price is the best available estimate of value.[105]] Verrecchia's model requires traders to make independent assessments of the value of risky securities based on their own facts and forecasts, which in the aggregate form a bounded, unbiased distribution around the hypothetical price that a fully informed trader would assign the security. The first of these conditions, that trader assessments be independent, requires an absence of collusion, "learning," or shared prejudice among traders that would render individual forecasting errors mutually reinforcing. . . .

The second condition of uninformed trading, that trader assessments be "bounded," merely requires that all such assessments fall in the same ball park. Traders with wildly-skewed personal assessments will impede price convergence -- reduce the relative efficiency of the uninformed trading mechanism -- and may even preclude it entirely in thinly-traded markets. [But] market discipline in the form of heavy trading losses will restrain idiosyncratic traders and may even eliminate them through a "Darwinian" process of natural selection.

---

[100] Note, however, that uninformed trading *never* leads to prices that reflect wholly optimal forecast data. Rather, this mechanism can lead to prices that reflect a *better approximation*, over the long run, of such hypothetical optimal forecasts than can the parallel assessments made by individual traders.

[105] Robert Verrecchia, *Consensus Beliefs, Information Acquisition, and Market Information Efficiency*, 70 Am.Econ.Rev. 874 (1980).

. . . [The third, no-bias condition] embraces the preceding two requirements, since either widely-shared forecasting errors or idiosyncratic trading can bias the aggregate-level distribution of trader assessments. But, in addition, the "no-bias" condition carries implications for the acquisition of new [information]. . . . Once *any* trader acquires a new key fact that renders hitherto uncertain contingencies more (or less) likely, the consensus forecast of uninformed traders, as embodied in existing price, is biased relative to the newly-available information. Moreover, it remains so until the market fully incorporates the new key information into price, through one of the three "informed" trading mechanisms previously described. . . .

[The uniformed and informed trading mechanisms are related]: traders themselves are acute observers of market behavior. If prices successfully aggregate all available information, including consensus forecasts and secondary facts, traders will begin to condition their trading activity on price as well as on their individual assessments of value. This conditioning on price adds "learning" to the basic aggregation mechanism of uninformed trading and is precisely the "weak learning" from price that we previously [discussed]. . . .

[Traders] only acquire an indication of whether the market disagrees with them, not of why it does. The force of such an indication depends on each trader's level of confidence. Individual estimates of value will move toward existing prices, and individual forecasts toward consensus predictions, in rough proportion to how highly each trader assesses the comparative quality of his or her own collection of information. . . [119]

Summary

The uninformed trading mechanism completes the array of capital market mechanisms that [contribute to market efficiency]. . . . Moreover, the four efficiency mechanisms are complementary; each functions over a characteristic segment of the continuum of initial distributions of information among traders.

As Figure 5-4 illustrates, if the mechanisms are portrayed in this fashion, they parallel the criterion for partitioning information sets that implicitly informed Fama's trichotomy of weak/semi-strong/strong form tests of market efficiency. Universally informed trading extends over all widely-disseminated information, including the

---

[119] If traders rely on price in roughly inverse proportion to the quality of their independent assests, the most poorly informed traders will rely most on price, thereby reducing the number of wildly skewed "outlier" trades. . . . On the other hand, weak learning can also generate inefficiency in uninformed trading by amplifying any systematic bias reflected in price. Weak learning cannot *create* biased prices, but if the forecasts of confident investors who trade heavily on their independent assessment are already biased, weak learning by less confident traders may transmit the bias and "freeze" it into price.

price-history information that underlies weak form tests. Professionally informed trading operates on all publicly available information, but it is particularly active where information is "semi-public" -- i.e., initially distributed or useful to only a minority of sophisticated trading professionals. . . . [D]erivatively informed trading acts most prominently on key trading facts over which very small numbers of traders exercise monopolistic access. . . . Finally uninformed trading acts on the "soft" information of forecasts and assessments that is not directly sampled by any of the other tests. . . .

Figure 5-4
Capital Market Efficiency Mechanisms

Traditional Categories of Efficiency	Weak Form	Semi-Strong Form	Strong Form	
Relative Efficiency	HIGH ←——————————————————————→ LOW			
Initial Distribution of Information Among Traders	BROAD ←——————————————————————→ NARROW			
Capital Market Mechanisms	Universally Informed Trading	Professionally Informed Trading	Derivatively Informed Trading	Uninformed Trading

The Information Market

. . . Given the operative capital market mechanisms, the relative efficiency of the market's response to particular information depends on the initial distribution of that information among traders. The question now is, what determines that initial distribution? To answer that question, the focus of our analysis shifts to the operation of a different market: the market for information. . . .

The lower the cost of particular information, the wider will be its distribution, the more effective will be the capital market mechanism operating to reflect it in prices, and the more efficient will be the market with respect to it. Understanding market efficiency, then, requires detailed analysis of the nature and dynamics of information costs.

A Taxonomy of Information Costs

Information costs may be divided into three categories. . . . The first category is costs of *acquisition*. These costs will differ in character depending on whether one is the originator of the information or only its subsequent recipient. For the originator, acquisition costs are the costs of producing the information in the first place (as with a discovery or innovation). For the subsequent recipient, acquisition costs are those of securing access to information produced by someone else. This may be done either with the originator's cooperation, as through purchase, or despite the originator's efforts to prevent access, as, at the extreme, through industrial espionage.

The second category is the cost of *processing* information once it is acquired. For both the originator and a subsequent recipient, processing costs are best exemplified by investment in human capital. Evaluation of information, whether self-produced or acquired from others, requires special skills, such as a facility in accounting, finance, or securities analysis, that can ordinarily be obtained only through investment in expensive professional training. The cost of such training is reflected in the wages of the skilled employee or in the opportunity costs of his or her principal.

The third category of information costs arises from the problem of *verification*. Here the task is to determine the quality of information. . . . For the originator, verification costs take the form of further investments to determine the accuracy of the existing information by, for example, hiring an expert to evaluate it. A subsequent recipient may undertake similar efforts, but its principal verification cost is that of determining the veracity of the originator. . . . [V]erification costs may take the form of a direct investigation by the subsequent recipient, similar in character to the efforts undertaken by an originator, or of alternative verification techniques such as bonding or the use of third party experts.[135]

Market Responses to Information Costs

Market participants shape the cost structure of the information market by their efforts to reduce each category of information costs. . . . [E]conomizing on information costs, [in turn] pushes the capital market in the direction of greater efficiency. . . .

[We see] market efforts to economize on acquisition costs through collectivization at both the private and public levels. At the private level, for example, organizations of securities professionals hold cooperative programs in which high company officials speak to many analysts at once, thus reducing the cost of access for any individual analyst. Indeed, the very existence of information intermediaries such as financial and securities experts reflects, in part, the potential for economics of scale and scope in efforts to economize on information costs.

---

[135] "Bonding" occurs when the originator of information puts at risk an asset that is forfeited if the information is less accurate than represented. . . . The general problem of verification costs, in relation to products as well as information, is surveyed in Yoram Barzel, *Measurement Cost and the Organization of Markets*, 25 J.L. & Econ. 27 (1982).

At the collective level, legislation such as the Securities Exchange Act of 1934, which requires continual disclosure of extensive current information by public companies, eliminates the repetitive cost of individual acquisition of information by each analyst. This form of mandatory disclosure collectivizes information acquisition by requiring the originators of information to distribute it and, in some cases, even requiring them to create it.

. . . [A] company that wishes to distribute information indicating favorable corporate prospects may do so at little cost merely by issuing a press release. The financial press as an institution functions to reduce the acquisition costs of information recipients, in large part by reducing the costs of voluntary distribution to the originators of information.

. . . [T]he specialized business of securities analysis . . . permits substantial economies of scale and scope in utilizing human capital. Similar economies are available in the use of the support equipment, such as computer hardware and software, that is increasingly necessary for performance of the analyst's task. As a result, there are specialists in information processing such as research firms and the research departments of brokerage firms, whose functional advantage is their ability to process information more cheaply than non-specialists.[152]

[Verification costs produce] the most interesting array of market techniques for reducing information costs. Consider the producer of a new financial product. The producer has an obvious incentive to supply the market with information indicating that the product is worth its asking price. . . . [But producers have incentives to exaggerate quality. If] the quality of the information is difficult to determine, its buyer has little choice but to assume that it, and the product it concerns, are of lower quality than represented. Only by discounting the information's accuracy can the buyer be certain that he or she has not unknowingly overpaid. The result is that sellers have too little incentive to provide better information, because "it won't be believed anyway." Poor quality information drives higher quality information from the market . . . .[154]

A broad range of market techniques has developed to deal with this problem by reducing verification costs. At the most costly end of the continuum are solutions that rely solely on buyer verification without the assistance of the originator. For example, buyers may employ experts, such as accountants, lawyers, or business consultants, to examine the offered information. . . .

---

[152] The financial press plays a similar role, offering almost continual analysis of corporate and economic prospects.

[154] This is an example of the "lemon problem." E.g., George Akerlof, *The Market for "Lemons": Quality Uncertainty and the Market Mechanism*, 84 Q.J. Econ. 488 (1970).

[Verification costs are reduced if sellers can] "signal" in a believable fashion that they offer high quality information. . . .   A typical but costly form of signaling is the investment by sellers in firm-specific capital, such as reputation and advertising, whose value would be reduced if the quality of the product were lower than represented. . . .

[In other situations], outside specialists acting as information intermediaries will offer their own reputation in lieu of the sellers' as a bond of quality. Examples of such specialists in the products market are the Underwriters Laboratory and the Good Housekeeping Seal; in the financial markets, the most obvious example is the role played by rating agencies such as *Standard & Poor's* and *Moody's*. A less obvious but similar role is also played by financial intermediaries, although the verification technique used by these information agents differs. Rather than demonstrating confidence in the accuracy of the seller's information by staking their reputation on it, these financial intermediaries signal their belief by purchasing the seller's offering for their *own* account, thereby staking *their* future directly on the accuracy of the seller's information.

A collective, and therefore potentially less expensive, solution to the problem is the legislative imposition of civil and criminal penalties on low quality producers. By imposing costs only on those producers who would exploit high buyer verification costs by falsely pretending to provide quality information, such legislation makes it more costly for producers of low quality goods to mimic the behavior of high quality producers. At the extreme, well-defined and energetically enforced legislation of this type turns the lemon problem on its head and drives low quality producers from the market. . . .

[In sum, from] the perspective of the capital market, market efficiency is a function of the initial distribution of information among traders; from the perspective of the information market, market efficiency is a function of the costs associated with particular information. The common factor is information costs. . . . As information costs decline, more -- and better -- information is available to more traders, and the market becomes more efficient, both because the information is better and because its wider distribution triggers a more effective capital market mechanism.

C. The Limits of Market Efficiency

Writing in 1984, when there was strong evidence for semistrong market efficiency, Gilson & Kraakman took their principal task to be explaining how markets become efficient. They note but do not pursue the argument that uninformed trading, if *not* random, can push prices away from efficiency. Since then, however, the evidence for various anomalies has multiplied. The next article on *noise trading* complements the Gilson & Kraakman reading by exploring how markets can become *inefficient* and discussing the principal anomalies.

Noise trading theory appears to have some explanatory power, but work on developing and testing the theory is still in its early stages.

The authors do not draw the distinction that we drew above between relative and absolute pricing efficiency. Consider as you read, though, which of the tests that they cite bear on relative efficiency, and which on the absolute level of stock prices.

ANDREI SHLEIFER & LAWRENCE SUMMERS, THE NOISE TRADER APPROACH TO FINANCE
4 J.Econ.Persp. 19 (1990)

If the efficient markets hypothesis was a publicly traded security, its price would be enormously volatile. . . . Michael Jensen was able to write in 1978 that "the efficient markets hypothesis is the best established fact in all of social sciences."[a] Such strong statements portend reversals, the efficient markets hypothesis itself notwithstanding. Stock in the efficient markets hypothesis lost ground rapidly following the publication of Shiller's (1981) and Leroy & Porter's (1981) volatility tests, both of which found stock market volatility to be far greater than could be justified by [subsequent] changes in dividends.[b] The stock snapped back following the papers of Kleidon (1986) and Marsh & Merton (1986) which challenged the statistical validity of volatility tests.[c] A choppy period then ensued, where conflicting econometric studies induced few of the changes of opinion that are necessary to move prices. But the stock in the efficient markets hypothesis -- at least as it has traditionally been formulated -- crashed along with the rest of the market on October 19, 1987. Its recovery has been less dramatic than that of the rest of the market.

This paper reviews an alternative to the efficient markets approach that we and others have recently pursued. Our approach rests on two assumptions. First, some investors are not fully rational and their demand for risky assets is affected by their beliefs or sentiments that are not fully justified by fundamental news. Second, arbitrage -- defined as trading by fully rational investors not subject to such sentiment -- is risky and therefore limited. The two assumptions together imply that changes in investor sentiment are not fully countered

---

[a] Michael Jensen, *Some Anomalous Evidence Regarding Market Efficiency*, 6 J.Fin.Econ. 95 (1978).

[b] Robert Shiller, *Do Stock Prices Move Too Much to be Justified by Subsequent Changes in Dividends?*, 71 Am.Econ.Rev. 421 (1981); Stephen Leroy & Richard Porter, *Stock Price Volatility: Tests Based on Implied Variance Bounds*, 49 Econometrica 97 (1981). Shiller's work on market efficiency is collected in Robert Shiller, *Market Volatility* (1989).

[c] Allan Kleidon, *Anomalies in Financial Economics*, 59 J.Bus. S285 (1986); Terry Marsh & Robert Merton, *Dividend Variability and Variance Bounds Tests for the Rationality of Stock Market Prices*, 76 Am.Econ.Rev. 483 (1986).

by arbitrageurs and so affect security returns. We argue that this approach to financial markets is in many ways superior to the efficient markets paradigm.

Our case for the noise trader approach is threefold. First, theoretical models with limited arbitrage are both tractable and more plausible than models with perfect arbitrage. The efficient markets hypothesis obtains only as an extreme case of perfect riskless arbitrage that is unlikely to apply in practice. Second, the investor sentiment/limited arbitrage approach yields a more accurate description of financial markets than the efficient markets paradigm. The approach not only explains the available anomalies, but also readily explains broad features of financial markets such as trading volume and actual investment strategies. Third, and most importantly, this approach yields new and testable implications about asset prices, some of which have been proved to be consistent with the data. . . .

The Limits of Arbitrage

We think of the market as consisting of two types of investors: "arbitrageurs" -- also called "smart money" and "rational speculators" -- and other investors. Arbitrageurs are defined as investors who form fully rational expectations about security returns. In contrast, the opinions and trading patterns of other investors -- also known as "noise traders" and "liquidity traders" -- may be subject to systematic biases. In practice, the line between arbitrageurs and other investors may be blurred, but for our argument it helps to draw a sharp distinction between them, since the arbitrageurs do the work of bringing prices toward fundamentals.

Arbitrageurs play a central role in standard finance. They trade to ensure that if a security has a perfect substitute -- a portfolio of other securities that yields the same returns -- then the price of the security equals the price of that substitute portfolio. If the price of the security falls below that of the substitute portfolio, arbitrageurs sell the portfolio and buy the security until the prices are equalized, and vice versa if the price of a security rises above that of the substitute portfolio. When the substitute is indeed perfect, this arbitrage is riskless. As a result, arbitrageurs have perfectly elastic demand for the security at the price of its substitute portfolio. . . .

Although riskless arbitrage ensures that relative prices are in line, it does not help to pin down price levels of, say, stocks or bonds as a whole. These classes of securities do not have close substitute portfolios, and therefore if for some reason they are mispriced, there is no riskless hedge for the arbitrageur. For example, an arbitrageur who thinks that stocks are underpriced cannot buy stocks and sell the substitute portfolio, since such a portfolio does not exist. The arbitrageur can instead simply buy stocks in hopes of an above-normal return, but this arbitrage is no longer riskless. If the arbitrageur is risk-averse, his demand for underpriced stocks will be limited. With a finite number of arbitrageurs, their combined demand curve is no longer perfectly elastic.

Two types of risk limit arbitrage. The first is fundamental risk. . . . Selling "overvalued" stocks is risky because there is always a chance that the market will do very well. Fear of such a loss limits the arbitrageur's original position, and keeps his short-selling from driving prices all the way down to fundamentals. The second source of risk that limits arbitrage comes from unpredictability of the future resale price. Suppose again that stocks are overpriced and an arbitrageur is selling them short. As long as the arbitrageur is thinking of liquidating his position in the future, he must bear the risk that at that time stocks will be *even more* overpriced than they are today. . . .

Japanese equities in the 1980s illustrate the limits of arbitrage. During this period, Japanese equities have sold at the price earnings multiples of between 20 and 60, and have continued to climb. Expected growth rates of dividends and risk premia required to justify such multiples seem unrealistic. Nonetheless, an investor who believes that Japanese equities are overvalued and wants to sell them short, must confront two types of risk. First, what if Japan actually does perform so well that these prices are justified? Second, how much more out of line can prices get, and for how long, before Japanese equities return to more realistic prices? Any investor who sold Japanese stocks short in 1985, when the price earnings multiple was 30, would have lost his shirt as the multiples rose to 60 in 1986.[d]

These arguments that risk makes arbitrage ineffective actually understate the limits of arbitrage. After all, they presume that the arbitrageur knows the fundamental value of the security. In fact, the arbitrageur might not exactly know what this value is, or be able to detect price changes that reflect deviations from fundamentals. . . . Are economists certain that Japanese stocks are overpriced at a price earnings ratio of 50?

Substantial evidence shows that, contrary to the efficient markets hypothesis, arbitrage does not completely counter responses of prices to fluctuations in uninformed demand. . . . Being added to the S&P 500 is not a plausible example of new information about the stock, since stocks are picked for their representativeness and not for performance potential. However, a stock added to the S&P 500 is subsequently acquired in large quantities by the so-called "index funds," whose holdings just represent the index. Both Harris & Gurel (1986) and Shleifer (1986) find that announcements of inclusions into the index are accompanied by share price increases of 2 to 3%. Moreover, the magnitude of these increases over time has risen, paralleling the growth of assets in index funds. . . .[e]

---

[d] See Kenneth French & James Poterba, *Are Japanese Stock Prices Too High*, 29 J.Fin.Econ. 337 (1991). American skepticism about Japanese stock prices in the late 1980s seems especially appropriate today, after the Nikkei 225 index dropped below 15,000 yen in 1992, down over 60% from a 1989 high of over 38,000 yen.

[e] Lawrence Harris & Eitan Gurel, *Price and Volume Effects Associated with Changes in the S&P 500: New Evidence for the Existence of Price Pressure*, 41 J.Fin. 851 (1986); Andrei Shleifer, *Do Demand Curves for Stocks Slope Down?*, 41 J.Fin. 579 (1986).

Further evidence on price pressure when no news is transmitted comes from Ritter's (1988) work on the January effect. The January effect is the name for the fact that small stocks have outperformed market indices by a significant percentage each January over the last 50 or so years. Ritter finds that small stocks are typically sold by individual investors in December -- often to realize capital losses -- and then bought back in January. These share shifts explain the January effect as long as arbitrage by institutions and market insiders is ineffective, since aggressive arbitrage should eliminate the price effects of temporary trading patterns by individual investors. . . .[f]

French & Roll (1986) look at a period when the U.S. stock market was closed on Wednesdays and find that the market is less volatile on these days than on Wednesdays when it is open [even though the supply of fundamental news is presumably the same].[g] [Roll (1988)] finds that individual stocks exhibit significant price movements unrelated to the market on days when there are no public news about these stocks.[h] A similar and more dramatic result is obtained for the aggregate stock market by Cutler, Poterba, & Summers (1989), who find that the days of the largest aggregate market movements are not the days of most important fundamental news and vice versa.[i] The common conclusion of these studies is that news *alone* does not move stock prices; uninformed changes in demand move them too.

Investor Sentiment

Some shifts in investor demand for securities are completely rational. . . . [But] some seem to be a response to changes in expectations or sentiment that are not fully justified by information. Such changes can be a response to pseudo-signals that investors believe convey information about future returns but that would not convey such information in a fully rational model. An example of such pseudo-signals is advice of brokers or financial gurus. We use the term "noise traders" to describe such investors. . . . Changes in demand can also reflect investors' use of inflexible trading strategies or of "popular models" . . . . One such strategy is trend chasing. Although these changes in demand are unwarranted by fundamentals, they can be related to fundamentals, as in the case of overreaction to news.

---

[f] Jay Ritter, *The Buying and Selling Behavior of Individual Investors and the Turn of the Year*, 43 J.Fin. 701 (1988).

[g] Kenneth French & Richard Roll, *Stock Return Variances: The Arrival of Information and the Reaction of Traders*, 17 J.Fin.Econ. 5 (1986).

[h] Richard Roll, R^2, 43 J.Fin. 541 (1988).

[i] David Cutler, James Poterba & Lawrence Summers, *What Moves Stock Prices?*, J. Portfolio Mgmt. 4 (Spr.1989).

These demand shifts will only matter if they are correlated across noise traders. If all investors trade randomly, their trades cancel out and there are no aggregate shifts in demand. Undoubtedly, some trading in the market brings together noise traders with different models who cancel each other out. However, many trading strategies based on pseudo-signals, noise, and popular models are correlated, leading to aggregate demand shifts. The reason for this is that judgment biases afflicting investors in processing information tend to be the same. Subjects in psychological experiments tend to make the same mistake; they do not make random mistakes. . . .

Many of these persistent mistakes are relevant for financial markets. For example, experimental subjects tend to be overconfident, which makes them take on more risk. Experimental subjects also tend to extrapolate past time series, which can lead them to chase trends. Finally, in making inferences experimental subjects put too little weight on base rates and too much weight on new information, which might lead them to overreact to news. . . .

A look at how market participants behave provides perhaps the most convincing evidence that noise rather than information drives many of their decisions. Investors follow market gurus and forecasters, such as Joe Granville and "Wall Street Week." . . . So-called "technical analysis" is another example of demand shifts without a fundamental rationalization. Technical analysis typically calls for buying more stocks when stocks have risen (broke through a barrier), and selling stocks when they fall through a floor. . . .

There can be little doubt that these sorts of factors influence demand for securities, but can they be big enough to make a difference? The standard economist's reason for doubting the size of these effects has been to posit that investors trading on noise might lose their money to arbitrageurs, leading to a diminution of their wealth and effect on demand. Noise traders might also learn the error of their ways and reform into rational arbitrageurs.

However, the argument that noise traders lose money and eventually disappear is not self-evident. First, noise traders might be on average more aggressive than the arbitrageurs -- either because they are overoptimistic or because they are overconfident -- and so bear more risk. If risk-taking is rewarded in the market, noise traders can earn higher expected returns even despite buying high and selling low on average. The risk rewarded by the market need not even be fundamental; it can be the resale price risk arising from the unpredictability of future noise traders' opinions. With higher expected returns, noise traders as a group do not disappear from the market rapidly, if at all. . . .

Learning and imitation may not adversely affect noise traders either. When noise traders earn high average returns, many other investors might imitate them, ignoring the fact that they took more risk and just got lucky. Such imitation brings more money to follow noise trader strategies. Noise traders themselves might become even more cocky, attributing their investment success to skill rather than luck. As noise traders who do well become more aggressive, their effect on demand increases.

The case against the importance of noise traders also ignores the fact that new investors enter the market all the time, and old investors who have lost money come back. These investors are subject to the same judgment biases as the current survivors in the market, and so add to the effect of judgment biases on demand. . . .

Explaining the Puzzles

When arbitrage is limited, and investor demand for securities responds to noise and to predictions of popular models, security prices move in response to these changes in demand as well as to changes in fundamentals. Arbitrageurs counter the shifts in demand prompted by changes in investor sentiment, but do not eliminate the effects of such shifts on the price completely.

In this market, prices vary more than is warranted by changes in fundamentals, since they respond to shifts in investor sentiment as well as to news. Stock returns are predictably mean-reverting, meaning that high stock returns lead to lower expected stock returns. This prediction has in fact been documented for the United States as well as the foreign stock prices by Fama & French (1988) and Poterba & Summers (1988). . . .[j]

This approach fits very neatly with the conventional nonacademic view of financial markets. On that view, the key to investment success is not just predicting future fundamentals, but also predicting the movement of other active investors. Market professionals spend considerable resources tracking price trends, volume, short interest, odd lot volume, investor sentiment indexes and numerous other gauges of demand for equities. Tracking these possible indicators of demand makes no sense if prices responded only to fundamental news and not to investor demand. They make perfect sense, in contrast, in a world where investor sentiment moves prices and so predicting changes in this sentiment pays. The prevalence of investment strategies based on indicators of demand in financial markets suggests the recognition by arbitrageurs of the role of demand.

Not only do arbitrageurs spend time and money to predict noise trader moves, they also make active attempts to take advantage of these moves. When noise traders are optimistic about particular securities, it pays arbitrageurs to create more of them. These securities might be mutual funds, new share issues, penny oil stocks, or junk bonds: anything that is overpriced at the moment. . . .

---

[j] Eugene Fama & Kenneth French, *Permanent and Temporary Components of Stock Market Prices*, 96 J.Pol.Econ. 246 (1988); James Poterba & Lawrence Summers, *Mean Reversion in Stock Prices: Evidence and Implications*, 22 J.Fin.Econ. 27 (1988).

When they bet against noise traders, arbitrageurs begin to look like noise traders themselves. They pick stocks instead of diversifying, because that is what betting against noise traders requires. They time the market to take advantage of noise trader mood swings. If these swings are temporary, arbitrageurs who cannot predict noise trader moves simply follow contrarian strategies. It becomes hard to tell the noise traders from the arbitrageurs. . . .

[Closed-end mutual fund discounts provide support for noise trading theories. An] investor who wants to liquidate his holdings of a closed-end fund must sell his shares to other investors; he cannot just redeem his shares as with an open-end fund. Closed-end funds present one of the most interesting puzzles in finance, because their fundamental value -- the value of the assets in their portfolios -- is observed, and tends to be systematically higher than the price at which these funds trade. The pervasiveness of discounts on closed-end funds is a problem for the efficient markets hypothesis: in the only case where value is observed, it is not equal to the price.

DeLong, Shleifer, Summers & Waldmann (1990) argue that investor sentiment about closed-end funds changes, and that this sentiment also affects other securities. When investors are bullish about closed-end funds, they drive up their prices relative to fundamental values, and discounts narrow or turn into premiums. When investors in contrast are bearish about closed-end funds, they drive down their prices and discounts widen. . . .

[Arbitrage] does not effectively eliminate discounts on closed-end funds. An arbitrageur who buys a discounted fund and sells short its portfolio runs the risk that at the time he liquidates his position the discount widens and so his arbitrage results in a loss. . . [k]

This theory of closed-end funds has a number of new empirical implications, investigated by Lee, Shleifer and Thaler (1991). First, it predicts that discounts on different closed-end funds fluctuate together, since they reflect changes in investor sentiment. This prediction is confirmed. Second, the theory predicts that new funds get started when investors are optimistic about funds, which is when old funds sell at a small discount or a premium. It is indeed the case that discounts on seasoned funds are much narrower in years when more new funds start. Perhaps most interestingly, the theory predicts that discounts on closed-end funds reflect the investor sentiment factor that also affects prices of other securities, which may have nothing to do with closed-end funds. Consistent with this prediction, Lee, Shleifer & Thaler find that when discounts on closed-end funds narrow, small stock portfolios tend to do well. . . .[l]

---

[k] J. Bradford DeLong, Andrei Shleifer, Lawrence Summers & Robert Waldmann, *Noise Trader Risk in Financial Markets*, 98 J.Pol.Econ. 703 (1990).

[l] Charles Lee, Andrei Shleifer & Richard Thaler, *Investor Sentiment and the Closed End Funds Puzzle*, 46 J.Fin. 75 (1991).

Implications of Positive Feedback Trading

One of the strongest investor tendencies documented in both experimental and survey evidence is the tendency to extrapolate or to chase the trend. Trend chasers buy stocks after they rise and sell stocks after they fall: they follow positive feedback strategies. Other strategies that depend on extrapolative expectations are "stop loss" orders, which prescribe selling after a certain level of losses, regardless of future prospects, and portfolio insurance, which involves buying more stocks (to raise exposure to risk) when prices rise and selling stocks (to cut exposure to risk) when prices fall.

When some investors follow positive feedback strategies -- buy when prices rise and sell when prices fall -- it need no longer be optimal for arbitrageurs to counter shifts in the demand of these investors. Instead, it may pay arbitrageurs to jump on the bandwagon themselves. Arbitrageurs then optimally buy the stocks that positive feedback investors get interested in when their prices rise. When price increases feed the buying of other investors, arbitrageurs sell out near the top and take their profits. . . . Although eventually arbitrageurs sell out and help prices return to fundamentals, in the short run they feed the bubble rather than help it to dissolve.

Some speculators indeed believe that jumping on the bandwagon with the noise traders is the way to beat them. George Soros, the successful investor and author of *Alchemy of Finance* (1987), describes his strategy during the conglomerate boom in the 1960s and the Real Estate Investment Trust boom in the 1970s precisely in these terms. The key to success, says Soros, was not to counter the irrational wave of enthusiasm about conglomerates, but rather to ride this wave for awhile and sell out much later. . . .

Positive feedback trading reinforced by arbitrageurs' jumping on the bandwagon leads to a positive autocorrelation of returns at short horizons. Eventual return of prices to fundamentals, accelerated as well by arbitrage, entails a negative autocorrelation of returns at longer horizons. Since news results in price changes that are reinforced by positive feedback trading, stock prices overreact to news.[m]

These predictions have been documented in a number of empirical studies. Cutler, Poterba and Summers (1989) find evidence of a positive correlation of returns at horizons of a few weeks or months and a negative one at horizons of a few years for several stock,

---

[m] *Autocorrelation* is a technical term that means that today's change in stock price predicts (correlates with) future stock price changes. *Positive* autocorrelation means that an increase today predicts a further increase in the future. *Negative* autocorrelation, also called *mean-reversion*, means that an increase in stock price today predicts a decrease in the future. Autocorrelation is inconsistent with the weak form of ECMH, under which stock prices should follow a random walk.

bond, foreign exchange, and gold markets. They report the average first order monthly serial correlation of more than .07 for 13 stock markets, and positive in every case. . . ."[n]

The presence of positive feedback traders in financial markets also makes it easier to interpret historical episodes, such as the sharp market increase and the crash of 1987. According to standard finance, the market crash of October 1987 reflected either a large increase in risk premiums because the economy became a lot riskier, or a large decrease in expected future growth rate of dividends. These theories have the obvious problem that they do not explain what news prompted a 22% devaluation of the American corporate sector on October 19. Another problem is that there is no evidence that risk increased tremendously - - volatility indeed jumped up but came back rapidly as it usually does -- or that expected dividend growth has been revised sharply down. . . . Perhaps most strikingly, Seyhun (1990) finds that corporate insiders bought stocks in record numbers during and after the crash, and moreover bought more of the stocks that later had a greater rebound. Insiders did not share the view that growth of dividends will slow or that risk will increase, *and they were right!*[o] Fully rational theories have a problem with the crash.

The crash is much easier to understand in a market with significant positive feedback trading. Positive feedback trading can rationalize the dramatic price increases during 1987, as more and more investors chase the trend. Positive feedback trading, exacerbated by possible frontrunning by investment banks, can also explain the depth of the crash once it has started. One still needs a theory of what broke the market on October 19, but the bad news during the previous week might have initiated the process, albeit with some lag.

Note on Noise Trading

1. *John Maynard Keynes on Investing as a Beauty Contest.* The Dean of the efficient market skeptics is John Maynard Keynes. In the book which laid the foundations for Keynesian economics, he stressed the difficulty of valuing securities from first principles, and argued that professional investors mostly didn't try. Keynes wrote:

> [Most professionals] are, in fact, largely concerned, not with making superior long-term forecasts of the probable yield of an investment over its whole life, but with foreseeing changes in the conventional basis of valuation a short time ahead of the

---

[n] David Cutler, James Poterba & Lawrence Summers, *Speculative Dynamics*, 58 Rev.Econ.Stud. 529 (1991).

[o] Nejat Seyhun, *Overreaction or Fundamentals: Some Lessons From Insiders' Response to the Market Crash of 1987*, 45 J.Fin. 1363 (1990).

general public. . . . For it is not sensible to pay 25 for an investment of which you believe the prospective yield to justify a value of 30, if you also believe that the market will value it at 20 three months hence. . . .

[P]rofessional investment may be likened to those newspaper competitions in which the competitors have to pick the six prettiest faces from a hundred photographs, the prize being awarded to the competitor whose choice most nearly corresponds to the average preferences of the competitors as a whole; so that each competitor has to pick, not those faces which he himself finds prettiest, but those which he thinks likeliest to catch the fancy of the other competitors, all of whom are looking at the problem from the same point of view.[6]

2. *If Prices are Inefficient, Why Don't Professionals Beat the Market?* Among the more important tests of ECMH are the many studies that show that market professionals don't consistently outperform the market. The efficient markets explanation is that professionals, all trying to find undervalued stocks, compete away each other's profitable opportunities. Noise trading proponents respond that this is well and good, *if* that's what market professionals are trying to do. But if, as Keynes believed, most professionals are trying to outguess each other on short-term price movements, it's not surprising, nor very probative on whether prices are efficient, that the average professional achieves average results.[7]

3. *Herd Behavior Models.* Finance economists have recently developed models of "herd behavior" by investors, which can lead to departures from efficient pricing. In these models: (i) some investors make valuation mistakes; (ii) all investors recognize that their information may be outdated or their beliefs inaccurate; and (iii) accordingly, all investors pay some attention to the market price, as evidence of the information or beliefs of other investors. In such a world, if enough investors make a common mistake, the mistake will be reinforced by the the efforts of other investors to learn from the (now incorrect) market price. Mistakes can be self-reinforcing, even if all investors are rationally trying to find

---

[6] John Maynard Keynes, *The General Theory of Employment, Interest, and Money* 154-56 (1936). To similar effect, though less colorful, is the description by Benjamin Graham and David Dodd, the founders of the field of security analysis. They described the stock market as a "voting machine" in the short run, and a "weighing machine" only over the long term. Benjamin Graham & David Dodd, *Security Analysis* 23 (1st ed.1934).

[7] See Louis Lowenstein, *What's Wrong With Wall Street: Short-Term Gain and the Absentee Shareholder* 52-53 (1988).

bargains.[8] Empirical studies, though, have thus far found little evidence of herd behavior by institutional investors.[9]

   4. *Rational Bubble Models*.   Shleifer & Summers discuss the possibility that arbitrageurs may sometimes find it profitable to buy an already overpriced stock, in the belief that it will become still more overpriced, and they will be able to sell ahead of the crowd.   Finance economists have recently developed theoretical models of "rational bubbles," in which once a price bubble forms, investors who expect the bubble to grow for a while, and then collapse at an unknown future time, will rationally act to reinforce the mispricing.[10]

   Rational bubble models are analytically similar to herd behavior models. Either way, informed investors act to reinforce the pricing errors of other investors. In herd behavior models, informed investors *unknowingly* reinforce price bubbles because they aren't sure of the quality of their own information.   In rational bubble models, informed investors *knowingly* reinforce price bubbles because they believe that the bubble will persist for a while. The skill to succeed at buying into a bubble and getting out before the crowd on a consistent basis, though, is likely as rare as the skill to outperform the market by analyzing fundamentals.

   5. *How Far From True Value Can Prices Go?* How far can noise trading push prices from fair value? Fischer Black, in the article that popularized the term *noise trading*, offers this suggestion:

> All estimates of value are noisy, so we can never know how far away price is from value. However, we might define an efficient market as one in which price is within a factor of 2 of value, i.e., the price is more than half of value and less than twice value. The factor of 2 is arbitrary, of course. Intuitively, though, it seems reasonable to me, in the light of sources of uncertainty about value and the strength of the forces tending to cause price to return to value. By this definition, I think

---

[8] See, e.g., Abhijit Banerjee, *A Simple Model of Herd Behavior*, 107 Q.J.Econ. 797 (1992); David Scharfstein & Jeremy Stein, *Herd Behavior and Investment*, 80 Am.Econ.Rev. 465 (1990); David Romer, *Rational Asset Price Movements Without News* (NBER Working Paper No. 4121, 1992).

[9] See Josef Lakonishok, Andrei Shleifer & Robert Vishny, *The Impact of Institutional Trading on Stock Prices*, 32 J.Fin.Econ. 23 (1992).

[10] See, e.g., J. Bradford DeLong, Andrei Shleifer, Lawrence Summers & Robert Waldman, *Positive Feedback Investment Strategies and Destabilizing Rational Speculation*, 45 J.Fin. 379 (1990).

almost all markets are efficient almost all of the time. "Almost all" means at least 90%.[11]

6. *Relative versus Absolute Efficiency.* We noted earlier in this chapter that the evidence for relative pricing efficiency of one stock relative to another is stronger than the evidence for absolute efficiency. Why might relative pricing be more efficient? Louis Lowenstein offers this explanation for the persistence of pricing errors, which has special force for the terribly difficult task of estimating the correct absolute level of stock prices:

> [Given] the overwhelming uncertainties affecting any long-term estimates of business and competition, given the lack of a sufficient basis for calculated mathematical projections, [we] take the next best course. We simply and conveniently assume that the current state of the world -- the economy, politics, war, climate, and so on -- represents a state of equilibrium and that the existing pattern or trend will continue indefinitely into the future until something happens to disturb it. Second, we assume that the stock market's valuations (and other markets' as well) reflect everything there is to know about business realities and prospects and that *they will change only as new information appears*.[12]

7. *How Strong is the Evidence for Noise Trading?* Some of the evidence that Shleifer & Summers offer in favor of noise trading can be questioned on statistical grounds, or interpreted in a way consistent with ECMH. For example, Shleifer & Summers cite evidence that multi-year stock prices show *mean-reversion* -- bull markets tend to be followed by bear markets and vice versa. They interpret this as evidence that the market overreacts to fundamental news. Eugene Fama, though, in a recent review, calls the mean-reversion studies "a statistical power failure."[13] Fama explains:

> [Shiller (1984) and Summers (1986)] present simple models in which stock prices take large slowly decaying swings away from fundamental values (fads, or irrational bubbles), but short-horizon returns have little autocorrelation. In the Shiller-Summers model, the market is highly inefficient, but in a way that is missed in tests on short-horizon returns. . . .[a]

---

[11] Fischer Black, *Noise*, 46 J.Fin. 529, 533 (1986).

[12] Louis Lowenstein, *Sense and Nonsense in Corporate Finance* 13 (1991) (emphasis in original) (citing John Maynard Keynes, *The General Theory of Employment, Interest and Money* (1936)).

[13] Eugene Fama, *Efficient Capital Markets: II*, 46 J.Fin. 1575, 1582 (1991).

[a] Robert Shiller, *Stock Prices and Social Dynamics*, 2 Brookings Papers on Econ. Activity 457 (1984), reprinted in Robert Shiller, *Market Volatility* ch. 1 (1989); Lawrence Summers, *Does the Stock Market Rationally Reflect Fundamental Values?*, 41 J.Fin. 591 (1986).

The Shiller-Summers challenge spawned a series of papers on the predictability of long-horizon returns from past returns. The evidence at first seemed striking, but the tests turn out to be largely fruitless. Thus, Fama & French (1988) find that the autocorrelations of returns on diversified portfolios of NYSE stocks for the 1926-1985 period have the pattern predicted by the Shiller-Summers model. The autocorrelations are close to 0 at short horizons, but they become strongly negative, around -0.25 to -0.4, for 3- to 5-year returns. Even with 60 years of data, however, the tests on long-horizon returns imply small sample sizes and low power. More telling, when Fama & French delete the 1926-1940 period from the tests, the evidence of strong negative autocorrelation in 3- to 5-year returns disappears.[b]

Similarly, Poterba & Summers (1988) find that, for N from 2 to 8 years, the variance of N-year returns on diversified portfolios grows much less than in proportion to N.[c] This is consistent with the hypothesis that there is negative autocorrelation in returns induced by temporary price swings. Even with 115 years (1871-1985) of data, however, the variance tests for long-horizon returns provide weak statistical evidence against the hypothesis that returns have no autocorrelation and prices are random walks.[14]

Fama also argues that mean-reversion, *if it exists*, could be consistent with market efficiency. Suppose that: (i) markets are efficient; (ii) the expected return that investors demand on stock portfolios varies randomly over time around a central value; and (iii) these fluctuations are unrelated to changes in investor expectations about future cash flows. In such a world, an increase in the expected return demanded by investors will cause stock prices to decline, relative to a long-term trend line. The price decline will be gradually erased by the higher returns that investors will now receive. Similarly, a decrease in the expected return demanded by investors will cause stock prices to increase, but the increase will gradually be erased by the lower returns that investors will now receive. In such a world, we will observe mean reversion, but the mean-reversion does not imply that investors are overreacting. Fama concludes:

> [A] ubiquitous problem in time-series tests of market efficiency, with no clear solution, is that irrational bubbles in stock prices are indistinguishable from rational time-varying expected returns.[15]

---

[b] Eugene Fama & Kenneth French, *Permanent and Temporary Components of Stock Market Prices*, 96 J.Pol.Econ. 246 (1988).

[c] James Poterba & Lawrence Summers, *Mean Reversion in Stock Prices: Evidence and Implications*, 22 J.Fin.Econ. 27 (1988).

[14] Fama (1992), *supra* note 13, at 1580-81.

[15] Id. at 1581.

8. *When Do Investors Overreact or Underreact?* The challenge for noise trading theories, as they develop, will be to explain *when* investors overreact, when they don't, and *why*. There are literally hundreds of event studies of market reaction to specific news events. Most do not find evidence of investor overreaction. Examples are the stock split study by Fama, Fisher, Jensen & Roll, discussed in the Lorie, Dodd & Kimpton excerpt above, and the many studies, discussed later in this book, of the reaction of target stock prices to takeover announcements. These studies must be weighed against the comparative handful of studies that find evidence of overreaction.[16]

9. *Investor Underreaction.* Do investors sometimes *underreact* to new information? A recent study suggests -- contrary to the popular wisdom that investors overreact to bad earnings reports -- that stock prices do not fully impound the implication of a single earnings announcement for future earnings. Instead, "the three-day price reactions to announcements of earnings for quarters $t + 1$ through $t + 4$ are predictable, based on earnings of quarter t."[17]

10. *Cognitive Errors as a Cause of Market Inefficiency.* Shleifer & Summers note that systematic human cognitive errors might lead to mispricing. These errors are discussed in the next section.

D. Systematic Errors in Human Cognition

Research in cognitive psychology demonstrates that human beings make a number of standard cognitive errors. Moreover, experimental subjects often fail to fully correct these errors *even when told about them*. These errors seem likely to affect the value assessments of *particular investors*, perhaps even *most* investors, in public securities markets. Because the errors are systematic, they won't average to zero across a large number of investors. But cognitive errors, if reflected in price, will also give rise to profitable arbitrage for

---

[16] See, e.g., Navin Chopra, Josef Lakonishok & Jay Ritter, *Measuring Abnormal Performance: Do Stocks Overreact?*, 31 J.Fin.Econ. 235 (1992).

[17] Victor Bernard & Jacob Thomas, *Evidence that Stock Prices Do Not Fully Reflect the Implications of Current Earnings for Future Earnings*, 13 J.Acct. & Econ. 305, 305 (1990). The earnings announcement anomaly may explain the long-standing *Value Line anomaly* -- the tendency for the timeliness rankings published by the Value Line Investment Survey (which depend in large part on earnings surprises) to predict stock price returns. See John Affleck-Graves & Richard Mendenhall, *The Relation Between the Value Line Enigma and Post-Earnings-Announcement Drift*, 31 J.Fin.Econ. 75 (1992).

investors who recognize them. The extent to which cognitive biases affect equilibrium prices will depend on the relative strength of the biases and of the correcting force of arbitrage.

Independent of their effect on security prices, cognitive errors may infect the judgments of the CEOs and financial advisors who must decide whether firm *A* should buy firm *B*, and at what price. These errors might explain why firms act *as if* accounting earnings affect stock prices, despite evidence to the contrary, or why bidders often overpay in acquisitions.

AMOS TVERSKY AND DANIEL KAHNEMAN, JUDGMENT UNDER UNCERTAINTY: HEURISTICS AND BIASES
185 Sci. 1124 (1974)[*]

[P]eople rely on a limited number of heuristic principles which reduce the complex tasks of assessing probabilities and predicting values to simpler judgmental operations. In general, these heuristics are quite useful, but sometimes they lead to severe and systematic errors. . . .

Representativeness

Many of the probabilistic questions with which people are concerned belong to one of the following types: What is the probability that object *A* belongs to class *B*? What is the probability that event *A* originates from process *B*? What is the probability that process *B* will generate event *A*? In answering such questions, people typically rely on the representativeness heuristic, in which probabilities are evaluated by the degree to which *A* is representative of *B*, that is, by the degree to which *A* resembles *B*. For example, when *A* is highly representative of *B*, the probability that *A* originates from *B* is judged to be high. On the other hand, if *A* is not similar to *B*, the probability that *A* originates from *B* is judged to be low. . . . This approach to the judgment of probability leads to serious errors, because similarity, or representativeness, is not influenced by several factors that should affect judgments of probability.

Insensitivity to Prior Probability of Outcomes

One of the factors that have no effect on representativeness but should have a major effect on probability is the prior probability, or base-rate frequency, of the outcomes. . . . If people evaluate probability by representativeness, therefore, prior probabilities will be neglected.

This hypothesis was tested in an experiment where prior probabilities were manipulated. . . . Subjects were shown brief personality descriptions of several individuals, allegedly sampled at random from a group of 100 professionals -- engineers and lawyers. The subjects were asked to assess, for each description, the probability that it belonged to an engineer rather than to a lawyer. In one experimental condition, subjects were told that the group from which the descriptions had been drawn consisted of 70 engineers and 30 lawyers. In another condition, subjects were told that the group consisted of 30 engineers and 70 lawyers. The odds that any particular description belongs to an engineer rather than to a lawyer should be higher in the first condition, where there is a majority of engineers, than in the second condition, where there is a majority of lawyers. . . . [In fact], subjects evaluated the likelihood that a particular description belonged to an engineer rather than to a lawyer by the degree to which this description was representative of the two stereotypes, with little or no regard for the prior probabilities of the categories.

. . . [P]rior probabilities were effectively ignored [even when the description] was totally uninformative. The responses to the following description illustrate this phenomenon:

Dick is a 30 year old man. He is married with no children. A man of high ability and high motivation, he promises to be quite successful in his field. He is well liked by his colleagues.

This description was intended to convey no information relevant to the question of whether Dick is an engineer or a lawyer. Consequently, the probability that Dick is an engineer should equal the proportion of engineers in the group, as if no description had been given. The subjects, however, judged the probability of Dick being an engineer to be .5 regardless of whether the stated proportion of engineers in the group was .7 or .3. . . .

Insensitivity to Sample Size

. . . [I]f probabilities are assessed by representativeness, then the judged probability of a sample statistic will be essentially independent of sample size. Indeed, when subjects assessed the distributions of average height for samples of various sizes, they produced identical distributions. For example, the probability of obtaining an average height greater than 6 feet was assigned the same value for samples of 1000, 100, and 10 men. Moreover, subjects failed to appreciate the role of sample size even when it was emphasized in the formulation of the problem. . . .

Misconceptions of Chance

People expect that a sequence of events generated by a random process will *represent* the essential characteristics of that process even when the sequence is short. In considering tosses of a coin for heads or tails, for example, people regard the sequence H-T-H-T-T-H to be more likely than the sequence H-H-H-T-T-T, which does not appear random, and also more likely than the sequence H-H-H-H-T-H, which does not represent the fairness of the coin. Thus, people expect that the essential characteristics of the process will be represented, not only globally in the entire sequence, but also locally in each of its parts. A locally representative sequence, however, deviates systematically from chance expectation: it contains too many alternations and too few runs.

Another consequence of the belief in local representativeness is the well-known gambler's fallacy. After observing a long run of red on the roulette wheel, for example, most people erroneously believe that black is now due, presumably because the occurrence of black will result in a more representative sequence than the occurrence of an additional red. Chance is commonly viewed as a self-correcting process in which a deviation in one direction induces a deviation in the opposite direction to restore the equilibrium. In fact, deviations are not "corrected" as a chance process unfolds, they are merely diluted. . . .

Insensitivity to predictability

People are sometimes called upon to make such numerical predictions as the future value of a stock, the demand for a commodity, or the outcome of a football game. Such predictions are often made by representativeness. For example, suppose one is given a description of a company and is asked to predict its future profit. If the description of the company is very favorable, a very high profit will appear most representative of that description; if the description is mediocre, a mediocre performance will appear most representative. The degree to which the description is favorable is unaffected by the reliability of that description or by the degree to which it permits accurate prediction. . . .

[For example], subjects were presented with several paragraphs, each describing the performance of a student teacher during a particular practice lesson. Some subjects were asked to *evaluate* the quality of the *lesson* described in the paragraph in percentile scores, relative to a specified population. Other subjects were asked to *predict*, also in percentile scores, the standing of each student teacher 5 years after the practice lesson. . . . [T]he prediction of a remote criterion (success of a teacher after 5 years) was identical to the evaluation of the information on which the prediction was based (the quality of the practice lesson). The students who made these predictions were undoubtedly aware of the limited predictability of teaching competence on the basis of a single trial lesson 5 years earlier; nevertheless, their predictions were as extreme as their evaluations.

The Illusion of Validity

As we have seen, people often predict by selecting the outcome (for example, an occupation) that is most representative of the input (for example, the description of a person). The confidence they have in their prediction depends primarily on the degree of representativeness (that is, on the quality of the match between the selected outcome and the input) with little or no regard for the factors that limit predictive accuracy. Thus, people

176

express great confidence in the prediction that a person is a librarian when given a description of his personality which matches the stereotype of librarians, even if [told that few people are librarians]. The unwarranted confidence [in predictions based on representativeness] may be called the illusion of validity. . . .

Misconceptions of Regression

Suppose a large group of children has been examined on two equivalent versions of an aptitude test. If one selects ten children from among those who did best on one of the two versions, he will usually find their performance on the second version to be somewhat disappointing. Conversely, if one selects ten children from among those who did worst on one version, they will be found, on the average, to do somewhat better on the other version. . . . These observations illustrate a general phenomenon known as regression toward the mean . . . .

In the normal course of life, one encounters many instances of regression toward the mean, in the comparison of the height of fathers and sons, of the intelligence of husbands and wives, or of the performance of individuals on consecutive examinations. Nevertheless, people do not develop correct intuitions about this phenomenon. First, they do not expect regression in many contexts where it is bound to occur. Second, when they recognize the occurrence of regression, they often invent spurious causal explanations for it. We suggest that the phenomenon of regression remains elusive because it is incompatible with the [representativeness heuristic].

The failure to recognize the import of regression can have pernicious consequences, as illustrated by the following observation. In a discussion of flight training, experienced instructors noted that praise for an exceptionally smooth landing is typically followed by a poorer landing on the next try, while harsh criticism after a rough landing is usually followed by an improvement on the next try. The instructors concluded that verbal rewards are detrimental to learning, while verbal punishments are beneficial, contrary to accepted psychological doctrine. This conclusion is unwarranted because of the presence of regression toward the mean. . . .

Availability

There are situations in which people assess the frequency of a class or the probability of an event by the ease with which instances or occurrences can be brought to mind. For example, one may assess the risk of heart attack among middle-aged people by recalling such occurrences among one's acquaintances. Similarly, one may evaluate the probability that a given business venture will fail by imagining various difficulties it could encounter. This judgmental heuristic is called availability . . . .

When the size of a class is judged by the availability of its instances, a class whose instances are easily retrieved will appear more numerous than a class of equal frequency whose instances are less retrievable. In an elementary demonstration of this effect, subjects heard a list of well-known personalities of both sexes and were subsequently asked to judge whether the list contained more names of men than of women. Different lists were presented to different groups of subjects. In some of the lists the men were relatively more famous than the women, and in others the women were relatively more famous than the men. In each of the lists, the subjects erroneously judged that the class (sex) that had the more famous personalities was the more numerous.

In addition to familiarity, there are other factors, such as *salience* [also called *vividness*], which affect the retrievability of instances. For example, the impact of seeing a house burning on the subjective probability of such accidents is probably greater than the impact of reading about a fire in the local paper. Furthermore, recent occurrences are likely to be relatively more available than earlier occurrences. It is a common experience that the subjective probability of traffic accidents rises temporarily when one sees a car overturned by the side of the road. . . .

Adjustment and Anchoring

In many situations, people make estimates by starting from an initial value that is adjusted to yield the final answer. The initial value, or starting point, may be suggested by the formulation of the problem, or it may be the result of a partial computation. In either case, adjustments are typically insufficient. . . . We call this phenomenon *anchoring*.

Insufficient Adjustment

In a demonstration of the anchoring effect, subjects were asked to estimate [the percentage of African countries in the U.N. A] number between 0 and 100 was determined by spinning a wheel of fortune *in the subjects' presence*. The subjects were instructed to indicate first whether [the randomly chosen] number was higher or lower than the [true percentage], and then to estimate the [true percentage] . . . . [T]he median estimates of the percentage of African countries in the United Nations were 25 and 45 for groups that received 10 and 65, respectively, as [random] starting points. Payoffs for accuracy did not reduce the anchoring effect. . . .

In a recent study by Bar-Hillel, subjects were given the opportunity to bet on one of two events. Three types of events were used: (i) *simple* events, such as drawing a red marble from a bag containing 50% red marbles and 50% white marbles; (ii) *conjunctive* events, such as drawing a red marble seven times in succession, with replacement, from a bag containing 90% red marbles and 10% white marbles; and (iii) *disjunctive* events, such as drawing a red marble at least once in seven successive tries, with replacement, from a bag containing 10% red marbles and 90% white marbles. In this problem, a significant majority of subjects preferred to bet on the conjunctive event (the probability of which is .48) rather than on the simple event (the probability of which is .50). Subjects also preferred to bet on the simple event rather than on the disjunctive event, which has a probability of .52.

[More generally], people tend to overestimate the probability of conjunctive events and to underestimate the probability of disjunctive events. These biases are readily explained as effects of anchoring. The stated probability of the elementary event (success at any one stage) provides a natural starting point for the estimation of the probabilities of both conjunctive and disjunctive events. Since adjustment from the starting point is typically insufficient, the final estimates remain too close to the probabilities of the elementary events in both cases. Note that the overall probability of a conjunctive event is lower than the probability of each elementary event, whereas the overall probability of a disjunctive event is higher than the probability of each elementary event. . . .

Biases in the evaluation of compound events are particularly significant in the context of planning. The successful completion of an undertaking, such as the development of a new product, typically has a conjunctive character: for the undertaking to succeed, each of a series of events must occur. Even when each of these events is very likely, the overall probability of success can be quite low if the number of events is large. The general tendency to overestimate the probability of conjunctive events leads to unwarranted optimism in the evaluation of the likelihood that a plan will succeed or that a project will be completed on time. . . .

Anchoring in the Assessment of Subjective Probability Distributions

[Suppose that a securities analyst is] asked to select a number, X_{90}, such that his subjective probability that this number will be higher than the value of the Dow-Jones average [at a specific future time] is .90. A subjective probability distribution for the value of the Dow-Jones average can be constructed from several such judgments corresponding to different percentiles. [If the analyst's judgment is sound], the true values should fall below X_{01} for 1% of the quantities and above X_{99} for 1% of the quantities. Thus, the true values should fall [below X_{01} or above X_{99} about 2% of the time].

[Investigators] have obtained probability distributions for [the Dow Jones average and many other] quantities from a large number of judges. These distributions indicated large and systematic departures from proper calibration. In most studies, the actual values of the assessed quantities are either smaller than X_{01} or greater than X_{99} for about 30% of the problems. That is, the subjects state overly narrow confidence intervals which reflect more certainty than is justified by their knowledge about the assessed quantities. This bias is common to naive and to sophisticated subjects . . . . [It] is attributable, at least in part, to anchoring.

179

To select X_{90} for the value of the Dow-Jones average, for example, it is natural to begin by thinking about one's best estimate of the Dow-Jones and to adjust this value upward. If this adjustment -- like most others -- is insufficient, then X_{90} will not be sufficiently extreme. A similar anchoring effect will occur in the selection of X_{10}, which is presumably obtained by adjusting one's best estimate downward. Consequently, the confidence interval between X_{10} and X_{90} will be too narrow, and the assessed probability distribution will be too tight. . . .

Note on Cognitive Biases

The literature on cognitive biases has exploded since Tversky & Kahneman wrote their review article in 1974. Additional biases documented in the literature that seem relevant to investor behavior include:

(i) *The endowment effect*: People insist on a higher price to sell something they already own, than to buy the same item if they don't own it.

(ii) *Loss aversion*: Most people are risk averse for *profit* opportunities. They are indifferent, say, between $450 for sure and a 50% chance of gaining $1,000. Economic theory predicts that risk aversion should be roughly the same for gains and losses. Someone who is indifferent between a sure gain of $450 and a 50% chance of gaining $1,000 also ought to be indifferent between losing $550 for sure and a 50% chance of losing $1,000, as long as $1,000 is a small fraction of their total wealth. Either way, they would pay $50 in expected value to avoid uncertainty.

People don't act that way, though. Instead, they tend to be highly risk-averse for profit opportunities, and much less risk-averse, or even risk-preferrers, when they must take a chance to avoid a loss. Someone might, for example, be indifferent between $450 for sure and a 50% chance of gaining $1,000, yet willing to accept a 50% chance of losing $1,000, to avoid a sure loss of only $400. This willingness to gamble to avoid a loss is called *loss aversion*. One can readily imagine loss aversion affecting the relative prices of stocks (which carry a high probability of loss), and high-grade bonds (which carry a low probability of loss if held to maturity, at least in nominal dollars).[18]

---

[18] See Amos Tversky & Daniel Kahneman, *Advances in Prospect Theory: Cumulative Representation of Uncertainty*, 5 J.Risk & Uncertainty 297 (1992).

(iii) *Insensitivity to small probabilities*: People have trouble distinguishing between *different* small probabilities, and also tend to systematically overweight small probabilities, in choosing a course of action. For example, they will pay almost as much to avoid a 1% chance of loss as to avoid a 5% chance of the same loss.

(iv) *Cognitive dissonance*: Cognitive dissonance is a catchall phrase for the tendency of people to like to think about some things, and avoid thinking about others. For example, people don't like thinking about bad outcomes, or remembering their own mistakes. Thus, for example, investors whose stock picks have beaten the market half the time and done worse half the time will tend to remember the successes, and forget the failures.

(v) *Self-confidence*: People believe in their own skill. For example, surveys routinely show that 80% of automobile drivers believe that they are more skilled than the average. Investors show similar tendencies. They interpret their successes as reflecting their own skill, and ascribe the losses to bad luck.

How might these various biases affect investor behavior? How might they lead to inefficient pricing, or acquisition mistakes?[16]

E. Summary

Thomas Kuhn argues that some scientific paradigms become so deeply embedded in scientific thought that scientists who grow up with a paradigm are often unable to discard it, even after its weakness becomes evident. A shift to a new paradigm must sometimes wait for a new generation of scholars, less wedded to old ways of thinking, to replace the old.[17] Is the efficient market hypothesis such a paradigm, already obsolete but surviving because today's scholars have grown up accepting it?[18]

---

[16] For a sampling of the literature on cognitive biases, see *Judgement Under Uncertainty: Heuristics and Biases* (Daniel Kahneman, Paul Slovic & Amos Tversky eds.1982); Richard Nisbett & Lee Ross, *Human Inference: Strategies and Shortcomings of Social Judgment* (1980); George Akerlof & William Dickens, *The Economic Consequences of Cognitive Dissonance*, 72 Am.Econ.Rev. 307 (1982); Daniel Kahneman, Jack Knetsch & Richard Thaler, *Anomalies: The Endowment Effect, Loss Aversion, and Status Quo Bias*, 5 J.Econ.Persp. 193 (1991).

[17] Thomas Kuhn, *The Structure of Scientific Revolutions* (1972).

[18] Donald Langevoort, *Theories, Assumptions, and Securities Regulation: Market Efficiency Revisited*, 140 U.Pa.L.Rev. 851 (1992), makes this argument.

Our judgment is no, especially if market efficiency is seen as a matter of *how much*, rather than yes or no. There is much evidence that stock prices are a good, even if not a perfect, estimate of value. And it seems unlikely that we will soon find another measure of value that works better, on average and over time, as a guide to investor behavior or legal policy.

In the words of an anonymous philosopher, "all things are difficult to predict, particularly the future." Investors in common stock face the incredibly difficult task of predicting dividends far into the future. The complexity of that task lays the seeds for departures from efficient pricing. But we cannot avoid the need to estimate value, and the difficulties do not disappear if we rely on other sources of value estimates. The consensus investor estimate of value reflected in price may sometimes reflect fads or other biases. But other plausible sources of value estimates -- such as judges in appraisal proceedings, regulators, or corporate managers, seem likely to produce worse value estimates, on average.

In particular, regulators and corporate managers often have incentives to reach systematically biased answers. For example, the managers of a takeover target often claim, and may really believe, that their company is worth more than the bidder is offering. The managers' strong self-interest provides reason to distrust such estimates. Sometimes, the managers are right. But as we will see in Part II, the market's estimate of value seems better on average, even though the managers have superior information about their company.

Problems to Accompany Chapter 5

1. You're on vacation, and you take a wrong turn while touring the wine country in upstate New York. You ask a local farmer for directions and are surprised by the trappings of great wealth on the farm. There's a late model Mercedes-Benz sedan in the driveway. The farmer greets you wearing a gold Rolex watch. After getting directions, you comment that your host must produce an extraordinary wine. He answers with a polite "no," and explains that he never was any good at making wine and hasn't made any for twenty years. Instead, he plays the stock market. Once a month, he lets his prize rooster eat of the market reporting section of the Wall Street Journal. Wherever the rooster pecks a hole through the paper, he buys the stock. His return has averaged 20% per year over the last 20 years, and he's never had two down years in a row. He would be happy to manage your money for you. Assume that the farmer's claims are true. Would you let the farmer manage your money? Why or why not?

2. As a guest at the Wealthy Acres Country Club, you are excited at the prospect of getting to meet new people with interests so similar to your own. While you are watching the polo match, one of the members pulls you aside, and blurts out that he must tell you

about the new account that his advertising agency just snagged away from another agency. He tells you that Dice Pizza is planning the greatest media blitz of all time. Everything is still in the planning stage now, but in three months time, when the campaign begins, he expects that pizza consumption around the world will increase dramatically, with Dice Pizza grabbing the lion's share of the global pizza market. You realize that the information you've just been given could be of great potential value to you. Dice Pizza is publicly held, and it would be easy to buy some stock, if you so choose. What factors should you consider in deciding whether or not to buy Dice stock? Specifically, what are your concerns about the efficiency of the market for Dice shares?

3. The stock of Street Corner Auto Parts Corp. has risen fifteen percent in the last week since a rumor that a major auto manufacturer was looking to buy the company circulated on Wall Street. Such an acquisition would probably involve a premium of at least 50% over the pre-rumor market price. What are your thoughts on whether purchasing shares of Street Corner would be a good idea at this point?

4. Corporate officers must report their purchases and sales of their company's stock to the SEC on a monthly basis. Several newsletters publish this information. One of these newsletters claims that it has a system for analyzing these reports and generating buy or sell signals from them. Historical analysis shows that following their monthly recommendations by buying the recommended stocks at the closing price on the date when each recommendation was made would have produced returns that exceed the market by an average of 3% per year.

a) If this pattern continues in the future, which form(s) of market efficiency would it call into question, and why?

b) Should you buy the newsletter? Why or why not?

5. *The Three Boxes*: You are asked to play the following two-stage game: There are 3 boxes on a table. One of them has a $100 bill under it; the others are empty. In stage 1, you must guess which box has the $100 bill. The game host, who knows which box has the bill, then opens the lid of *another* box (not the one you have chosen), and *always* opens an *empty* box. The host can always do this because at least one of the other boxes *must* be empty. At this point in the game, there are two closed boxes, one of which contains the $100 bill. In stage 2, you must decide whether to stick with your initial choice, or to switch and choose the other closed box.

a) Should you keep your initial choice or switch? What is the best strategy?

b) What is the chance that you will win, under the best available strategy?

6. *The AIDS Test*: Lifeco requires all applicants for life insurance to take an AIDS test. A particular applicant has a positive AIDS test. You have no other information about the applicant. You are told that:

- The test produces the correct result 87% of the time -- both for subjects with and without the disease.
- The incidence of the disease in the population is 1%.

(a) How likely is it that an applicant who tests positive really has AIDS?

(b) How likely is it that an applicant who tests negative really does not have AIDS?

7. *The Juror's Fallacy*: A cab was involved in a hit and run accident at night. Two cab companies, the Green and the Blue, operate in the city. You are told that:

- 85% of the cabs are Green and 15% are Blue.
- A witness identified the cab as Blue.
- The witness can correctly identify the cab's color under the circumstances that existed on the night of the accident 80% of the time.

What is the probability that a Blue cab was involved in the accident? If you can't compute a precise answer, pick a range (0-20%; 20-40%; 40-60%; 60-80%; 80-100%).

CHAPTER 6: EVENT STUDIES:
MEASURING THE IMPACT OF INFORMATION

In a semistrong efficient market, market prices provide an unbiased forecast of the present value of a firm's cash flows, based on all publicly available information. If new information becomes available, market prices respond rapidly and without bias to the new information. This leads to an important class of tests of semistrong efficiency called *event studies*. An event study involves identifying *when* information about a company is released and observing the stock price response. A rapid and unbiased response is consistent with semistrong efficiency.

In Figure 6-1, a particularly important piece of news about firm X is released on day 0, which is called the *announcement date* or the *event date*. This leads to an immediate stock price jump. The stock price fluctuates randomly, in response to other information, or perhaps due to noise trading, both before and after day 0. This response is consistent with semistrong market efficiency.

Figure 6-1
Efficient Market Response to New Information

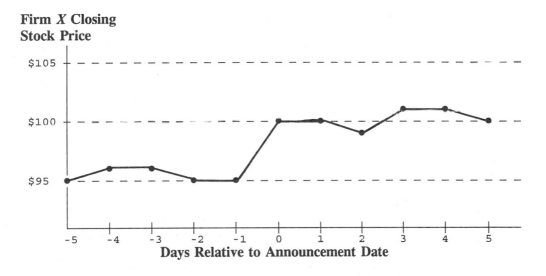

Firm X Closing Stock Price

Days Relative to Announcement Date

In contrast, the stock price response shown in Figure 6-2 is inconsistent with semistrong market efficiency because it is too *slow* -- it takes several days for the price to move to the new equilibrium level. Arbitrageurs could buy firm Y's stock right after the announcement and profit from the gradual move to the new equilibrium price.

Figure 6-2
Slow (*Inefficient*) Market Response to New Information

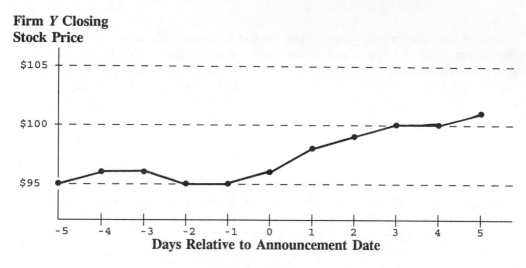

The stock price response shown in Figure 6-3 is also inconsistent with semistrong market efficiency. The immediate response is not *unbiased*. Instead, the stock price overshoots the new equilibrium value of $100, and then settles back to $100 over several days. Arbitrageurs could sell firm Z's stock short after it shoots up in response to the announcement and profit from the gradual decline back to the new equilibrium price.

Figure 6-3
Biased (*Inefficient*) Market Response to New Information

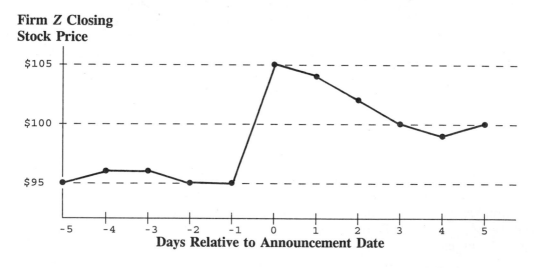

A second use of event studies *assumes* that the stock market is semistrong efficient. In an efficient market, the market price is an unbiased estimate of the present value of the firm's expected future cash flows, *given* a publicly available information set. This is true at all times, including just before and just after new information is released. Thus, the market's response to new information is an unbiased measure of *how important* the information is. A large response means that the information was important; a small change means that the information was unimportant.

For example, in Figure 6-1, investors value firm X at $95 before the announcement, and $100 after the announcement. The $5 per share increase measures how much more investors *think* firm X is worth after the announcement, relative to other firms. The announcement may involve a new event that increases the present value of firm X's expected cash flows by $5. Or the announcement may change investor *beliefs* about firm X's value, while actual value doesn't change at all. Or the price change may reflect a combination of (i) change in firm X's actual value, and (ii) change in investor beliefs about value, independent of actual change in value.

Some announcements appear mostly to affect actual value. For example, there is evidence that takeover bids don't change investor beliefs about the target's value as a stand-alone firm.[1] This suggests that the takeover premium reflects an actual increase in the target's value due to the takeover. Other announcements mostly affect investor beliefs about value. For example, the Fama, Fisher, Jensen & Roll study described in Chapter 5 suggests that stock split announcements affect price because they signal good news about the firm, not because investors value low-priced shares more highly.

Event studies can also provide information on *when* information is released to the market. For example, the target's stock price often creeps up *before* the formal announcement of a takeover bid. Examples of this are shown in Figures 5-3 and 6-8. This provides evidence of news leakage, perhaps through insider trading amplified by the trade and price decoding efforts of market professionals.[2]

Both uses of event studies -- as a *test* of semistrong market efficiency, and as a *measure* of the impact of new information -- are central to evaluating the motives for acquisitions, understanding how acquisitions affect the value of particular firms, and

---

[1] See Chapter 14.

[2] See Gregg Jarrell & Annette Poulsen, *Stock Trading Before the Announcement of Tender Offers: Insider Trading or Market Anticipation?*, 5 J.L. Econ. & Organization 225 (1989); John Pound & Richard Zeckhauser, *Clearly Heard on the Street: The Effect of Takeover Rumors on Stock Prices*, 63 J.Bus. 291 (1990). The statistical tests used to measure the significance of stock price returns require the investigator to first specify an announcement date, and then assess whether the announcement has significantly affected stock prices. One can work backwards -- inferring the release of information by observing a price runup -- only if prior studies clearly establish the importance of the information that has been released.

assessing legal policy toward takeovers. Section A of this Chapter introduces techniques for measuring the value of new information. Section B develops the statistical techniques underlying event studies. Section C provides an example of how event studies can be used to measure the impact of new information. Section D discusses the limits on what event studies can tell us, including the central problem of determining when information is *new*, and the often insoluble problem of determining *why* the market price has reacted to new information when there are competing explanations. Finally, section E discusses methodological issues in conducting event studies, and some common variations in the ways that event studies are conducted.

A. The Expected Value of Information

CHARLES HOLLOWAY, DECISION MAKING UNDER UNCERTAINTY
348-359 (1979)[*]

What is the value of information in a particular setting? The basic principle is that *information only has value in a decision problem if it results in a change in some action to be taken by a decision maker.* . . . The value of information can be calculated using the [decision tree] techniques already developed. An *information alternative* is created and included in the decision diagram like any other alternative. The *cost* [of obtaining the information] that makes the information alternative equivalent to the *best alternative without the information* is called the *value* of the information. Two cases are usually considered: . . . .

Expected Value of Perfect Information

Definition: Expected Value of Perfect Information (EVPI) =
(expected value if perfect information could be obtained) −
(expected value of the best alternative without information)

Expected Value of Sample Information

Definition: Expected Value of Imperfect or Sample Information (EVSI) =
(expected value of the information alternative) −
(expected value of the best alternative without information)

Expected Value of Perfect Information (EVPI)

Perfect information about a given event means complete elimination of all uncertainty about the event's outcomes. That is, *after* receiving the information, you will know exactly which outcome will occur. In some cases perfect information *is* obtainable. For instance, if the uncertain event involved the decision of a customer to let a contract, it might be possible to find out what the decision is by offering the customer an incentive for telling you. In other cases perfect information is not possible but is a useful concept. It is useful because it provides an *upper bound* on the value of information in a particular decision, and because the calculations [of the value of perfect information] usually can be done easily.

There are several ways to visualize and calculate the EVPI. To illustrate the methods, consider the following example.

Example 6-1

A construction contract must be completed prior to [a specified date] to avoid a significant penalty. There are three different plans that can be used for the construction [and four different expected weather types: good (type n_1); hot (type n_2); cold (type n_3); and rainy (type n_4)]. The plans differ primarily in their ability to provide flexibility in the face of varying weather conditions. Plan 1 will be the most profitable if good weather exists during the construction period; however, it is the worst under other conditions. Plan 2 [does relatively well] under all conditions. Plan 3 is good [in good weather and adequate in cold weather] but poor under the other two possible weather types. The plans and their net [profit] in thousands of dollars for the four possible weather types are shown in Table 6-1 along with the assessed probabilities for the weather possibilities. . . .

Table 6-1
Profit Under Varying Weather Conditions

Weather	Plan 1	Plan 2	Plan 3	Probability
Good (n_1)	48	24	40	0.4
Hot (n_2)	16	24	16	0.2
Cold (n_3)	16	32	24	0.2
Rainy (n_4)	16	24	16	0.2
[Expected Profit]	28.8	25.6	27.2	1.0

In this example . . . the expected [profit if you have] *perfect advance information* is $35,200. [If the weather is good, you will choose Plan 1 and earn $48,000; otherwise

189

you will choose Plan 2, and earn either $24,000 or $32,000. The calculation is shown in Table 6-2.] Note that the decision to obtain perfect information does *not* eliminate all uncertainty. You are still (until the perfect information is received) uncertain about what the information will reveal. Without perfect information Plan 1 will yield the maximum expected monetary value of $28,800. Therefore, the value of the perfect information must be the difference between $35,200 and $28,800, or $6,400. . . .

Table 6-2
Net Profit With Perfect Information

Weather	Choice with Perfect Information	[Profit]	Probability
Good (n_1)	Plan 1	48	0.4
Hot (n_2)	Plan 2	24	0.2
Cold (n_3)	Plan 2	32	0.2
Rainy (n_4)	Plan 2	24	0.2
[Expected Profit]		35.2	1.0

Another method of visualizing EVPI is to consider how much perfect information would be worth to you for each possible weather state. For instance, what if the information transmitted were that weather type n_1 would occur? Without this information you would choose Plan 1. With this information you would still choose Plan 1. Therefore, the information *weather type n_1* would result in no change in your choice and it would not be worth anything to you. However, if the signal were *weather type n_2*, you would switch to Plan 2, increasing your payoff by $24,000 − $16,000 = $8,000. Table 6-3 displays your actions and the difference in payoff for each state of weather.

Table 6-3
Value of Information Under Varying Weather Conditions

Weather	Current Choice	Choice [with Perfect Information]	Change in [Profit]	Probability
Good (n_1)	Plan 1	Plan 1	0	0.4
Hot (n_2)	Plan 1	Plan 2	8	0.2
Cold (n_3)	Plan 1	Plan 3	16	0.2
Rainy (n_4)	Plan 1	Plan 4	8	0.2
[Additional Profit			6.4	1.0

Now place yourself back at a point in time before the information on which weather state will occur has been transmitted, and ask: "How much would I be willing to pay for the information?" The amount clearly depends upon which signal (i.e., weather type) is transmitted. All you have available are the probabilities of various weather types, and therefore you can calculate the EVPI as $(0 \times 0.4) + (\$8,000 \times 0.2) + (\$16,000 \times 0.2) + (\$8,000 \times 0.2) = \$6,400$.

Expected Value of Imperfect or Sample Information

When the information available is not perfect but still offers the potential for reducing the uncertainty associated with a decision problem, its expected value can sometimes be calculated. . . .

Example 6-2

Faced with a difficult technological problem, the manager of an engineering and development laboratory was considering bringing in an outside expert to help determine whether the process under development would be a technological success. It was impossible to know for sure if the process would be a success until the research was completed. However, the expert he had in mind was more knowledgeable than anyone on his staff on the crucial part of the project. If the process turns out to be a success, the payoffs will be large -- approximately $10,000,000. On the other hand, a failure will result in a substantial loss, estimated to be $5,000,000. The manager currently assesses the chances of success at only 30%. When considering the expert, he feels confident the assessment provided after the investigation will be a probability of success of 60%, 40%, 20%, or 0%. Moreover, he feels that each possibility is equally likely. As a matter of fact, this assessment on the expert's response, which corresponds to an overall probability of success of 30% $[(.25)(.60) + (.25)(.40) + (.25)(.20) + (.25)(0) = .30]$, just confirms his opinion about the success of the project. . . .

[Without the expert's advice, the manager should terminate the project. Continuing would have an expected value of $(.30)(\$10,000,000) + (.70)(-\$5,000,000) = -\$500,000$. If the expert believes that the odds of success are 20% or 0%, the best option is still to terminate the project. But if the expert believes that the odds of success are 60%, the project has a positive expected value: $(.60)(\$10,000,000) + (.40)(-\$5,000,000) = \$4,000,000$. If the expert believes that the odds of success are 40%, the project also has positive expected value: $(.40)(\$10,000,000) + (.60)(-\$5,000,000) = \$1,000,000$. Thus, the best strategy -- proceed or stop -- depends on the expert's estimate.

Table 6-4
Value of Expert's Opinion About Project Success

Expert's Predicted Chance of Success	Current Choice	Choice with Expert's Imperfect Information	Change in Profit	Probability
60%	Stop	Proceed	$4,000,000	0.25
40%	Stop	Proceed	$1,000,000	0.25
20%	Stop	Stop	0	0.25
0%	Stop	Stop	0	0.25
Additional Profit			**$1,250,000**	**1.0**

Table 6-4 shows how the expert's opinion affects the choice of strategy, and the increased value from having the opinion available. The expected value of the expert's opinion, with the decision *proceed* if the expert predicts 60% or 40% chance of success and *stop* if the expert predicts 20% or 0% chance of success, is $1,250,000.]

The Relationship Between Value of Information and Amount of Uncertainty

The value of information depends on both the amount of uncertainty [before the information is received] and the payoffs. To demonstrate, consider the following simplified example.

Example 6-3

As an investor you are convinced that XYZ Company's earnings have an equal chance to be either $2 per share or $2.50 per share for last year. Furthermore you believe the stock price will be 10 times last year's earnings per share (EPS) in either case. The stock is now selling for $22 per share and the earnings are to be reported in 1 month. . . . Although you are not sure if you can obtain "perfect" information, you realize that it would be possible to get close to perfect information by talking with company officials. Since this would be a time-consuming and expensive process, you want to get a feel for the value of the information. . . .

[Without the information, you expect a profit of $0.50 per share from the investment (a total of $500 if you buy 1,000 shares). Half the time, the earnings will be $2.50, and the stock will rise to $25, for a profit of $3 per share. The other half the time, the earnings will be $2.00, and the stock will drop to $20, for a loss of $2 per share. The expected per share profit is $(.50)(\$3) + (.50)(-\$2) = \$0.50$. Table 6-5 shows how your strategy changes if you can obtain perfect information about the expected earnings.

Table 6-5
Value of Information About Future Earnings

Actual Earnings	Current Choice	Choice with Perfect Information	Change in Profit	Probability
$2.50	Invest	Invest	0	0.50
$2.00	Invest	Don't Invest	$2,000	0.50
Additional Profit			**$1,000**	**1.0**

In this case, perfect information about XYZ's earnings is worth $1,000.] This value is based on the prior assessment $P_{EPS=\$2} = 0.5$, $P_{EPS=\$2.50} = 0.5$. If the prior probabilities were changed from 0.5, the EVPI would change. Figure 6-4 displays how EVPI changes for this particular problem as $P_{EPS=\$2.50}$ varies from 0 to 1.0. At either extreme the EVPI is low because the *amount* of uncertainty is not great. In the middle ranges the additional uncertainty is reflected in a higher EVPI.

Figure 6-4
Variation in EVPI with Prior Assessment of Probability

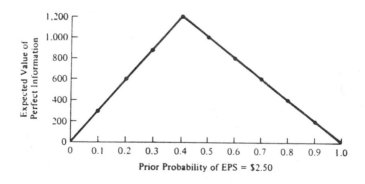

B. The Event Study Methodology

An event study seeks to measure the impact of new information. A central problem is isolating a *single* release of information. Investors are constantly bombarded with information -- about particular companies, inflation, unemployment, interest rates, political decisions, and so on. If stock prices move, which information they have reacted to? We need a way to hold everything else constant, so that we can measure the impact on asset value of a single event, such as a takeover announcement.

Financial economists have developed a statistical technique -- *cumulative abnormal returns analysis* -- that, in appropriate circumstances, lets us do precisely that for publicly traded common stock. The idea is to predict the return from holding the stock in the absence of the information in question, so that we can compare the predicted return to the actual return. The difference is a measure of the impact of the information. In this section, we describe a common way to conduct an event study.

1. Measuring Abnormal Returns

Cumulative abnormal returns analysis begins with the *market model* of stock returns that we developed in Chapter 3. The market model of the percentage return $R_{i,t}$ on an investment in the stock of firm i, on day t, is:

$$R_{i,t} = \alpha_i + \beta_i \cdot R_{m,t} + \epsilon_{i,t} \qquad \qquad \textbf{(6-1)}$$

Where:

$R_{m,t}$ is the percentage return on the overall stock market on day t

β_i is the slope of the best fit straight line in a regression analysis of the relationship between the daily returns on firm i's stock and the returns on the stock market as a whole.

α_i is the intercept of the best fit regression line

$\epsilon_{i,t}$ is the residual portion of the change in Company i's stock price -- the part that *cannot* be explained by the change in the market price $R_{m,t}$

Equation 6-1 is identical to Equation 3-5, except that we have added subscripts to indicate that the equation applies to the returns on a particular stock, for a particular day.

In Chapter 3, we focused on β_i, which we interpreted as a measure of the *systematic risk* of Company i. The final term in the market model -- $\epsilon_{i,t}$ -- was unimportant. It was a measure of *unsystematic risk*. In a regression analysis intended to measure systematic risk, unsystematic risk merely adds *noise* (statisticians call $\epsilon_{i,t}$ an "error" term). Since unsystematic risk could be eliminated by holding a diversified portfolio, it didn't matter much how large the error term was for a particular firm on a particular day.

In an event study, in contrast, we care about unsystematic risk. We want to know how a news announcement that is specific to firm i affects firm i's stock price. $\epsilon_{i,t}$ is a measure of that effect. $\epsilon_{i,t}$ measures the change in the price of firm i's stock that is *independent* of what we would expect based on what happens to the rest of the market. An announcement that affects only firm i will affect $\epsilon_{i,t}$, but will not affect the other elements of the market model -- α_i or $\beta_i \cdot R_{m,t}$. Conversely, news that affects *all* stocks will be largely captured by $\beta_i \cdot R_{m,t}$, and will have only a limited effect on $\epsilon_{i,t}$.

Because of its importance to event studies, financial economists give $\epsilon_{i,t}$ a special name -- they call it the *abnormal return* on firm i's stock on day t. This is to distinguish $\epsilon_{i,t}$ from the *normal* return on firm i's stock, which is the return that is expected based on what happens to the rest of the market. From Equation 6-1, we have:

Total Return	=	Normal Return	+	Abnormal Return
$R_{i,t}$	=	$[\alpha_i + \beta_i \cdot R_{m,t}]$	+	$\epsilon_{i,t}$

$$(6\text{-}2)$$

Figure 6-5 shows an example of abnormal returns for Allied-Signal for a 21-day period during 1991. The most obvious feature of Figure 6-5 is the large positive abnormal return on the day labelled "day 0" (actually June 27, 1991). It appears that something important happened that day. In fact, Allied-Signal announced on June 27 that it's CEO, Edward Hennessy, had been forced to resign by the board of directors, and would be replaced by an outsider. Investors apparently didn't think much of Hennessy's ability, and reacted with glee to the news of his departure. The 12.5% abnormal return translates into a $500,000,000 increase in the value of Allied-Signal's shares.[3]

---

[3] The Allied-Signal example is taken from Joseph Grundfest, *Just Vote No: A Minimalist Strategy for Dealing with Barbarians Inside the Gates*, 45 Stan.L.Rev. 857 (1993). Figures 6-5 and 6-7 were prepared by Cornerstone Research.

Figure 6-5
Allied-Signal Abnormal Returns: June 13 - July 12, 1991

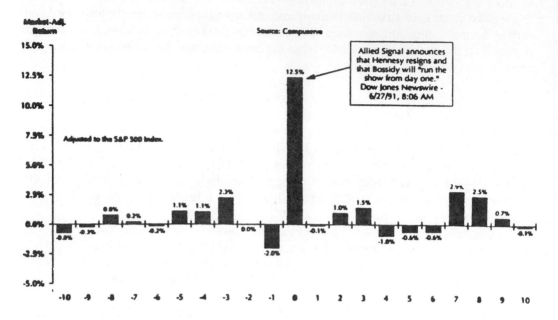

Days Relative to Announcement Date

In Figure 6-5, the abnormal returns on the days surrounding the announcement date, though much smaller than 12.5%, *are not zero*. There are many possible reasons for this, including: (i) the division of total return into normal and abnormal components is based on an *estimate* of Allied-Signal's β, which may not equal the true β; (ii) as we learned in Chapter 4, there may be systematic factors that affect security prices which are not captured by β, and which therefore show up as part of the abnormal return $\epsilon_{i,t}$; (iii) other news bearing on the value of Allied-Signal stock may have been released on those days; (iv) some trades will occur at the *bid* price (the price at which market professionals stand ready to *buy* Allied-Signal stock), while other trades occur at the higher *asked* price (the price at which market professionals stand ready to *sell* Allied-Signal stock); and (v) possible noise trading.

In other words, $\epsilon_{i,t}$ is not a *clean* measure of the impact of a single piece of new information. Instead, it is contaminated by other sources of stock price fluctuations. How then do we tell whether a stock price change is a response to a *particular* piece of information, or a response to these other "background" sources?

2. The Statistical Significance of Abnormal Returns

We can't ever know for sure what caused a stock price change, but standard statistical techniques let us ask *how likely* it is that the change was a response to particular event. One way to do this is as follows. As part of the regression analysis used to estimate β_i, we can also compute abnormal returns for each day in the time period used to estimate β_i. We can then compute the mean and the standard deviation of these abnormal returns.

The mean of the daily abnormal returns $\epsilon_{i,t}$ is uninteresting -- it equals zero. That is guaranteed by the regression procedure used to estimate β_i. The standard deviation, (which we will call σ_i) is important. It gives us a measure of how big $\epsilon_{i,t}$ is on an average day -- a day when nothing special is happening (at least nothing that we can identify).

We can also study the *distribution* of the daily abnormal returns around zero. Abnormal returns on common stocks *approximately* follow the *normal* or *bell curve* distribution discussed in Chapter 3. The terminology is confusing but the result is important: *abnormal* returns are *normally* distributed! This means that the abnormal returns fall within one standard deviation from zero about 68% of the time, and within two standard deviations from zero about 95% of the time (see Table 3-1). The standard deviation of Allied-Signal's daily abnormal returns is about 1.88%. This means that the 12.5% spike when Edward Hennessy was fired is *6.65 standard deviations from zero*. The odds that this would happen by chance, on an ordinary day when there was no special news about Allied-Signal, are infinitesimal -- less than 1 in 10,000.

But suppose that the market response to Hennessy's firing was less clear-cut. When are we confident *enough* that the market response was not mere chance so that we can say that this new information caused Allied-Signal's stock price to increase? Statisticians use *confidence intervals* to express the likelihood that an event happened by chance. For abnormal returns, the 95% confidence interval runs from slightly less than two standard deviations below zero to slightly less than two standard deviations above zero (more precisely it runs from $-1.96\sigma_i$ to $+1.96\sigma_i$). In a large sample, 95% of the daily abnormal returns will fall inside the 95% confidence interval. Thus, if an abnormal return falls *outside* this confidence interval, we can be 95% confident that this was not by chance. For Allied-Signal, the 95% confidence interval runs from -3.7% to 3.7%.

Ninety-five percent confidence is a standard measure of *statistical significance*. If we are 95% confident that a stock price change didn't happen by chance, we say that the change is *statistically significant at the 95% confidence level*. Other common measures of statistical significance are the *90% confidence level* (returns falling outside the 90% confidence interval, which runs from $-1.65\sigma_i$ to $1.65\sigma_i$) and the *99% confidence*

197

level (returns falling outside the 99% confidence interval, which runs from $-2.6\sigma_i$ to $2.6\sigma_i$). These confidence intervals are shown in Figure 6-6. The cross-hatched areas *outside* the confidence intervals shows the corresponding areas of statistical significance.

Figure 6-6
Statistical Significance: 90%, 95%, and 99% Confidence Levels

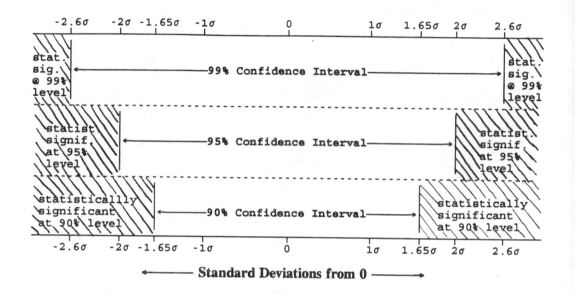

In this book, we will generally treat empirical results as statistically significant if they are significant at the 95% confidence level. We will generally treat all other empirical results as *statistically insignificant*. Sometimes, we will refer to results that are significant at the 90% confidence level as *marginally significant*.

To evaluate whether abnormal returns are statistically significant, researchers often convert them to a *standard normal* or *z* distribution, which is a normal distribution with mean = 0 and standard deviation = 1. To do this, we define a *standardized abnormal return (SAR)*, which is just the abnormal return divided by its standard deviation:

$$SAR_{i,t} = \epsilon_{i,t}/\sigma_i \qquad (6\text{-}3)$$

$SAR_{i,t}$ is a *test statistic* for the significance of the abnormal return $\epsilon_{i,t}$. Over the period used to estimate σ_i, the *SAR*s are (approximately) normally distributed and have mean = 0 and standard deviation = 1. The *SAR* tells us if a result is statistically significant simply by inspection -- an *SAR* greater than about $+2$ or less than about -2 indicates statistical significance at the 95% confidence level. For example, the *SAR* for Allied-Signal on June 27, 1991 was 6.65 (12.5%/1.88%). This is clearly significant.

To further illustrate the important concept of statistical significance, we have redrawn Allied-Signal's abnormal returns in Figure 6-7, together with dotted lines showing the 95% confidence interval. Over this 21-day period, the abnormal returns for all days except day 0 fell within the 95% confidence interval. Most of the abnormal returns *should* fall within the 95% confidence interval, but it wouldn't be surprising if one or two fell outside this confidence interval, *strictly by chance*.

Figure 6-7
Allied-Signal Abnormal Returns and 95% Confidence Interval
(June 13, 1991 - July 12, 1991)

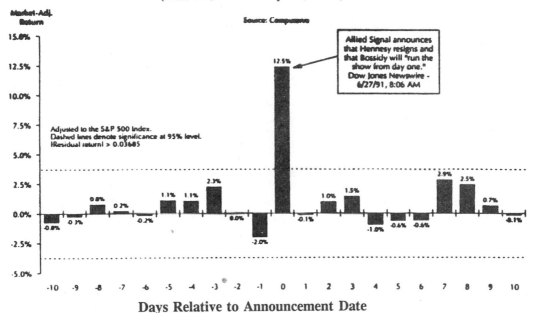

Days Relative to Announcement Date

3. Cumulating and Averaging Abnormal Returns

Sometimes, information is released gradually over a period of time. At other times, we aren't sure exactly when information has been released. In both cases, we need to cumulate abnormal returns over time and test whether these *cumulative abnormal returns (CARs)* are statistically significant. We also often want to determine the response of a sample of firms that have received a similar announcement. For example, we may want to know how the market reacts, *on average*, to an announcement that a CEO has

199

been fired, or that a firm has become a takeover target. Thus, we need to measure the *average abnormal return (AAR)* for a number of firms and test the statistical significance of the *AAR*. Finally, we often want to both average abnormal returns over a number of firms and cumulate them over time, and test the statistical significance of the *cumulative average abnormal return (CAAR)*.

This subsection develops the necessary statistical tools. Although the mathematical steps are complicated, each type of cumulation involves the same basic steps. First, we measure a desired quantity (either a *CAR*, or an *AAR*, or a *CAAR*). Second, we convert the measured quantity to the standard normal distribution. The standardized quantity is a *test statistic* that lets us measure statistical significance. Table 6-6, at the end of this subsection, summarizes the results and should help those who struggle with the mathematical details.

Cumulating Abnormal Returns Across Time. We first consider cumulating returns across time for a single firm. To cumulate returns, we just add them up. The cumulative abnormal return on firm i's stock over a k trading day period (called an *event window*), running from day d_1 to day d_2, is:

$$CAR_i = \sum_{t=d_1}^{d_2} \epsilon_{i,t} \qquad (6\text{-}4)$$

To determine the statistical significance of the *CAR*, we first need to compute its standard deviation. Probability theory tells us that if k events are (i) *normally* distributed; (ii) *independent* of each other; and (iii) *identically* distributed with mean = 0 and standard deviation = σ, then the *sum* of the events is normally distributed with mean = 0 and standard deviation proportional to *the square root of the number of events*:

$$\sigma_{\text{sum of } k \text{ events}} = \sigma \cdot k^{1/2} \qquad (6\text{-}5)$$

Applying this general formula to the specific case of abnormal returns, the standard deviation of a k-day *CAR* is:

$$\sigma_{k\text{-day } CAR} = \sigma_i \cdot k^{1/2}$$

Once we know the k-day CAR and its standard deviation, we can define a *standardized CAR (SCAR)* as a test statistic for the statistical significance of the *CAR*. For 1-day returns, we divided the abnormal return by its standard deviation to obtain a standardized abnormal return (*SAR*). Similarly, the *SCAR* is just the *CAR* divided by its standard deviation:

$$SCAR_i \;\; = \;\; CAR_i/\sigma_{k\text{-day } CAR} \;\; = \;\; CAR_i/(\sigma_i \cdot k^{1/2}) \qquad\qquad \textbf{(6-6)}$$

Like the *SAR*, the *SCAR* has a standard normal or z distribution over the period used to estimate σ_i. An *SCAR* greater than about $+2$ (or less than -2) indicates statistical significance at the 95% confidence level.

The factor $k^{1/2}$ in the denominator of Equation 6-6, which does not appear in the definition of the 1-day *SAR* in Equation 6-3, means that a multiday *CAR* must be *larger* than a 1-day abnormal return to be statistically significant. Moreover, the longer the event window, the larger the *CAR* must be to be statistically significant. This is because each extra day adds more *noise* -- more sources of stock price movement in addition to the response to the information release that we're trying to study.

The extra noise introduced by using a long event window makes it important for researchers to measure as carefully as they can *when* information is released to the market. The narrower the event window, the easier it is to tell if and how investors have responded to the information release.

Averaging Abnormal Returns Across Firms. Often, we want to average abnormal returns across a sample of n firms that have experienced a similar event, such as a takeover bid, on *different* calendar days. Computing the average abnormal return is straightforward. For each firm, we use the market model to compute the abnormal return $\epsilon_{i,t}$ on the day of interest. Since the events occur on different calendar days, we measure t in *event time -- relative to that firm's announcement date*. It is common, as in the Allied-Signal example, to call the announcement date *day 0*. The *average abnormal return* for the sample for day t is:

$$AAR_t \;\; = \;\; (1/n) \; \cdot \; \sum_{i=1}^{n} \epsilon_{i,t} \qquad\qquad \textbf{(6-7)}$$

The next step is to assess statistical significance. Recall from equation (6-5) that the *sum* of n normally distributed, independent, and identically distributed events (with mean $= 0$ and standard deviation $= \sigma$) is normally distributed with standard deviation proportional to the square root of the number of events. Similarly, the *average* of n such events is normally distributed with a standard deviation that is *inversely* proportional to the square root of the number of events:[4]

$$\sigma_{\text{avg. of } n \text{ events}} = \sigma/n^{1/2} \qquad\qquad \textbf{(6-8)}$$

---

[4] This is because the average is simply the sum divided by n. The variance for the coin flip example developed in Chapter 3 is a specific example of the general result shown in Equation 6-5.

Unfortunately, the abnormal returns for different firms are *not* identically distributed. Instead, each firm's abnormal returns have their own standard deviation σ_i. Fortunately, there is a cure for this problem. We can divide each firm's abnormal return $\epsilon_{i,t}$ by that firm's σ_i to obtain a standardized abnormal return ($SAR_{i,t} = \epsilon_{i,t}/\sigma_i$). The average *SAR* for the sample of n firms on day t is:

$$ASAR_t \quad = \quad (1/n) \quad \cdot \quad \sum_{i=1}^{n} \epsilon_{i,t}/\sigma_i$$

The *SAR*s all have the same standard deviation ($\sigma = 1$). Thus, from Equation 6-8, the standard deviation of the average *SAR* is:

$$\sigma_{ASAR} \quad = \quad 1/n^{1/2}$$

We can now compute, as a test statistic for statistical significance, a *standardized average SAR (SASAR)*, which has the standard normal or z distribution. As usual, we divide the quantity of interest (here $ASAR_t$) by its standard deviation:

$$SASAR_t \quad = \quad ASAR_t/\sigma_{ASAR} \quad = \quad (1/n^{1/2}) \quad \cdot \quad \sum_{i=1}^{n} \epsilon_{i,t}/\sigma_i \qquad \textbf{(6-9)}$$

The *SASAR* has the usual interpretation in terms of statistical significance. If it is greater than about $+2$ (or less than -2), the event is statistically significant at the 95% level of confidence.

The most important feature of the *SASAR* is that it *increases* as the number of firms in the sample increases. The sum in equation (6-9) involves adding n abnormal returns. We then divide by $n^{1/2}$, so the *SASAR* increases roughly in proportion to $n^{1/2}$. Thus, the *larger* the sample, the easier it is to assess whether an information release is statistically significant. For example, a 1-day abnormal return for Allied-Signal must be greater than 3.7% (or less than -3.7%) to be statistically significant at the 95% confidence level. In contrast, a 1-day return for a sample of 100 firms similar to Allied-Signal will be statistically significant if the average abnormal return is greater than about 0.4% (or less than -0.4%). *Event studies that use a large sample of firms are much more powerful than event studies that focus on a single firm.*

The confidence interval gets narrower as n increases because factors that influence stock price, *other than the event of interest*, tend to average out. Good things will happen to some firms in the sample on the event date, but bad things will happen to other firms. The response to the event of interest is the only common influence on stock price. The factor $1/n^{1/2}$ tells us how fast this averaging process occurs as sample size increases.

The methodology for averaging returns across firms must be modified if all of the firms in the sample have the *same* event date. This might be the case if we are studying the market response to new legislation -- for example, an antitakeover statute affecting all firms incorporated in New York. Because the firms have the same event date, their abnormal returns may not be *independent*. We can solve this problem by forming a portfolio consisting of the firms in the sample, and then estimating the market model and computing an abnormal return and standard deviation for the *portfolio*. In effect, we treat the portfolio as a single firm.[5]

Averaging Abnormal Returns Across Firms and Cumulating Them Across Time. Lastly, researchers doing event studies often want both to average abnormal returns over a sample of firms and cumulate them across time. This is straightforward. We first compute an average abnormal return AAR_t for the sample for each day t in the event window. As before, we measure t *relative* to each firm's announcement date. We also compute the associated $SASAR_t$, which measures the statistical significance of the average abnormal return.

Next, we add the daily AARs to obtain a cumulative AAR for the sample over the event window. Suppose, for example, that the event window runs for k days -- from day d_1 to day d_2. The cumulative AAR is:

$$CAAR = \sum_{t=d_1}^{d_2} AAR_t = \sum_{t=d_1}^{d_2} (1/n) \cdot \sum_{i=1}^{n} \epsilon_{i,t}$$

The common factor $(1/n)$ can be brought out of the sum to give:

$$CAAR = (1/n) \cdot \sum_{t=d_1}^{d_2} \sum_{i=1}^{n} \epsilon_{i,t} \qquad \textbf{(6-10)}$$

To measure the statistical significance of the *CAAR*, we cumulate the *SASARs* (which meausre the significance of the daily *AAR*s) over the k-day event window. Each daily *SASAR* is (approximately) normally distributed with mean $= 0$ and $\sigma = 1$. Thus, from equation 6-5, the sum of k *SASARs* is (approximately) normally distributed with mean $= 0$ and $\sigma = k^{1/2}$. To get back to a standard normal distribution with $\sigma = 1$, we divide by $k^{1/2}$. Thus, the test statistic (which we will simply call z) is:

---

[5] See Stephen Brown & Jerold Warner, *Using Daily Stock Returns: The Case of Event Studies*, 14 J.Fin.Econ. 3 (1985). Many studies use this procedure -- forming a portfolio of all sample firms, and measuring the significance of the portfolio abnormal return -- even when event dates are not correlated. There is nothing wrong with this, but the resulting statistical tests are less powerful than tests that use firm-specific *SARs*, because the portfolio tests don't fully use the information in the firm-specific values of σ_i.

$$z \quad = \quad (1/k^{1/2}) \quad \cdot \quad \sum_{t=d_1}^{d_2} SASAR_t \quad = \quad (1/n{\cdot}k)^{1/2} \cdot \sum_{t=d_1}^{d_2} \sum_{i=1}^{n} \epsilon_{i,t}/\sigma_i$$

As usual, a z value greater than about $+2$ (or less than -2) indicates statistical significance at the 95% confidence level. The *larger* the sample, and the *narrower* the event window, the larger z will be, and the more likely that the study will detect a statistically significant response to new information when such a response is present.[6]

And we're done! Table 6-6 summarizes the different measures of abnormal returns, and the test statistic for each. The names we have given to the various measures and test statistics are not important. In some cases, standard names have developed; in others, we have invented our own names. What matters is: (i) the different ways to sum and average abnormal returns; (ii) the *availability* of a test statistic for each; (iii) the *decrease* in noise as the number of firms increases; and (iv) the *increase* in noise as the number of days in the event window increases.

Table 6-6
Abnormal Returns and Test Statistics

Type of Return	Measure of Abnormal Returns	Test Statistic (standard normal or z distribution)
abnormal return: 1 firm, 1 day	$\epsilon_{i,t}$	$SAR_{i,t} = \epsilon_{i,t}/\sigma_i$
cumulative abnormal return: 1 firm, k days	$CAR_i = \sum_{t=d_1}^{d_2} \epsilon_{i,t}$	$SCAR_i = (1/k^{1/2}) \cdot \sum_{t=d_1}^{d_2} \epsilon_{i,t}/\sigma_i$
average abnormal return: n firms, 1 day	$AAR_t = (1/n) \cdot \sum_{i=1}^{n} \epsilon_{i,t}$	$SASAR_t = (1/n^{1/2}) \cdot \sum_{i=1}^{n} \epsilon_{i,t}/\sigma_i$
cumulative average abnormal return: n firms, k days	$CAAR = (1/n) \cdot \sum_{t=d_1}^{d_2} \sum_{i=1}^{n} \epsilon_{i,t}$	$z = (1/n{\cdot}k)^{1/2} \cdot \sum_{t=d_1}^{d_2} \sum_{i=1}^{n} \epsilon_{i,t}/\sigma_i$

---

[6] We developed the *CAAR* and the z test for the significance of *CAAR*s by first averaging daily abnormal returns across firms and then summing the average abnormal returns over time. But the measure of abnormal returns and the related test statistic would be exactly the same if we first cumulated abnormal returns over time for each firm, and then averaged these returns across firms.

C. An Event Study Example

The development of the statistical tools used in event studies was hard going for most readers, we suspect. It's time to see how these statistical techniques are used in an actual empirical study.

MICHAEL BRADLEY, ANAND DESAI, & E. HAN KIM, **SYNERGISTIC GAINS FROM CORPORATE ACQUISITIONS AND THEIR DIVISION BETWEEN THE STOCKHOLDERS OF TARGET AND ACQUIRING FIRMS,** 21 J.Fin.Econ. 3 (1988)

Abstract: This paper documents that a successful tender offer increases the combined value of the target and acquiring firms by an average of 7.4%. We also provide . . . empirical evidence that competition among bidding firms increases the returns to targets and decreases the returns to acquirers . . . and that changes in the legal/institutional environment of tender offers have had no impact on the total (percentage) synergistic gains created but have significantly affected their division between the stockholders of the target and acquiring firms.

There is empirical evidence that corporate acquisitions effected through tender offers are wealth-increasing transactions for the stockholders of both the target and acquiring firms [Dodd & Ruback (1977) and Bradley (1980)].[a] Moreover, Bradley, Desai & Kim (1983) show that these gains are not due to the market's reassessment of previously undervalued securities. They document that the positive revaluation of the target's shares is permanent only if the offer is successful, i.e., only if the resources of the two firms are combined.[b] This evidence is consistent with the synergy theory of tender offers, which posits that the acquisition of control over the target enables the acquirer to redeploy the combined assets of the two firms toward higher-valued uses.

None of the above studies, however, documents the magnitude of the synergistic gains that result from successful acquisitions achieved through tender offers. Indeed, whether or not such acquisitions result in synergistic gains is still a contentious issue in the literature. For example, Roll (1986) has proposed the *Hubris Hypothesis*, which posits that the gains to target shareholders represent wealth transfers from acquiring

---

[a] Peter Dodd & Richard Ruback, *Tender Offers and Stockholder Returns*, 5 J.Fin.Econ. 351 (1977); Michael Bradley, *Interfirm Tender Offers and the Market for Corporate Control*, 53 J.Bus. 345 (1980).

[b] Michael Bradley, Anand Desai & E. Han Kim, *The Rationale Behind Interfirm Tender Offers: Information or Synergy?*, 11 J.Fin.Econ. 183 (1983).

firms' shareholders and not necessarily synergistic gains.[c] To test this hypothesis, it is necessary to measure synergistic gains using matched pairs of target and acquiring firms. None of the earlier studies impose this requirement on their samples.

In this paper, we estimate the magnitude of the synergistic gains [from successful tender offers], using the revaluation of the combined wealth of target-firm and acquiring-firm shareholders as a basis. We also examine the factors that determine the division of these gains between the stockholders of the two firms and document how the division and the total gains created have changed with the changing environment of the tender offer process. . . .

Synergistic Gains

. . . We define the total synergistic gain from a successful tender offer as the sum of the change in the wealth of the stockholders of the target and acquiring firms . . . . This definition assumes that corporate acquisitions effected through interfirm tender offers have no effect on the wealth of the senior claimants (e.g., bondholders and other creditors) of the firms involved. Kim & McConnell (1977) and Asquith & Kim (1982) provide evidence that is consistent with this assumption for a sample of firms involved in corporate mergers.[d]

[The sample for the study consists of 236 successful tender offers between 1963-1984 for which the shares of both the target and acquiring firms were traded on the New York or the American Stock Exchange]. Of the 236 acquiring firms, 155 held no target shares prior to the offer. The 236 acquiring firms sought, on average, 66.2% of the target shares. The mean as well as the median fraction of target shares ultimately purchased in our total sample is in excess of 50%. Thus the "typical" acquiring firm in our sample held no target shares prior to the offer but held a majority of the outstanding target shares upon successful execution of the offer.

Methodology

Our estimates of the gains created by tender offers are based on market model prediction errors. Under the assumption of multivariate normality [of stock price returns], the abnormal return (prediction error) to firm i on day t can be written as:

$$\epsilon_{i,t} = R_{i,t} - \alpha_i - \beta_i \cdot R_{m,t}$$

[c] Richard Roll, *The Hubris Hypothesis of Corporate Takeovers*, 59 J.Bus. 197 (1986).

[d] E. Han Kim & John McConnell, *Corporate Merger and the "Co-Insurance" of Corporate Debt*, 32 J.Fin. 349 1977); Paul Asquith & E. Han Kim, *The Impact of Merger Bids on the Participating Firms' Security Holders*, 37 J.Fin. 1209 (1980).

where:

$\epsilon_{i,t}$ = abnormal return to firm i on day t
$R_{i,t}$ = realized return to firm i on day t
α_i, β_i = market model parameter estimates
$R_{m,t}$ = return to the equally-weighted CRSP market portfolio on day t.

The market model parameter estimates for each target firm are obtained using a maximum of 240 trading days of daily returns data beginning 300 days before the announcement of the first tender offer bid in the contest. Estimates for the acquiring firms are obtained using 240 trading days of returns data beginning 300 days before the first bid made for the target by this firm.

For each of the 472 firms in our sample, we cumulate the daily abnormal return over a contest-specific interval to obtain the cumulative abnormal return (CAR). The CAR is computed from five trading days before the announcement of the first bid through five days after the announcement of the ultimately successful bid. We begin to cumulate the CAR five days before the announcement of the initial bid in order to capture any anticipatory price behavior (leakage of information) that may occur before the actual public announcement.

Ideally, we would like to extend our CAR window until the day just before the offer is executed. Reliable execution dates are not available, however, for most of the offers in our sample. . . . We do not extend the CAR window through the execution of the offer because this would cause a downward bias in the measured returns to target shareholders. This downward bias stems from the necessary condition for a successful tender offer that the [tender] offer price, P_T, be greater than the expected postexecution price of the remaining target shares, P_E. [Otherwise, the target firm's shareholders will not tender their shares.] . . . [4]

---

[4] We recognize that our CAR statistic is but one measure of the increase in the wealth of target stockholders. An alternative measure has been proposed by Jensen (1985) and Comment & Jarrell (1987). These authors employ what has become known as the blended premium (BP), which is defined as:

$$BP = [f(P_T - P_O) + (1 - f)(P_E - P_O)]/P_O,$$

where [f = fraction of target shares purchased; P_T = tender offer price; P_O = pre-offer target stock price; and P_E = post-tender price of the shares that aren't purchased. Michael Jensen, *When Unocal Won Over Mesa, Shareholders and Society Lost*, 9 Financier 30 (1985); Robert Comment & Gregg Jarrell, *Two-Tier and Negotiated Tender Offers: The Imprisonment of the Free-Riding Shareholder*, 19 J.Fin.Econ. 283 (1987)].

[The mean BP for the 52 tender offers between 1981-1984 is 43.03%, compared to a CAR of 35.34%. There] are at least two computational reasons why CAR is systematically less than BP, and these

Our *CAR* algorithm generates an 11-day [event] window for all but 15 [of the 163] tender offers in which there is only one bidder. For tender offer contests in which there is more than one bidder, the window for targets varies, with a mean of 43 trading days and a standard deviation of 52 trading days. Using these variable-window *CARs*, we estimate the dollar gain to the target and acquiring firms in each tender offer contest i as

$$\delta W_{T,i} = W_{T,i} \cdot CAR_{T,i} \qquad\qquad \delta W_{A,i} = W_{A,i} \cdot CAR_{A,i}$$

where:

$W_{T,i}$	=	market value of the target equity as of the end of six trading days prior to the first announcement for the target, minus the value of the target shares held by the acquirer
$CAR_{T,i}$	=	cumulative abnormal return to the target firm . . .
$W_{A,i}$	=	market value of the acquiring firm as of the end of six days prior to the first announcement made by the acquiring firm
$CAR_{A,i}$	=	cumulative abnormal return to the acquiring firm . . .

. . . [O]ur estimate of the total percentage synergistic gains [$CAR_{C,i}$] is based on the *CAR* to a value-weighted portfolio of the ith target and the ith acquiring firm, where the weights used are $W_{T,i}$ and $W_{A,i}$ . . . . $CAR_{C,i}$ is measured by cumulating the abnormal returns to this portfolio from five trading days before the announcement of the first bid through five days after the announcement of the ultimately successful bid. Using this percentage measure, we estimate the total dollar synergistic gain, $\delta W_{C,i}$, as:

$$\delta W_{C,i} = W_{C,i} \cdot CAR_{C,i}$$

where:

$$W_{C,i} = W_{T,i} + W_{A,i}$$

---

explanations can easily account for the 7.7% difference. First, *CAR* is, by design, net of market movements, The average duration of the offers in this sample is 22 trading days or one trading month. The average monthly return to the CRSP equally-weighted market portfolio between 1981 and 1984 is roughly 1.7%. [Thus], 1.7% of the 7.7% difference between *BP* and *CAR* can be attributed to general market movements. [Second, *CAR*] is a sum of (abnormal) returns whereas [*BP*] is essentially a continuously compounded return. Given that the returns to the targets are predominantly positive over the tender offer period, it follows that the sum of the daily (abnormal) returns will be strictly less than a continuously compounded return. For example, the sum of 2% per day for 22 days is 44%, whereas the continuously compounded return of 2% [per day] for 22 days is 55%.

Estimate of Synergistic Gains

Table 6-7 reports our measures of the synergistic gains created by tender offers, as well as the changes in the wealth of the stockholders of the target and acquiring firms. The data in the last column of the top panel of Table 6-7 (labeled *Combined Returns*) show that the combined value of the target and acquiring firms increased, on average, by 7.43%, with 75% of the combined revaluations being positive. Our estimate of this percentage synergistic gain is statistically greater than zero ($z = 19.95$).[5]

Table 6-7
Mean Percentage and Dollar Gains from Successful Tender Offers
(dollar figures in millions of 1984 dollars)

	Subperiod			Total
	7/63-6/68	7/68-12/80	1/81-12/84	7/63-12/84
Number of Contests	51	133	52	236
Combined Returns				
CAR_C (%)	7.78[a]	7.08[a]	8.00[a]	7.43[a]
δW_C ($)	91.1	87.5	218.5	117.1
% positive	78	74	73	75
Target Returns				
CAR_T (%)	18.92[a]	35.29[a]	35.34[a]	31.77[a]
δW_T ($)	70.7	71.6	233.5	107.1
% positive	94	98	90	95
Acquirer Returns				
CAR_A (%)	4.09[a]	1.30	-2.93[a]	0.97[a]
δW_A ($)	25.0	31.8	-27.3	17.3
% positive	59	48	35	47

[a] Significantly different from zero at the 0.01 level.

The mean total dollar gain created by the acquisitions in our sample is $117 million (expressed in December 1984 dollars). Since the distribution of our dollar measure $\delta W_{C,i}$ is extremely leptokurtic and skewed to the right (the skewness and kurtosis coefficients are 6.70 and 62.38, respectively), we conduct the nonparametric Wilcoxon

---

[5] This z-statistic is computed following [the techniques described in Section B of this Chapter].

Signed Rank test to test if the median $\delta W_{C,i}$ of \$26.9 million for the total sample is statistically greater than zero. This test yields a z-statistic of 9.30, which is significant at the 1% level.[e]

Table 6-7 also reports data for three subperiods: 1963-1968, 1968-1980, and 1981-1984. Although this division is somewhat arbitrary, there have been some dramatic changes in the tender offer process during the 22-year period under study, and these three subperiods correspond roughly to the three distinct regimes that have existed in the legal and institutional environment of tender offers since 1963.

The first period (1963-1968) is important because before 1968, cash tender offers were free of government regulation. They were considered private transactions between the acquiring firm and the stockholders of the target firm. In July 1968 Congress passed the Williams [Act], which brought the tender offer within the purview of the Securities and Exchange Commission (SEC). In the same year, Virginia enacted the first state antitakeover statute; by 1978, 36 states had enacted their own takeover regulations. By isolating the offers that occurred in the unregulated period, we can examine the effects of government regulation on the magnitude and division of the synergistic gains from tender offers.

The last period (1981-1984) is distinguished by three factors that have drastically changed the environment in which tender offers take place. First is the avowed laissez-faire attitude of the Reagan Administration toward corporate takeovers in general. Second is the development of sophisticated tactics to repel takeovers (poison pills, targeted share repurchases, lock-up provisions, and supermajority and fair-price amendments). The third factor is the advent of investment banking firms that specialize in raising funds to finance corporate takeovers. We are interested in how these recent developments in the market for corporate control have affected the gains created by tender offers.

The data in the top panel of Table 6-7 indicate that the percentage synergistic gains created by tender offers have remained remarkably constant, between 7% and 8%, over the three subperiods. The dollar gains, however, have increased dramatically from the first two subperiods to the third; expressed in December 1984 dollars, the average synergistic gain has grown from \$91 million and \$87 million in the first two subperiods to \$219 million in the 1981-1984 subperiod. This increase in the dollar synergistic gains, but not in the percentage synergistic gains, is due to the increase in the size of target

---

[e] The authors' references to statistical significance at the "1% level" or the "0.01 level" have the same meaning as what we called, in section A, the *99% confidence level*. Similarly, statistical significance at what we called the *95% confidence level* can also be called the 5% level or the 0.05 level.

210

firms. . . . [This] may be due to the laissez-faire attitude of the Reagan Administration and innovative financing methods of investment banking firms. . . .

The overwhelming conclusion is that target stockholders capture the majority of the gains from tender offers. Ninety-five percent of the targets in the total sample experienced a positive abnormal return. The average abnormal return is 32% and the ratio of the mean dollar gain to targets to the mean dollar total gain ($\delta W_T / \delta W_C$) is 91%. In contrast, the average abnormal return to acquiring firms is 0.97%, only 47% of the observations are positive, and the ratio of the mean dollar gain [to acquirers] to the mean total gain ($\delta W_A / \delta W_C$) is 15%. Whether measured as rates of return or dollar gains, the lion's share of the gains from tender offers is captured by target shareholders.[f]

The data in Table 6-7 also indicate that the returns to acquiring firms have decreased over time, whereas the returns to targets have increased. The mean abnormal return to acquiring firms is 4.09% ($z = 5.88$) in the first period and -2.93% ($z = -2.79$) in the last. In contrast, the mean abnormal return to targets has increased from 18.92% ($z = 26.2$) to 35.34% ($z = 26.2$).

In sum, the data in Table 6-7 compel the following conclusions:

(1) Successful tender offers generate significant synergistic gains and lead to a more efficient allocation of corporate resources.[8] . . .

(3) Both the rate of return and dollar gains to target stockholders have increased over time, whereas the returns to the stockholders of acquiring firms have decreased. In fact, in the most recent subperiod, acquiring firms actually suffered a significant abnormal loss. . . .

---

[f] The ratio of target dollar gains to total dollar gains (91%) and the ratio of acquirer dollar gains to total dollar gains (15%) do not sum to 100% because the event window for measuring total gains differs from the acquirer's event window for tender offers involving multiple bidders.

[8] We recognize that, theoretically, the gains from tender offers may stem from the creation of market power and not necessarily from increased allocative efficiency. However, the work of Eckbo (1983, 1985) and Stillman (1983) indicates that corporate acquisitions have no measurable effect on the degree of market power in the economy. [B. Espen Eckbo, *Horizontal Mergers, Collusion, and Stockholder Wealth*, 11 J.Fin.Econ. 241 (1983); B. Espen Eckbo, *Mergers and the Market Concentration Doctrine: Evidence from the Capital Market*, 58 J.Bus. 325 (1985); Robert Stillman, *Examining Antitrust Policy Towards Horizontal Mergers*, 11 J.Fin. Econ. 225 (1983).]

Empirical Evidence on the Determinants of the Division
of the Gains from Tender Offers

[We examine] the time series of cumulative abnormal returns (*CARs*) to the portfolios of 236 targets and 236 acquiring firms, classified by the observed level of competition among bidding firms. . . . The time series of *CARs* are [plotted in Figure 6-8] for three portfolios of the target firms: 163 targets of single-bidder tender offers, 73 targets of multiple-bidder tender offer contests, and the total sample of 236 targets. . . .

The *AR* and the *CAR* of the single-bidder subsample on day 0 (14.67% and 23.95%) are approximately equal to those of the multiple-bidder subsample (14.12% and 25.98%). Thus when a target receives an initial offer, the average value of this offer does not depend on whether it will be followed by other bids. Only when competing bids are actually announced do additional returns accrue to the targets of multiple-bidder contests. The additional returns are reflected in the gradual rise of the *CAR* series for the multiple-bidder sample. The difference in the *CAR* between the multiple-bidder and single-bidder subsamples reaches about 20% by day +40. Clearly, target shareholders earn greater returns from multiple-bidder contests than from single-bidder offers. These findings are not consistent with the alternative hypothesis that multiple-bidder contests arise because the initial bid was too low. . . .

Figure 6-8
CARs for *Targets* in Single and Multiple Bidder Tender Offers

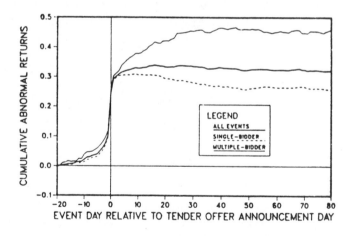

The *CAR* series for the three portfolios of *acquiring* firms are plotted in Figure 6-9. Event day 0 is the day of the announcement of the first offer made by the acquiring firm. The *CAR* to the portfolio of all 236 acquiring firms from event day -5 through +5 is 0.79% with a *t*-statistic of 1.69. This is not significantly different from zero at the 5%

level. However, the *CAR* from day -5 through day +20 is 1.70% ($t = 2.36$), which is significant at the 5% level. Thus, unlike for target firms, there is mixed evidence concerning the returns to acquiring firms.[g]

Classifying the portfolios of acquiring firms by the level of competition reveals that the *CAR* from day -5 through day +20 to the single-bidder portfolio is 2.8% ($t = 2.94$), whereas the return to the multiple-bidder portfolio is -0.70% ($t = -0.56$) over the same period. Thus, significant positive returns accrue to the stockholders of acquiring firms in single-bidder tender offers but not in multiple-bidder contests.

Figure 6-9
CARs for *Acquirers* in Single and Multiple Bidder Tender Offers

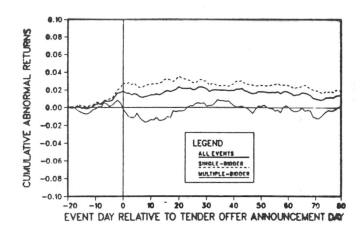

To examine the behavior of the *CARs* to the multiple-bidder portfolio more closely, we divide the sample into two groups: first-bidder, ultimately successful acquirers, and those acquirers who entered the contest after some other firm initiated the bidding process. Of the 73 acquirers in the multiple -bidder portfolio, 24 are first-bidder acquirers, and 49 are late-bidder acquirers. The *CAR* from day -5 to day +1 for the portfolio of first-bidder acquirers is 2.0%, whereas the *CAR* for the portfolio of late-bidder acquirers is -2.5% over the same interval. Apparently, the market's reaction to the first bid of first-bidder acquirers in multiple-bidder contests is similar to its

---

[g] The *t* statistic has essentially the same interpretation as the *z* statistic for large samples. Technically, the *t* statistic is appropriate when the sample mean and standard deviation must be *estimated from the sample*, while the *z* statistic is appropriate when the sample mean and standard deviation are *already known*. The confidence intervals for the *t* statistic are somewhat larger for small samples. In section B of this Chapter, we used a *z* statistic because the mean and standard deviation of the abnormal returns *in the event window* were measured during the *separate* period used to estimate β, and thus were assumed to be known. It isn't clear why Bradley, Desai & Kim switch from *z* to *t* in mid-article.

reaction to bids made in single-bidder tender offers. Thus the negative *CAR* from day -5 to day +1 to the portfolio of acquirers in multiple-bidder contests is due primarily to the negative returns to late-bidder acquirers, more commonly known as *white knights*. In other words, our data indicate that the average white knight pays 'too much' for the target it acquires.

In sum, our time-series analysis indicates that the net effect of multiple-bidder contests is to increase the returns to target firms and decrease the returns to acquiring firms. The market's average reaction to the bid that initiates a tender offer contest does not depend on whether the bid eventually leads to a multiple-bidder contest. This is true for both target and bidding firms. Only when competing bids are actually made do we observe greater returns to target shareholders and a dissipation of the initial gains to the stockholders of bidding firms. . . .

[To separate the] effects of regulation and competition on the returns to acquiring firms, we report the CAR_A by time period and our multiple/single-bidder classification in Table 6-8. The data show that acquiring firms gained most (4.62%, $z = 5.99$) in single-bidder contests effected during the unregulated period of 1963-1968; they lost the most (-5.10%, $z = -2.87$) in multiple-bidder contests effected in the most recent period (1981-1984).

Perhaps the most notable of the data reported in Table 6-8 is that the 52 acquiring firms in the most recent period (1981-1984) realized a significant abnormal loss of -2.93% ($z = -2.79$). This period is associated with an increase in the extent and degree of Congressional regulations, the tolerance of [the] Reagan Administration towards large-scale mergers, the advent of investment banking firms that specialize in raising funds to finance takeover battles, and the development of sophisticated defensive tactics. We believe that all of these factors have contributed to an increase in competition among bidding firms. Consistent with this conjecture, the data in the table indicate an increasing trend in the relative frequency of multiple-bidder contests over time; 18%, 30%, and 46%, in subperiods 1963-1968, 1968-1980, and 1981-1984, respectively. Obviously, an increase in competition among bidders does not explain *negative* returns to acquirers. However, if every successful bidder is pushed to its maximum valuation of the target, there is a greater probability that overvaluations will occur and the acquirer's shareholders will suffer a capital loss. . . .

Table 6-8
CARs to Acquirers by Time Period and Single/Multiple Bidder Classification

	Subperiod			Total
	7/63-6/68	7/68-12/80	1/81-12/84	7/63-12/84
Number of Contests	51	133	52	236
Single Bidder	4.62[a]	1.74[b]	-1.08	2.00[a]
	(z = 5.99)	(z = 2.04)	(z = -1.14)	(z = 4.11)
	n = 42	n = 93	n = 28	n = 163
Multiple Bidder	1.62	0.27	-5.10[a]	-1.33
	(z = 1.05)	(z = 0.22)	(z = -2.87)	(z = -1.44)
	n = 9	n = 40	n = 24	n = 73
Total	4.09[a]	1.30	-2.93[a]	0.97[a]
	(z = 5.88)	(z = 1.58)	(z = -2.79)	(z = 2.61)
	n = 51	n = 133	n = 52	n = 236

[a] Significantly different from zero at the 0.01 level.
[b] Significantly different from zero at the 0.05 level.

Summary and Conclusions

This paper provides a theoretical and empirical analysis of interfirm tender offers. We analyze the mechanics of the tender offer process and demonstrate how this capital market transaction allocates corporate resources to their highest-valued use. Our empirical analysis documents the synergistic gains created by tender offers and how these gains are divided between the stockholders of the target and acquiring firms. . . .

We find that target stockholders have captured the lion's share of the gains from tender offers, and their share of the gains has increased significantly since the passage of the Williams Amendment in 1968. Acquiring firms, on the other hand, realized a significant positive gain only during the unregulated period 1963-1968 and, in fact, suffered a significant loss during the most recent subperiod, 1981-1984. We also find that the total percentage synergistic gains from tender offers have remained remarkably constant over time. Thus, government regulations and other changes that have occurred in the tender offer environment have been a zero sum game: the increase in the gains to the target stockholders has come at the expense of the stockholders of acquiring firms. . . .

We find that competition among bidding firms reduces the average gain to acquirers to a level that is not significantly different from zero. This adverse effect of competition is most severe for late-bidder acquirers, more commonly known as white knights. On average, the white knights in our sample pay 'too much' for the targets they acquire. . . .

In sum, our theoretical analysis implies that interfirm tender offers are efficient mechanisms to channel corporate resources to higher-valued uses. Our empirical results are consistent with this implication. We therefore see no justification for the continuing efforts by those in Washington to "reform" the tender offer process. Rather, we believe that public policy should be directed toward facilitating this capital market transaction.

Note on Bradley, Desai & Kim

1. Our main purpose in including the Bradley, Desai & Kim article at this point in this book is to illustrate the use of the event study methodology. We will consider in later chapters the implications of the evidence they develop for the sources of takeover gains, and for legal policy toward takeovers. Still, you should be skeptical about bold statements such as "[Our] data *compel*" the conclusion that "successful tender offers generate significant synergistic gains and lead to a more efficient allocation of corporate resources."

That conclusion may well be right *on average*. But it is surely not true in every case, and it may not be true in every time period. As discussed in Chapter 9, there is reason to question the existence of efficiency gains for their 1963-1968 subperiod. Moreover, we can reach such a strong conclusion only after carefully winnowing out alternative explanations for the stock price gains. No one study can do that.

2. In their summary, Bradley, Desai & Kim state that "competition among bidding firms reduces the average gain to acquirers to a level that is not significantly different from zero." This is technically true for their 21-year sample *as a whole*. But is it a fair statement, given that acquirers realized significant losses in the most recent period, 1981-1984, and these losses were concentrated in transactions where there was overt competition?

One reason to develop the skills needed to read event studies is so that you can assess the evidence yourself, and not just rely on what researchers *say* they found. Computing abnormal returns requires statistical skill. Interpreting them calls for analytical skill and openness to alternative explanations.

D. Issues in Interpreting Event Studies

Event studies are a powerful tool for exploring the causes and consequences of takeovers. Otherwise, we wouldn't spend so much time on them. But event studies also have important limitations. This section discusses the principal issues in interpreting event studies.

Absolute Versus Relative Pricing Efficiency. Event studies, *as a test of market efficiency*, are useful as a test of *relative* efficiency. They cannot test whether stock prices as a whole are too high or too low. This is inherent in a test that relies on *abnormal* returns -- returns measured relative to market returns.

Similarly, event studies, *as a measure of change in value*, are useful principally in measuring relative changes in value. Often, this limitation is not very important. If the market as a whole is 50% above true value, this may have little effect on the *percentage* change in value due to a particular event, and no effect on the *direction* of the change -- positive or negative. On the other hand, if we want to convert a percentage change in price into a change in *dollar value*, then absolute mispricing will affect our dollar estimates.

Gradual Release of Information. A second problem with interpreting event studies is that it is not always clear *when* information has been released to the market. Consider, for example, a tax bill that, *if adopted*, will reduce after-tax cash flows for some firms. Investors will react when they first learn of the bill -- say when it is first introduced into the House Ways and Means Committee. The stock price impact, though, will be discounted by the probability that the bill will pass. If investors judge that the bill has a 10% chance of passage, and will reduce firm X's cash flows by 10% (relative to other firms), firm X's stock should immediately decline by 1% relative to the market (one-tenth of the 10% drop in relative value if the bill becomes law). If the bill is approved by the Ways and Means Committee, investors will increase their estimate of the likelihood that the bill will become law -- say to 30%. This will result in a further 2% relative drop in firm X's stock price. If the offending provision is dropped in the Senate, the likelihood that it will become law may drop to 20% (the provision could still be reintroduced in the Conference Committee). And so on.

In a situation like this, no single event date captures the full impact of the tax bill. There may be a few relatively clean dates on which important information about the bill's prospects is released. But investors will also revise their estimate that the provision will pass almost daily, as the bill is marked up, as important Representatives and Senators come out for or against it, as the President makes and withdraws veto threats. To measure the bill's impact, we can try to measure cumulative abnormal returns over the entire period when the bill is pending, but this will introduce a lot of noise into the *CAR* estimate.[7]

Anticipation. Investors do not always wait passively for news to be released. When important news is expected, investors will try to guess in advance what the announcement will say. If they guess right, stock prices will not move at the time of announcement, even if the announcement is very important.

A recent Supreme Court decision on the tort liability of tobacco companies illustrates both the speed of the market response to new information and the effect of anticipation. The U.S. Court of Appeals had found that tobacco companies were not liable *at all* to smokers for harm caused by cigarettes purchased after 1966, when federal law first required warning labels on cigarette packages. The federal warning law was deemed to preempt state tort law that might require a stronger warning. The Supreme Court granted certiorari to decide the preemption question.

The stakes were huge. If the Supreme Court affirmed the Court of Appeals, this would drastically shrink the pool of potential plaintiffs. If the Supreme Court reversed, tobacco companies could be driven into bankruptcy by smoker lawsuits. Billions of dollars in value were riding on the decision. How were investors to value tobacco stocks?

Investors could begin with a known pattern. The Supreme Court rarely grants certiorari to affirm a decision by a lower federal court. Usually, there is something in the lower court opinion it finds troubling. Thus, complete affirmance was unlikely. Next, investors could analyze the case. They could hire legal experts to advise them on the likely outcome in light of the lower court opinion, the prior positions on preemption taken by individual Justices, and the questions asked at oral argument. Investors still had to guess, but they could at least make an educated guess.

The Supreme Court reversed the Court of Appeals, but only in part. The Court held that smokers could sue tobacco companies for fraud, but not (for cigarettes smoked after 1966) for failure to warn. The following story describes what happened next:

---

[7] For an effort to measure the impact of tax legislation where it was possible to find a few reasonably clean event dates, see Mark Mitchell & Jeffry Netter, *Triggering the 1987 Stock Market Crash: Antitakeover Provisions in the Proposed House Ways and Means Tax Bill?*, 24 J.Fin.Econ. 37 (1989).

SETH FAISON, CIGARETTE RULING: HOUR OF CONFUSION
N.Y. Times, June 26, 1992

For a long hour on Wednesday morning, a big news event threw Wall Street into the kind of uncertainty that traders love and analysts hate. The first news of the Supreme Court's ruling on a case concerning cigarette makers' product liability was an eight-word electronic headline on the Bloomberg News Service that seemed to be bad news for tobacco stocks: *"High Court Says Smokers May Sue Tobacco Companies."*

As traders leaped into action, responding to an avalanche of sell orders in tobacco stocks, analysts who had tried to prepare for this moment for weeks were left grasping for more information. Was the ruling uniformly in favor of the plaintiffs, the analysts wondered, or was it split on different components?

Initial Response: Tumbling

The big tobacco stocks tumbled as soon as the news came at 10:20, except for the Philip Morris Companies, which was so overwhelmed with [sell] orders that trading was suspended at 10:21. Philip Morris was one of the companies sued; the others were the Loews Corporation and the Liggett Group. About an hour later, after analysts got copies of the decision, and were able to talk to big investors, the tobacco stocks rebounded.

It was a complex case concerning whether companies could be sued on the ground that they had withheld information about potential health dangers and whether they had responsibilities to disclose more than mandated by the 1966 Federal law requiring health warnings on cigarette packets. The Court in part reversed an appeals court ruling in a case brought by the family of Rose Cipollone, a Little Ferry, N.J., woman who died of lung cancer in 1984.

By the end of the day, most stocks closed only slightly down. Philip Morris was even up 62.5 cents, to $73.75. "Millions were lost by people panicking on the news," said Max Holmes, director of bankruptcy research at Solomon Brothers. "And millions were made by people who caught it going back up." Mr. Holmes called the first headlines on news tickers "grossly misleading," and argued that subsequent flashes were little better, exaggerating the risk to tobacco companies. . . .

Lawrence Adelman, a tobacco analyst at Dean Witter Reynolds, lamented the way that a complex legal decision could be squeezed into a short news headline, provoking confusion. "We had explained to our traders and our retail operation that it could be a multilayered decision," he said. "This was definitely one of the most complex decisions on a business-related issue that I've ever seen."

Hired Two Lawyers

Rebecca Barfield, a tobacco analyst at First Boston, had gone to her firm's equities trading floor because she knew the decision might be announced Wednesday morning, and she wanted to be on hand when it came. She had already hired two lawyers to help her interpret court decisions, as well as a law student, who for the last month and a half went to the Supreme Court on each day that a decision might be announced.

When she first saw the news on the Bloomberg News Service, Ms. Barfield said, it appeared to signal that the Court had reached a split decision. But moments later, she saw what appeared to be a different message on the Dow Jones ticker, indicating that the Court had decided fully in favor of the plaintiffs. "It was total confusion," said Ms. Barfield, who was besieged with calls and requests for information. "Everybody was shouting and screaming." Only after she heard from the law student, who called and then faxed a copy of the decision, and from one of the legal experts she had hired, was she able to start telling clients that she thought the decision did not present a great new risk of liability.

First Boston convened a conference call with about 200 listeners at 1 P.M., and Morgan Stanley and Salomon Brothers held similar calls in the early afternoon. RJR Nabisco and American Brands had begun to recover shortly after 11 A.M., while Philip Morris remained suspended; it [reopened and] began its own tumble just before noon, and [then] rose gradually through the afternoon. . . .

Philip Morris ended Wednesday with a volume of 9.7 million shares traded. RJR Nabisco traded a whopping 14.7 million shares, closing down 12.5 cents at $9.375. American Brands ended down 12.5 cents, to $45.375, on 1.5 million shares.

Figure 6-10 shows the intraday abnormal returns to a portfolio consisting of the three tobacco companies discussed in the story above -- American Brands, Philip Morris, and RJR Nabisco. The figure shows the sharp impact of the initial, misleading headlines, and then the gradual rebound during the afternoon as investors digested the significance of the opinion. Between 10:20 and noon, Philip Morris stopped trading altogether because of an imbalance of buy and sell orders. For this period, Figure 6-10 shows the returns to Philip Morris and American Brands.

For the day as a whole, the three tobacco companies did not experience significant abnormal returns. Investors decided that their pre-decision guesses about the Court's ruling weren't far off. The next day, after investors had time to read the opinion more carefully, and reflect on its implications, most tobacco companies were down slightly, but again, not significantly.

220

Figure 6-10

Value Of $100 Invested Equally In American Brands, Philip Morris and RJR Nabisco At the Open Of Trading On June 24, 1992

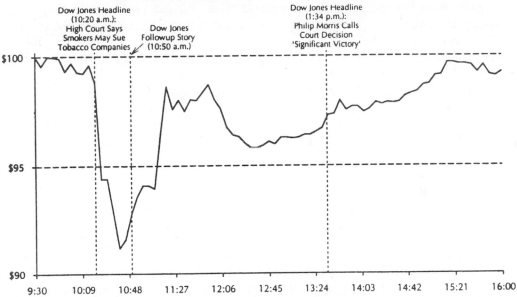

Source: Fitch Group. Returns computed every five minutes. Trading in Philip Morris was suspended from 10:20 to 11:27 a.m. For this period, the chart shows the value of $100 invested in American Brands and RJR Nabisco. For the day, RJR Nabisco, Philip Morris and American Brands ranked 1,2, and 11 on the NYSE list of most actively traded stocks.

Were investors wrong to dump tobacco stocks after the first misleading headline came out? Not in an efficient market. Instead, the initial price plunge probably reflected the sellers taking a calculated gamble that the headlines were mostly accurate, while buyers gambled that the news wasn't all bad. This time, the sellers lost their gamble. But if the full story had been as dismal for tobacco firms as the headlines, the sellers could profit by selling when they did, because tobacco stocks would probably have dropped even further.

Learning Over Time. A firm's stock price at any point in time reflects investor *estimates* of the firm's future cash flows, and the riskiness of those cash flows. In a semistrong efficient market, those estimates are *unbiased*, but they aren't necessarily *right*. In the tobacco example, the initial estimates were wrong, and were soon corrected.

Other mistakes aren't corrected as quickly. An example is the conglomerate merger wave of the 1960s. At the time, investors reacted favorably to conglomerate mergers -- the combined value of bidder and target increased sharply. The consensus view today is that most of these mergers were mistakes. In hindsight, the *estimate* was wrong.[8]

This is one reason to be skeptical about the claim by Bradley, Desai & Kim that the gains from tender offers didn't change between 1963 and 1984, and the only change was in the division of gains between bidders and targets. In hindsight, there wasn't much value added by the conglomerate acquisitions of the 1960s. Investors only *thought* there would be. By the 1980s, conglomerate acquisitions were out of favor, and many tender offers involved horizontal acquisitions (two firms in the same industry joining together). Some major takeovers involved busting up conglomerates that had been formed in the 1960s and 1970s.

Was investor enthusiasm for conglomerate firms an irrational fad, inconsistent with ECMH? Or was it just a garden variety mistake, albeit a large one? It's hard to say, even with the benefit of hindsight.

Did the Sample Firms Really Experience a Similar Event? Should an event study treat conglomerate and horizontal acquisitions as the same type of event, or as two different types of events? Should it treat mergers and tender offers, or friendly and hostile acquisitions, as the same type of event, or as two different types of events? There are almost limitless ways to subdivide samples based on various characteristics of the sample firms, and no clear answer as to when an event study should subdivide and when not. Researchers must use their best judgment, taking into account the questions the study is trying to answer, the loss of statistical power that comes from dividing a sample more finely, and -- most critically -- whether, *if the sample is divided*, there are significant differences between subsamples.

In interpreting an event study, one must always be sensitive to the possibility that the researcher has collapsed two different types of events into one (say, conglomerate and horizontal tender offers into an undifferentiated pool of tender offers, or tender offers and mergers into an undifferentiated pool of acquisitions). If so, then the full sample results are really an average over distinct subclasses. A significant result for the full sample could reflect abnormal returns to only one subclass. Conversely, an insignificant result could reflect a mix of positive abnormal returns to one subclass and negative abnormal returns to another subclass.

The danger of unwittingly combining distinct subclasses is especially strong when an event study uses a sample collected over an extended period of time. The problem

---

[8] Chapter 9 discusses the evidence on conglomerate acquisitions.

is that the nature of the event being studied may change over time. For example, most tender offers in the 1960s involved conglomerate acquisitions; this was no longer the case in the 1980s. This makes it important to subdivide the sample into shorter time periods, to see if the results are different in the subperiods. Bradley, Desai & Kim do this, but don't fully appreciate the implications of change over time in the nature of the acquisitions they are studying.

Multiple Explanations. An event study can tell us that something happened, but it can't tell us *why*. To explain positive or negative abnormal returns, we must closely examine the events and institutions involved. If the market's response was based on a strategy which the investigator does not understand, the *CAR* results, though technically accurate, will be used to support an inaccurate explanation of what occurred. The event study technique does not eliminate the need to assess cause through deductive reasoning; it only -- though this is substantial -- helps delineate what needs to be explained.

Sometimes, there will be two or more plausible explanations for why a firm's stock price changes in response to new information. For example, when firms raise cash by issuing additional common stock, their stock price usually drops.[9] One explanation is that firm value has not changed, but the stock issuance sends a *signal* to investors that the firm needs cash, and hence is in worse shape than investors had previously realized, or a signal that the managers think the firm's stock is overpriced, and hence think that this is an opportune time to sell some (overpriced) shares. An alternate explanation is that per share value declines *in fact* because cash-rich firms tend to waste cash, so existing shareholders won't get $1 of value for each $1 in funds raised.[10] An event study of stock issuances can't tell us which explanation is correct. Sometimes, other studies will indicate that one explanation is more likely, but in this case, both the *signalling* and the *free cash flow* explanation are supported by other studies. We simply don't know which is right; perhaps they both are.

The Relationship Between CAPM and Event Studies. Event studies use the market model to separate abnormal from normal returns. CAPM is also related to the market model. Yet Chapter 4 suggested that CAPM doesn't predict expected returns very well. If CAPM falls, do event studies fail as well? To answer this question, we need to

---

[9] See Clifford Smith, *Investment Banking and the Capital Acquisition Process*, 15 J.Fin.Econ. 3 (1986).

[10] See Michael Jensen, *The Takeover Controversy: Analysis and Evidence*, in *Knights, Raiders & Targets: The Impact of the Hostile Takeover* 314 (John Coffee, Louis Lowenstein & Susan Rose-Ackerman eds. 1988).

consider separately the two uses of event studies -- as a *measure of the impact of information*, and as a *test of market efficiency*.

Event studies as a measure of the impact of information survive largely intact. The abnormal returns procedure tests whether daily returns are *unusual* -- different than one would expect on a normal day. For that statistical test, it is perfectly appropriate to remove *usual* influences on stock prices. The market model does that. It's unfortunate that we lack a better model of stock prices. If we had such a model, we could do a better job of removing *systematic* factors that affect stock prices from the daily abnormal returns $\epsilon_{i,t}$. Noise would be lower, and statistical tests would be more powerful. But that doesn't mean that there is anything wrong with removing the influences we know about. And even if β_i doesn't predict the future rate of return on firm i's stock very well, it does predict how firm i's stock varies day to day with changes in overall stock market prices.

CAPM and the market model are also not identical. In CAPM, the return on firm i's stock can be written as:

$$R_{i,t} = (1 - \beta_i)R_f + \beta_i \cdot R_{m,t} + \epsilon_{i,t}$$

See Equation 4-3. Thus, CAPM requires that the constant term α_i in the market model equal $(1 - \beta_i)R_f$ for all firms. The market model, in contrast, lets α_i take whatever firm-specific value emerges from the regression analysis used to determine β_i. Systematic factors other than β that affect asset prices may be partly reflected in α_i, and thus will have less effect on $\epsilon_{i,t}$.

For short-window event studies, we can take further comfort from the tendency for event study results not to be sensitive to the details of the model used to separate normal from abnormal stock price returns. Even simple techniques, such as techniques that don't use β to adjust for risk, work reasonably well.

For long-window studies, the situation is less clear. Such studies are sometimes sensitive to the details of model specification. We might reach different conclusions if we had a better asset pricing model. Thus, one should be cautious about relying heavily on long-window studies where the degree of statistical significance is only moderate.

Short-window event studies *as tests of market efficiency* are probably also reliable. The studies are not sensitive to model specification, so it is unlikely that a better model would produce different results. This makes short-window event study tests of market efficiency *less subject* than other studies to the joint-hypothesis problem -- the need to always test market efficiency jointly with an asset pricing model. But long-window event studies, such as studies that test for overreaction or underreaction to news followed by gradual relaxation to true value, or studies that test the performance of takeover bidders and targets after a takeover bid, *are* sensitive to the particular model used to estimate abnormal returns.   If we find an anomaly, such as early studies that showed that acquiring firms underperform the market after an acquisition, we don't know whether to attribute the anomaly to inefficient pricing or to use of an incorrect asset pricing model.[11]

An increasing number of event studies respond to the limitations of CAPM by using a multifactor asset pricing model (often using both **B** and size adjustments) to measure abnormal returns.   Over time, we should learn which event study results are robust to model specification and which are not.

The Implications of a Negative Result.   Suppose that an event study fails to find a statistically significant result.   That does *not* mean that the announcement being studied had no effect, nor even that the announcement was unimportant.   All it does is give us a *rough upper bound* on how important and unexpected the announcement was.

Lawyers and policymakers sometimes treat the absence of a *significant* change as equivalent to *no change in value*.   This is simply wrong.   The noise in stock prices can hide even important results.   Recall, for example, the Allied-Signal example in Figure 6-7.   Suppose that on the day when its CEO was fired, Allied-Signal's stock had climbed 3% relative to the market, instead of 12.5%.   This would have been a change in value of $125 million, but it would not be statistically significant at the 95% confidence level.

Just as there can be multiple explanations for a statistically significant result, there can be multiple causes for the absence of a significant result.   We noted earlier that investors react negatively to stock price issuances designed to raise cash.   Consider now a stock-for-stock merger, in which the acquirer issues stock to buy another company.   Suppose that the acquirer's stock price does not change significantly.   This could reflect two offsetting effects -- a positive reaction to the merger, and a negative reaction to the issuance of stock.   *If*, that is, investors react to the issuance of stock in a merger in the same way as to the issuance of stock to raise cash.   We don't know whether they do or not, because we can't separate the multiple reasons why a stock-for-stock merger may affect the acquirer's stock price.

---

[11] See Julian Franks, Robert Harris & Sheridan Titman, *The Postmerger Share Price Performance of Acquiring Firms*, 29 J.Fin.Econ. 81 (1991).

E. Variations and Methodological Issues

This Chapter has developed one common way to conduct an event study. Ther methodology we developed, though, is not the only possible one. This section discusses some variations in event study techniques, and some methodological issues in conducting event studies that drive the choice among the available techniques.[12]

1. *Event Studies for Preferred Stock and Debt.* The event study technique is used principally for common stock. It can be adapted for use with other securities, such as preferred stock and debt. This is important in assessing how takeovers affect creditors as well as stockholders. For leveraged buyouts and leveraged recapitalizations, which involve large increases in debt, we will want to ask whether stock price gains reflect net increases in firm value, or whether some of the stock price gains come at the expense of creditors. Other transactions may reduce firm-specific risk, and thus produce positive abnormal returns to creditors. If so, then the gains to common stockholders will understate the increase in firm value.[13]

2. *Event Studies Using Monthly Returns.* We have described the event study methodology for *daily returns*. Some event studies use *monthly returns*, especially for time periods prior to 1962, for which the CRSP data base contains only monthly returns. The methodology can be used for other time intervals as well, as long as stock price returns over the chosen interval are approximately normal.[14]

3. *Nonnormality of Stock Price Returns.* The confidence intervals described in section B apply to returns that perfectly follow the normal distribution. Since abnormal returns are only approximately normal, the true confidence intervals are slightly larger (and theory doesn't tell us exactly what they are). The confidence intervals are also not perfectly symmetric around zero, due to skewness in the actual return distribution

---

[12] For a recent, relatively nontechnical survey of event study methodology, see Glenn Henderson, *Problems and Solutions in Conducting Event Studies*, 57 J. Risk & Ins. 282 (1990).

[13] For an example of the use of event studies to measure returns to preferred stock and debt, see Debra Dennis & John McConnell, *Corporate Mergers and Security Returns*, 16 J.Fin.Econ. 143 (1986). Chapter 15 discusses the evidence on gains or losses to holders of preferred stock and debt from leveraged buyouts and other takeovers.

[14] For a careful discussion of event studies using monthly returns, see Stephen Brown & Jerold Warner, *Measuring Security Price Performance*, 8 J.Fin.Econ. 205 (1980).

(slightly more than half of daily abnormal returns are negative, but there are more large positive than large negative abnormal returns). Departures from normality are important mostly for studies that use small samples. The *AAR*s for large samples come closer to following the normal distribution (this is a special case of a general result in probability theory called the Central Limit Theorem).[15]

4. *One-Tail Versus Two-Tail Tests*. We have discussed statistical significance for the usual situation where we want to assess whether the response to information is *significantly different from zero*, against the null hypothesis that the response equals zero. In this situation, a so-called *two-tailed test* is appropriate. Sometimes, we want to assess whether the response is significantly *greater than zero*, against the null hypothesis that the response is less than or equal to zero. In this situation a *one-tailed* test must be used. In a one-tailed test, the likelihood that the quantity being measured will be 2 or more standard deviations abov zero is 2.5% -- exactly half as large as for a two-tailed test.

5. *Correction for Finite Estimation Period*. The market model parameters α_i and β_i, and the standard deviation of abnormal returns σ_i, are estimated over a finite measurement period and are then used to compute a test statistic for returns *outside* the estimation period. Because of this, σ_i slightly underestimates the true standard deviation of the abnormal returns during the event period. The correction factor is on the order of $2/n$, where n is the number of days in the estimation period. Some event studies adjust σ_i to correct for the finite measurement period, but others do not.[16]

6. *Choosing the Market Model Estimation Period*. Most event studies estimate the market model parameters α_i and β_i, and the standard deviation of the abnormal returns σ_i, over a period of 120-240 trading days *preceding* the event window. Some studies estimate these parameters both before and after the event window, and average the two, to take into account the possibility that the event being studied has changed either the market model parameters α_i and β_i, or the standard deviation of the abnormal returns σ_i. One can also estimate the market model over a time period that includes the event window, though this adds some statistical complexity. The choice of estimation period can be important for event study results that use long event windows, and in situations where the event being studied changes the variance of the abnormal returns.

---

[15] Brown & Warner (1985), *supra* note 5, discuss the statistical properties of daily abnormal returns, and their implications for event studies.

[16] James Patell, *Corporate Forecasts of Earnings Per Share and Stock Price Behavior: Empirical Tests*, 14 J.Acct.Res. 246 (1976), develops the correction factor.

7. *Dealing with Variance Shifts*. A problem with event studies, including short-window studies, is that the event being studied may change the distribution of abnormal returns, either temporarily (while investors are absorbing the new information) or permanently. Suppose, for example, that the event causes the standard deviation of a firm's abnormal returns to increase. A test statistic, such as the *SAR*, that is computed by dividing daily abnormal returns by the *pre-event* standard deviation σ_i will make too many post-event returns appear to be statistically significant. There are techniques for measuring statistical significance that are less sensitive to a variance shift, or other forms of model misspecification, than the standard method we have described. The tradeoff is that these techniques generally have less power to detect statistical significance when a variance shift doesn't take place. These techniques are beyond the level of this book, but you should know that they exist.[17]

8. *Sign tests and other nonparametric tests*. The z test for *CARs* developed in section B is a *parametric* test -- it depends on knowing a particular *parameter* -- the standard deviation σ_i. One way to reduce the problems caused by a variance shift (or other model misspecification) is to use a *nonparametric* test that does not depend on σ_i. One simple nonparametric test is the sign test: Is the percentage of positive abnormal returns significantly different from the (approximately) 50% positive abnormal returns we would expect when nothing special is happening?

For example, Bradley, Desai & Kim report in Table 6-7 that 75% of the completed tender offers in their sample produced positive combined bidder and target abnormal returns. We will use this result as an example of how a sign test can be used. For a large sample, the test statistic for the percentage of positive returns is:

$$z_{\text{sign test}} = (p - 0.5)/[p(1 - p)/n]^{1/2}$$

where:

p	=	fraction of positive returns
n	=	sample size

---

[17] One simple technique for handling variance shifts involves estimating the reduced model $R_{i,t} = \beta_i \cdot R_{m,t} + \epsilon_{i,t}$ *during* the event period. One measures the *average* standard deviation σ of the event period abnormal returns for the firms in the sample, and uses this standard deviation to compute a t-statistic. The drawback of this method is that one can no longer factor the constant term α_i out of the daily returns, nor measure a firm-specific standard deviation of abnormal returns σ_i. This causes some loss of statistical power. For a more sophisticated effort to deal with variance shift at the event date, see Sanjai Bhagat & Richard Jefferis, *Voting Power in the Proxy Process: The Case of Antitakeover Charter Amendments*, 30 J.Fin.Econ. 193 (1991). Tim Bollersev & Robert Hodrick, *Financial Market Efficiency Tests* (NBER Working Paper No. 4108, June 1992), survey various statistical techniques for testing market efficiency.

For the Bradley, Desai & Kim sample, $p = 0.75$, and $n = 236$, so:

$$z_{\text{sign test}} \qquad = \qquad (0.25)/[(0.75)(0.25)/236]^{1/2} \qquad = \qquad 8.87$$

Statistical significance is apparent.[18]

9. *Abnormal Performance Index*. Bradley, Desai & Kim discuss one problem with *CAR*s -- when positive returns are realized over a number of days in an event window, the *CAR* understates the total percentage gain over the event window. This can be avoided by an alternative measure called the *Abnormal Performance Index*, which is a product of the daily abnormal returns:

$$API \quad = \quad \prod_{t=d_1}^{d_2} (1 + \epsilon_{i,t})$$

Here the capital Greek letter Π means that one takes the product of the quantities $(1 + \epsilon_{i,t})$ over the indicated time period.[19]

10. *Event Studies of Market-Wide Returns*. The event study methodology can be adapted to measure whether *market-wide* returns on a day when a news announcement is made -- say a discount rate cut by the Federal Reserve Board -- is made are significantly larger than on an average day. Such studies, though, are uncommon. The announcement must be important enough to move the whole market, and must be recurring for us to have much confidence that it was *this* announcement, rather than the many others on the same day, that moved prices. But important, recurring announcements are especially vulnerable to anticipation. Investors may approve of a discount rate cut, yet the market may drop because they had anticipated a larger cut.

---

[18] By way of comparison, the authors report a z statistic of 19.95 for their event study of the combined abnormal returns. This reflects the greater power of the parametric test discussed in section B, compared to the nonparametric sign test, when abnormal returns are large. This is because the parametric test uses information about *how far* the abnormal returns are from zero, while the sign test only uses the fact that an individual abnormal return is positive or negative. It is also possible for the average abnormal return to be positive, even if more than half of the individual abnormal returns are negative.

[19] Steve Cantrell, Michael Maloney & Mark Mitchell, *On Estimating the Variance of Abnormal Stock Market Performance* (working paper, 1987) discuss the *API*, and show that statistical tests are at least as well specified as the standard tests for the significance of *CAR*s.

Problems to Accompany Chapter 6

1. Is the response of Allied-Signal's stock to the announcement that it's CEO had been fired, shown in Figures 6-5 and 6-7, consistent with semistrong market efficiency? Why or why not?

2. For the 1981-1984 period, Bradley, Desai & Kim report that 35% of the tender offers in their sample produced positive abnormal returns for the acquiring firm. Is this result statistically significant, compared to the null hypothesis of 50% positive abnormal returns? If so, at what confidence level?

3. (a) Suppose that news about a pending takeover comes out gradually over a 5-day period. In response, the target's stock price increases 5% per day relative to the market on each of the five days. What is the CAR for the five-day period?

   (b) What is the abnormal performance index (API) for the five-day period?

   (c) Which is a better measure of the increase in the value of the target's shares during the period, and why?

4. Sometimes, it is useful to compute results in a different way than the authors of a study. Based on Table 6-8 in the Bradley, Desai & Kim study, what is the average CAR to bidders in multiple bidder tender offers, for the period from July 1968 through December 1984 (their second and third subperiods)?

5. Buyback Corp. announces that it will conduct a self-tender offer, under which it will buy 25% of its outstanding shares at $150 per share. Each shareholder can tender some or all of her shares. If more than 25% of the shares are tendered, Buyback will buy stock prorata from each shareholder in proportion to the number of shares tendered. In response, the market price of Buyback stock jumps from $100 to $120 per share. Why might Buyback's stock price have increased? After all, the company's business has not changed. Suggest as many (reasonable) explanations as you can think of.

6. What value do investors expect Buyback's stock to have after the tender offer is completed? Ignore the time value of money for the time needed to complete the tender offer. Assume that all investors will tender their shares.

CHAPTER 7: THE OPTION PERSPECTIVE

Some of the most important recent developments in financial theory have concerned the valuation of *options* to acquire or dispose of other assets. The modern theory of option pricing begins with the development in 1973 of the Black-Scholes model of the value of an option to buy common stock. This model has become one of the major paradigms in modern financial theory.[1]

Our principal interest in option theory involves not the mathematical formula for determining an option's value, but instead the insight, also originating with Fischer Black and Myron Scholes, that much can be learned about various securities, including common stock and bonds, by seeing these securities as containing options, and exploring the factors that makes those options more or less valuable. Option theory tells us, for example, that in some circumstances common stock is really more like an option than like a fractional share in a business. Option theory also tells us that some corporate actions -- such as large, risky investments -- are good for stockholders but bad for creditors, because they increase the value of the stock (seen as an option) and decrease the wealth of the party that has sold the option (in this case, creditors).

If so, then stockholders can behave *strategically* or *opportunistically* -- for example, by making risky investments that benefit themselves at the expense of creditors -- even if those investments have a negative net present value for the company. Option theory also offers insight into when the stockholders' incentives to take such actions are especially strong.

Identifying incentives to act strategically is the first step in transaction planning. If you know when stockholders and creditor interests will diverge, you can structure a transaction to reduce the divergence, and write a contract that limits the other side's ability or incentive to act strategically. Such transaction planning can increase company value, with the gains split between shareholders and creditors. Anticipating and controlling strategic behavior is among the principal ways that advisors can add value when they participate in business transactions. And option theory is central to understanding how to anticipate strategic behavior.

With this brief introduction as motivation for why option theory is worth studying, we begin in Section A by introducing simple options on common stock in their standard context. Section B discusses the factors that affect option value. Section C

---

[1] Fischer Black & Myron Scholes, *The Pricing of Options and Corporate Liabilities*, 81 J.Pol.Econ. 637 (1973); see also Robert Merton, *Theory of Rational Option Pricing*, 4 Bell J.Econ. 141 (1973).

applies the option perspective to two important situations: the conflict between shareholders and creditors over the firm's investment strategy; and efforts to develop compensation contracts that give managers the right risk-taking incentives.

A. The Basics of Put and Call Options

A *call option* is a contract that gives the holder the right to *buy* an underlying asset -- for example, a share of common stock -- at a fixed price, on or before a specified date. A *put option* gives the holder the right to *sell* an underlying asset at a fixed price on or before a specified date. The fixed price for buying or selling the underlying asset is called the option *strike price* or *exercise price*. The last date when the option can be exercised is called its *maturity date* or *expiration date*. The seller of the option is also known as an *option writer*. The price that the option buyer pays to the option writer for the option is called the *option premium*.

If the price of the underlying security *exceeds* the exercise price of a call option, the call option is *in the money*. If this relationship still holds at expiration, the call option holder will exercise the option and make a profit. Suppose, for example, that you hold a call option to buy IBM stock at $70, and on the expiration date, IBM sells for $77 per share. You can make an immediate $7 profit by exercising your option to buy the stock for $70, and then selling the stock in the market for $77.

If the price of the underlying security is *less than* the call option exercise price, the call option is *out of the money*. If this relationship holds at expiration, the option holder will let the call option expire without exercising it. For example, if you hold a call option to buy IBM stock at $70, and on the expiration date, IBM sells for $63 per share, the call option is worthless. You would not exercise an option to buy IBM for $70 when you can buy IBM for $63 in the market.

If the price of the underlying security *exactly equals* the exercise price of a call option, the call option is *at the money*. If this relationship holds at expiration, you would be indifferent (before transaction costs) between exercising and not exercising. Either way, you make no profit and incur no loss.

Figure 7-1 shows the relationship *at expiration* between the value of a call option V_c and the value of the underlying asset V_a. The call option is worth zero whenever the the underlying asset is worth less than the exercise price X: that is, whenever $V_a < X$. As the value of the underlying asset increases above the exercise price X, the call option gains value dollar for dollar: Its value is $V_c = V_a - X$.

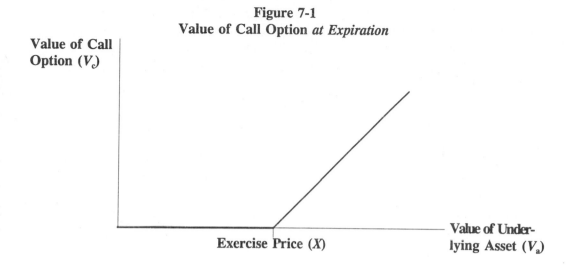

Figure 7-1
Value of Call Option *at Expiration*

Value of Call Option (V_c)

Exercise Price (X)

Value of Under-lying Asset (V_a)

For a put option, these relationships are reversed. A put option is *in the money* if the price of the underlying security is *less than* the option exercise price. If this relationship still holds at expiration, the put option holder will exercise the option and make a profit by selling the underlying security for more than its market value. Suppose, for example, that you hold a put option to sell IBM stock at $70, and on the expiration date, IBM sells for $63 per share. You can make an immediate $7 profit by buying IBM for $63 in the market, and then using the put option to sell IBM to the option writer for $70.

If the price of the underlying security *exceeds* the put option exercise price, the put option is *out of the money*. If this relationship holds at expiration, the put option will expire worthless. You would not sell IBM stock for $70 using a put option if you can sell it for $77 in the market. Finally, if the price of the underlying security equals the put option exercise price, the put option is *at the money*. If this relationship holds at expiration, you would be indifferent (before transaction costs) between exercising and not exercising.

Figure 7-2 shows the relationship *at expiration* between the value of a put option (V_p) and the value of the underlying asset (V_a). The put option is worth zero whenever the the underlying asset is worth *more* than the exercise price X: that is, whenever $V_a > X$. As the value of the underlying asset *decreases* below the exercise price X, the put option gains value dollar for dollar: Its value is $V_p = X - V_a$.

233

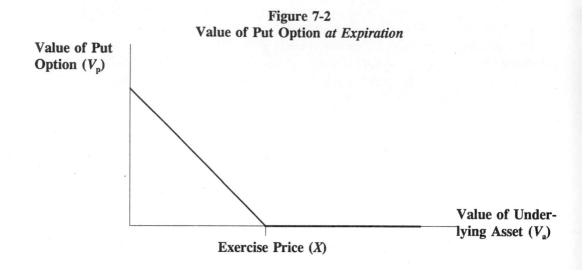

Figure 7-2
Value of Put Option *at Expiration*

Value of Put
Option (V_p)

Value of Under-
lying Asset (V_a)

Exercise Price (X)

For both puts and calls, the option holder exercises if doing so is profitable, and lets the option expire otherwise. Before expiration, when the value of the underlying security at expiration is uncertain, the *expected value* of a call or put option is positive. In some states of the world, the holder gains by exercising the option; in all others, the holder throws the option away and breaks even. The option writer, in contrast, can only lose and never gain at expiration. The option writer's compensation comes up front, when the writer sells the option. In an efficient market, the sale price will equal the expected value of the option to the holder.

The next reading discusses how investors use publicly traded put and call options, as substitutes for or complements to investing in the underlying common stock.

MYRON SCHOLES, OPTIONS -- PUTS AND CALLS,
in *Encyclopedia of Investments*
559-578 (Marshall Blume & Jack Friedman eds.1982)

Since 1973, call options and, more recently, put options have been trading on organized secondary markets. Investors have become familiar with the characteristics of these contracts, which are relatively simple contracts with set maturity dates and exercise prices. They may be unaware, however, that other commonly traded securities are first cousins to options. Warrants, executive stock options, and even the common stock and bonds of a corporation are examples of securities that are closely related to put and call options.

The common stock of a corporation with bonds in its capital structure is [a call] option because the shareholders have the right to buy back the assets of the firm from the bondholders by paying off the face amount of the debt (its fixed price) at the maturity of the bond (the expiration date of the contract). Since many financial instruments have characteristics similar to those of put and call options, a detailed knowledge of put and call options may be helpful in understanding these other contracts, and vice versa. . . .

[A put] option contract is similar to an insurance policy. The asset being insured is the underlying common stock. Investors insure against possible loss in return on the holdings of common stock by buying put options on their stock; a put option with the same exercise price as the current stock price insures against a decline in the stock price for the term of the put option. Loss . . . is limited to the premium paid for the put option; on a fall in price the investor puts the stock to the put seller, the insurer, and receives the exercise price in return. Naturally, if the stock increases in price, the put is not exercised; the insurance is not used. . . .

As an insurance policy on a home insures against the loss from a fire, holding put options on common stock insures against the loss from a drop in the price of the stock. Using options, investors can sell off part of the risk -- insure part of the risk of common stock investments. The sellers of options, like insurers generally, expect that the option premiums will cover the costs of the insurance they sell to the buyers of the options. If [the option price is] actuarially fair, neither the buyer nor the seller expects to earn an above-normal rate of return at the expense of the other side of the trade.

. . . [O]ptions have been confused with futures contracts and with forward contracts. The confusion arises because the terms are similar. Several concepts [first] used in the marketing of futures contracts were [adapted] for use in the trading of options. Buyers of futures [or forward] contracts for July wheat have *bought* the July wheat, although they will not take delivery until July. . . . Buyers of [call] options for July IBM, in contrast, have not bought IBM, but only the *right to buy* IBM at a fixed price. . . .

Since buyers match sellers and no new money is raised by corporations, [future and option] contracts have been compared to side bets and to gambling, contracts without an economic purpose. Futures and options both have economic purposes; they help investors with portfolio planning, thereby facilitating the functioning of the primary and secondary markets in the [underlying] commodities or securities. . . .[a]

---

[a] The critics of option trading, to whom Scholes is responding, argue that options *can* be used to insure a stock portfolio against loss, but they don't *have to* be used this way. For example, one can buy a put option without owning the underlying stock. In contrast, you can't buy fire insurance on a house you don't own. Buying a put option on stock you don't own can be seen as a side bet on the future performance of the stock, in which the option buyer wagers against the option seller. Transaction costs

Reduction of Risk in Investment Portfolios

The attractive characteristics of options become evident when options are combined with other securities. Combining options with other securities transforms the returns and risks of an option into the returns and risks of an investment strategy: options combine with other investments to produce patterns of returns for a portfolio of investments.

There are several important ways to limit the risk of investing in securities. Diversification is one of the main ways to limit the risk of holding securities. The larger the number of assets held in a portfolio, the smaller will be an investor's exposure to the risks of any one of the securities within the portfolio; the risk of the portfolio approaches the risk of the market portfolio. Another approach to limiting the risk of holding securities is to invest a percentage of the assets in bonds. By holding a larger fraction of the portfolio in bonds or money market funds, the investor unlevers the portfolio. The percentage changes in the value of the total portfolio will be less than the percentage changes in the value of the risky securities. With options, investors can limit risk by insuring against adverse changes in the prices of their holdings of securities, or against adverse changes in the value of a portfolio of assets. . . .

Use as Investment Insurance

Put options as insurance. A put option is like a term insurance policy in which the term or maturity is the length of time between the purchase of the put and its expiration date; the item being insured is the value of the underlying stock. The face value of the policy, or the maximum claim that is paid in the event that the underlying stock becomes worthless, is equal to the number of shares specified in the contract times the exercise price. For partial losses, the amount received is equal to the number of shares times the difference between the exercise price and the market price of the underlying security at the time that the put is exercised.

Moreover, depending upon the relation between the strik[e] price and the price of the underlying stock when the put is purchased, the put option will have features quite similar to an insurance policy with a deductible amount. If investors own 100 shares of stock with a market value of $100 per share, and if they buy a put with a strik[e] price of $100, they insure totally against any decline in the price of the stock during the life of the option. If, however, investors buy instead a put on the stock with an exercise price of $90 per share, they are not insured against the first 10 point decline (i.e., the

---

aside, the wager is a zero-sum game. Once we include transactions costs, the wager is negative sum. Critics of options trading believe that most trading involves this sort of negative-sum gamble. In contrast, supporters like Scholes believe that most options trading involves investor efforts to adjust the risk and return characteristics of an investment portfolio, with the potential for net gains in *risk-adjusted* value.

first $1,000 in losses), although they are covered against any additional losses resulting from a decline below $90; therefore, the put has a $1,000 deductible. It is even possible to buy the insurance with a negative deductible: The investor purchases a put option with an exercise price of $110, thereby insuring against the event that the stock price does not appreciate by at least 10 percent. Unlike traditional insurance, however, the investor can buy the insurance without owning the asset.

Call options as insurance. Call options are also akin to insurance policies. Consider the following investment strategy: (1) Buy one share of a non-dividend-paying security; (2) take out a [loan under which you must] pay $X, the strik[e] price, at the maturity of the option, t months in the future. The loan, if prepaid, is prepayable at face value; (3) buy a put option on one share of the stock with a strik[e] price of $X and an expiration date t months in the future. If, at the end of t months, the stock [is worth] $$V_a$$ per share, the value of the position would be as follows. If V_a were less than X, the put would be exercised [and] the stock delivered, for $X. The face amount of the loan, $X, however, must be repaid. The net value of the position is zero. On the other hand, if V_a were greater than X, the put would expire, the stock would be sold for $$V_a$$, and the loan [would be] repaid from the sale of the stock. The net value of the position would be $$(V_a - X)$. . . .

Suppose the investment strategy [instead] consisted of buying a call option on one share of the stock with an exercise price of $X and an expiration date t months in the future. If, at the end of t months, the stock were selling for $$V_a$$ per share, with V_a less than X, the call would expire unexercised; the value of the position would be zero. If V_a, however, were larger than X, the call would be exercised, paying $X for the stock, [and then] selling the stock for $$V_a$$; the value of the position would be $$(V_a - X)$. [The payoff is exactly the same].

Since the payoffs to both strategies are the same for every possible price of the underlying security at the maturity of the contracts, the two are functionally equivalent: *Call options are equivalent to [(i) owning] the underlying security; [(ii) being obligated to repay] a term loan with a face value of $X; plus [(iii) owning] an insurance policy against declines in the stock price below $X per share.* While the leverage component of a call option is its most commonly known characteristic, the insurance characteristic distinguishes call-option strategies from simple stock strategies such as buying stocks on margin. . . .

[Selected] Glossary

Black-Scholes	Pricing model for options used by practitioners.
call option	Right to buy a security for a fixed price on or before a given date.
exercise value	Value of the option if it was to be exercised.
expiration date	Last day on which the option can be exercised.

fully covered	Writing an option on stock held by the writer.
futures contract	Buying an asset today for delivery in the future.
hedging	Reducing risk by selling an asset similar to the one held.
in-the-money call	Stock price is above the strik[e] price of the option.
in-the-money put	Stock price is below the strik[e] price of the option.
leverage	Borrowing money to buy an asset.
naked option	Writing an option to deliver a security that is not owned.
option buyer	One who has the right to exercise the option.
option writer	Person who sells the right of exercise to the buyer of the option.
out-of-the-money	For a call option, the stock price is below the strik[e] price; for a put option, the stock price is above the strik[e] price.
premium	Price paid for the option to the writer by the buyer.
put option	Right to sell a security for a fixed price on or before a given date.
strik[e] price	Price at which the option can be exercised.

B. The Factors that Determine Option Value

The Scholes reading describes some of the investment strategies that can be pursued using options. We turn next to the factors that determine the value of an option. We will consider only call options, but the same factors determine the value of put options. For simplicity, we assume that all cash flows from the underlying asset will be received after the option expires. Thus, the call option holder can capture all the cash flows from the underlying asset at expiration, and has no reason to exercise before the expiration date.

At expiration, valuing a call option is easy. The value of an in-the-money call option equals the value of the underlying asset V_a minus the exercise price X. The value of an out-of-the-money call option is zero. Valuing the option become complex, though, when there is time remaining until expiration, and the value of the underlying asset *at expiration* is uncertain. Before expiration, an out-of-the-money option has value because the option *may* become in-the-money by the time it expires.

Five fundamental factors determine call option value:

(1) The *current* value V_a of the underlying asset;

(2) The exercise price X;

(3) The risk-free rate of interest r_f, which tells us the time value of money;

(4) The variability in the value of the underlying asset, measured by the standard deviation of price σ_a; and

(5) The time t remaining until the option expires.

We will consider each factor in turn.

1. Current Value

Other things equal, the value of a call option increases with an increase in the current value V_a of the underlying asset. In an efficient market, the higher today's asset price is, the higher the *expected* price at expiration. And the higher the asset price at expiration, the more the *option* will be worth. Today's value and the value at expiration are linked, *for both the option and the underlying asset*, by the time value of money.

An increase in current asset value V_a will make a call option worth more even if the option is out of the money. An increase in current value makes it more likely that the option will be in the money at expiration. *How much* more likely the option is to be in the money, and how far in the money it is likely to be, depends on how far out of the money the option currently is, the time t remaining until expiration, and the standard deviation σ_a of the asset's value.

2. Exercise Price

The lower the exercise price X, the more likely a call option is to be in the money at expiration, and the further in the money it will be. Thus, an option with a *lower* exercise price is worth more than an otherwise identical option with a higher exercise price. Option value depends largely not on current value alone, nor exercise price alone, but the difference between the two: $V_a - X$. If $V_a < X$, the option is out of the money. The further out of the money the option is, the less it is worth. If $V_a > X$, the option is in the money. The further in the money the option is, the more it is worth.

3. Time Value of Money

To exercise a call option, the option holder must pay the option writer the exercise price $X on the expiration date. To have $X available at expiration, the option

239

holder today needs only a smaller amount, which can be invested to return X on the expiration date. That amount is simply the present value of X:

$$PV(\$X \text{ at time } t) \;=\; \$X/(1 + r_f)^t$$

The longer the time until expiration, and the higher the interest rate r_f, the more valuable the option, because the holder needs less money today to be able to exercise the option at expiration.[2] The size of the discounting effect depends on the likelihood that the option will be exercised, since only then is the exercise price paid. The more likely an option is to be exercised, the more important the factors -- r_f and t -- that determine the present value of the exercise price.

4. Variability in Asset Value

A central factor in valuing an option is the variance in value of the underlying asset. The *greater* the variance in the value of the underlying asset, *holding constant the value of the asset*, the more the option is worth. At first glance, this seems counterintuitive. For the asset itself, higher systematic risk means that investors demand a higher expected rate of return. Thus, an increase in systematic risk, *holding constant the expected cash flows from the asset*, means that those cash flows have a lower *discounted present value*. But when an option on that asset is being sold, an increase in variance *increases* the value of the option.

This is due to the differences between the payoff to the holder of a call option and the payoff to the holder of the underlying asset. Consider first an option which is *at the money in present value terms*. The two curves in Figure 7-3 show the probability distributions of the value *at expiration* of the stock of two companies, Stableco and Variableco. Each has an expected value at expiration of X. The heavy black line shows the payoff at expiration to a call option with an exercise price of X -- the gain on exercise of the option and sale of the underlying common stock.

By "at the money *in present value terms*" we mean that the expected value of each company's stock *at expiration* equals the option exercise price. The Stableco and Variableco options illustrated in Figure 7-3 are slightly out-of-money giving the term its usual meaning, which ignores the time value of money. If an asset's expected value is X sometime in the future, its current value must be less than X.

---

[2] The present value formula works for any time period -- day, week, month, or year. If the time period is measured in, say, months, then the risk-free interest rate is the *monthly* rate.

To keep the example simple, we will assume that the extra variance in Variableco stock results solely from *unsystematic* risk. Thus, Stableco and Variableco stock will will sell at the same price in an efficient market.

Variableco stock has both greater upside and greater downside than Stableco stock. A call option holder, though, only cares about the upside. In bad states of the world, the option holder will let the option expire worthless. The holder *cannot do worse than zero*, no matter how badly the stock performs. Holding a Variableco option, rather than Variableco stock, preserves the extra upside and eliminates the extra downside. This makes the Variableco option worth more than a Stableco option, even though the stocks are worth the same and the options have the same exercise price and expiration date.

In Figure 7-3, the option holder neither gains nor loses if the share price is below the exercise price. The only part of the probability distribution that matters is the part where the share price at expiration exceeds the exercise price. Greater variance in the value of the underlying common stock shifts *that portion of the distribution* to the right. This increases the probability of a high stock price and, therefore, of a high option value.

Figure 7-3
Effect of Variance in Asset Value on Option Value

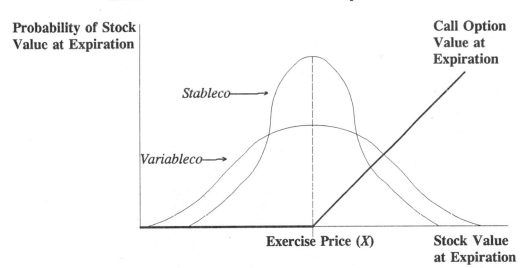

Figure 7-4 shows the probability distribution of value at expiration *for the option holder*. The left half of the bell curves in Figure 7-3 has been collapsed to the heavy black line at a value of zero, because zero is the option holder's outcome whenever the stock price at expiration is less than or equal to the exercise price $X.

In Figure 7-4, the mean of the option holder's probability distribution curve is greater for Variableco than for Stableco. The striped area under the Stableco curve and the cross-hatched area under the Variableco curve are equal in size -- they represent equal probabilities. But the cross-hatched area is at a higher price than the striped area. Thus, the Variableco stock has a higher expected value than the Stableco option.

<h3 style="text-align:center">Figure 7-4
Option Value Probability Distribution</h3>

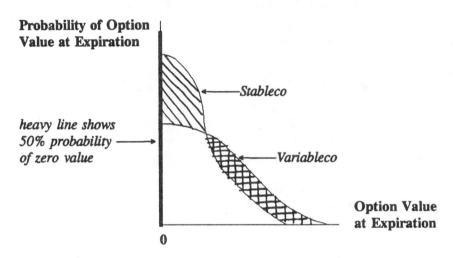

The same result -- greater stock price means greater option value -- holds *even more strongly* for an option that is out of the money in present value terms. It also holds, *though less strongly*, for an an option that is in the money in present value terms. The holder of such an option sees all of the increased upside, and *only some* of the increased downside. Thus, the Variableco option is still worth more than the Stableco option. But as we steadily reduce the exercise price toward zero, the difference in value becomes less and less. In the extreme case where the option is so deep in the money that it is almost certain to be exercised, the option value will equal the stock value V_a minus the present value of the exercise price $PV(\$X)$. Since Stableco and Variableco have the same stock price, their options will also have the same value in this extreme case. In effect, as an option becomes deeper and deeper in the money, its return characteristics approach those of the underlying asset.

The effect of increased variance on option value is more complex if the increased variance results from *systematic*, rather than unsystematic, risk. For an option that is at the money or out of the money in present value terms, the same analysis applies. Investors will now pay less for Variableco stock than for Stableco stock, because Variableco promises the same expected return but has higher systematic risk. But investors will still pay more for a Variableco option, because the option holder sees only the greater upside. The positive effect on value of the greater upside potential outweighs the negative effect of the increase in systematic risk.

For an option that is *in the money* in present value terms, we need more information to know how option value changes as systematic risk increases. The increase in systematic risk will make the option worth less; the increase in total variance will make the option worth more. The sign of the change in value will depend on which effect is larger. The deeper in the money the option is, the more stock-like the return on the option, and thus the weaker the second, value-increasing factor will be.

Finally, if the systematic variance of the underlying asset increases and expected return also increases just enough so that the *value* of the underlying asset doesn't change, the value of a call option on the asset increases, *even if* the option is in the money. This is the situation considered in the Black-Scholes option pricing model, which gives option value as a function of the variance of the underlying asset, holding asset value constant.

To summarize: An increase in variance, *holding asset value constant*, increases call option value. If we instead hold *expected return* constant, then: (i) an increase in *unsystematic risk* increases option value; (ii) an increase in systematic risk increases the value of an option that is *at the money* or *out of the money* in present value terms; and (iii) an increase in systematic risk has an uncertain effect on the value of an option that is *in the money* in present value terms. The further out of the money a call option is, the stronger the effect of asset value variance on option value. Conversely, the deeper in the money an option is, the weaker the variance effect. The value of a deep-in-the-money option tracks the value of the underlying asset, nearly dollar for dollar.

This relationship between variance and option value yields an insight that will be of substantial value. Suppose you are a Stableco shareholder and have to decide whether it will make a major acquisition. After studying the issue, you decide not to make the acquisition because the expected return is insufficient to compensate Stableco for the associated risk. Would your conclusion change if you held an option on Stableco's stock rather than the stock itself? A change in risk has a very different impact on an option holder than it does on the holder of the underlying security. We will return to this point in Section C of this Chapter.

5. Time Remaining Until Expiration

The last factor that affects call option value is time remaining until expiration. Time to expiration affects option value in two ways. The first, considered in subsection 3, involves the need to discount the exercise price to present value. The second effect involves variability in the value of the underlying asset. The longer the time remaining until expiration, the more time there is for the value of the underlying asset to change.

If asset values follow a random walk over time, the variance in expected value on a future date is proportional to the time between today and the future date. The standard deviation is proportional to the *square root* of the time remaining. All that is needed to change the distribution of expected future returns for Stableco into a distribution more like Variableco is to increase the time remaining until expiration.

Figure 7-5 shows the effect of time to expiration on the distribution of expected value of the underlying asset *at expiration*. If the option expires in a week, the probability distribution is very narrow. There isn't enough time for much to happen to change asset value. Thus, a deep out-of-the-money option will be nearly worthless. As the time to expiration increases, the probability distribution flattens out more and more. This makes an option, especially an out-of-the-money option, worth more. More specifically, in the Black-Scholes option pricing formula, the standard deviation of the return on the underlying asset σ_a is estimated for a specified time period (such as one month or one year), and then multiplied by $t^{1/2}$.

Figure 7-5
Effect of Time to Expiration on Option Value

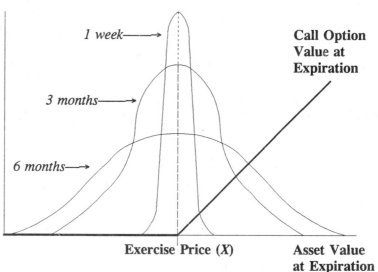

Probability of Asset Value at Expiration

1 week⟶

3 months⟶

6 months⟶

Call Option Value at Expiration

Exercise Price (*X*)

Asset Value at Expiration

C. Applying the Option Perspective

Understanding the factors that affect option value, can help in understanding a broad range of events. Many common relationships can be recharacterized as involving the grant and receipt of an option. This can provide insight into the factors that bear on the value of the interests held by each party to the relationship and, as a result, each party's incentives. We will use this perspective often in later chapters. Here we offer two examples: (i) the conflict between bondholders and stockholders; and (ii) the conflict between management and stockholders.

1. An Option Perspective on the Conflict Between Debt and Equity

Assume that Firm X has a capital structure made up of only debt and equity, and that the debt has a specified face value and is repayable on a specified date in a single lump sum. The value of the equity then equals the firm's total value minus the value of the debt. If the debt is not repaid when due, the firm will go into bankruptcy, with the result (we will assume for simplicity) that the stockholders are wiped out and the debtholders become the owners of the firm. Thus, the value of the debt on the repayment date is either: (i) its face value if it is repaid; or (ii) the value of Firm X's assets if the debt is not repaid and the debtholders take over the firm.

This arrangement can be recharacterized as an option. The stockholders can be seen as having sold an *unlevered* firm X to the debtholders in return for: (i) the proceeds from issuing the debt; (ii) a management contract; and (iii) most importantly, a call option to repurchase the unlevered firm by paying off the debt (face value plus interest). On the repayment date, if the firm's assets are worth more than the repayment price, the stockholders will "exercise their option" to repurchase the unlevered firm by repaying the debt. If the firm's assets are worth less than the repayment price, the equity holders won't exercise their option. They do this by defaulting on the debt.

Given this recharacterization of the relationship between debtholders and equity holders as involving a call option, how do the factors that determine option value affect the incentives of both parties? We would expect the debtholders to negotiate an interest rate that reflects their view of the risk of default at the time the terms of the debt are negotiated. But now consider the stockholders' incentives once the debt has been sold. The stockholders hold, in effect, a call option on an unlevered firm X. A major determinant of the value of that option is the variance in the future value of firm X. The stockholders thus have an incentive to cause firm X to make *riskier* investments than would be optimal for an unlevered firm.

Stockholders in a highly levered firm (say a firm worth $100, with outstanding debt with a face value of $90) hold a slightly in-the-money call option. The stockholders get all of the increased upside potential from taking a large risk. Much of the increased downside is borne by the debtholders, who suffer all losses that drop the firm's value below $90. A highly risky project that has zero net present value, and thus doesn't change the value of the firm as a whole, will increase the value of the stock and decrease the value of the debt.

This can be shown with a simple numerical example. Suppose that Firm X has assets of $100, all invested in Treasury bills, and outstanding debt of $90. If the firm keeps its funds in Treasury bills, it will be able to pay the debt for sure, so the debt will be worth $90 and the stock will be worth $10. Suppose though, that the stockholders find a project that requires a $100 investment, and has a 50% chance of returning $200 and a 50% chance of returning $0. The expected return on the $100 investment is $100.

The expected payoff to the stockholders from this investment is strongly positive. If the investment pays off, they repay the debt and are left with stock worth $110. If the investment doesn't pay off, the stockholders default on the debt and are left with $0. Since both outcomes are equally likely, the expected payoff is $55. This is shown in Table 7-1:

Table 7-1
Value of Levered Firm's Stock and Debt Before and After a Risky Investment

	Before Risky Investment	After Risky Investment
Stock Value	$ 10	$(.50 \times \$110) + (.50 \times \$0) = \$ 55$
Debt Value	$ 90	$(.50 \times \$90) + (.50 \times \$0) = \$ 45$
Firm Value	$100	$(.50 \times \$200) + (.50 \times \$0) = \$100$

The stockholders' gain, though, is the debtholders' loss. If the investment pays off, the debtholders receive $90. If the investment doesn't pay off, they are left with a claim on a worthless firm, worth $0. Since both outcomes are equally likely, the expected payoff is $45. This is also shown in Table 7-1.

Bond Covenants. The debtholders will anticipate such risk-increasing behavior when the terms of the debt were negotiated. They will demand some combination of (i) covenants that limit the stockholders' ability to make risky gambles, and (ii) an interest rate that reflects the anticipated increase in risk (taking the covenants into account). If the stockholders want to limit the interest rate they must pay, they will agree to covenants that prohibit the firm from, for example, substantially altering its investment portfolio, incurring additional debt, or taking other actions that would increase the risk of default. The more highly levered the firm, the more important such covenants will be.

The option perspective focuses attention on the importance of variance in the value of the underlying asset. Thus, it highlights the stockholders' incentives to take risks, and hence the debtholders' need for protection, by contract, a higher interest rate, or some of both.[3] A similar analysis is possible with respect to the conflict between preferred and common stockholders.

One might think that, if the debtholders are compensated through a higher interest rate for risk-increasing behavior by stockholders, the two parties would be indifferent between a high interest rate loan that allowed such strategic behavior, or a lower interest rate loan plus strong covenants. In fact, the problem is not zero sum. Often, an option holder can gain from a risky investment even if the investment has a negative net present value. Thus, viewed *ex ante*, covenants that limit strategic behavior can increase the total value of the firm. Stockholders benefit from this increase in firm value. The lower interest rate on the firm's debt more than offsets the lost opportunity to act strategically once debt has been issued.

Many terms in debt contracts are standardized, but opportunities for innovation remain. For example, the growth in leveraged buyouts and leveraged recapitalizations in the 1980s led to the development of "event risk" covenants, which give bondholders the right to "put" their bonds back to the issuing firm if the firm takes one of the leverage-increasing actions described in the covenant.[4] But many early event risk covenants were not very effective, perhaps because the legal and financial advisors who developed them did not fully understand the stockholders' incentives to increase leverage. Identifying the options implicit in the relationship, and how those implicit options affect

---

[3] Option-sensitive efforts to analyze bond covenants include Clifford Smith & Jerold Warner, *On Financial Contracting: An Analysis of Bond Covenants*, 7 J.Fin.Econ. 117 (1979), reprinted in *The Modern Theory of Corporate Finance* 167 (Clifford Smith ed. 2d ed. 1990); Kose John & Avner Kalay, *Costly Contracting and Optimal Payout Constraints*, 37 J.Fin. 457 (1982); Avner Kalay, *Stockholder-Bondholder Conflict and Dividend Constraints*, 10 J.Fin.Econ. 211 (1982) (evaluating American Bar Foundation, *Corporate Debt Financing Project: Commentaries on Model Debenture Indenture Provisions* (1971)).

[4] See, e.g., Leland Crabbe, *Event Risk: An Analysis of Losses to Bondholders and "Super Poison Put" Bond Covenants*, 46 J.Fin. 689 (1991); Steven Zimmer, *Event Risk Premia and Bond Market Incentives for Corporate Leverage*, Fed. Reserve Bank N.Y.Q.Rev. 15 (Spr.1990). These covenants are also called "poison put" covenants because they can be structured to increase the cost of a hostile takeover, whether or not accompanied by an increase in leverage.

the parties' incentives, could have offered a systematic way to identify the actions that an event-risk covenant should cover.

Strategic Behavior in Bankruptcy. The option perspective on the conflict between debt and equity is especially important when a firm is in or near bankruptcy. In a bankrupt firm, there are conflicts not only between stockholders and debtholders, but also between senior creditors, who are entitled to be paid first, and junior creditors, who get what's left over after the senior creditors are paid. Often, the common stock and one or more classes of junior debt may be worthless, or nearly so, if the firm were liquidated or sold today. This gives them strong incentives to delay a liquidation or sale, in the hope that the firm's prospects will improve. In effect, stockholders and junior debtholders hold an out-of-the-money call option on the firm's assets, and want to stretch out the time to maturity of their option.

The incentives for some classes of claimants to delay do much to explain why bankruptcy is often a costly and protracted process. In most cases, the value of the *firm* is maximized by a quick restructuring and exit from bankruptcy. But that might wipe out stockholders and junior creditors. As a result, they may litigate (or threaten to litigate) every issue in order to delay the resolution of the bankruptcy. Unfortunately, bankruptcy law leaves ample room for protracted litigation. Scholars have argued that society would be better served by a bankruptcy process that emphasized speed, and limited the parties' ability to delay the needed financial restructuring. *Ex ante*, shareholders and creditors would be better off under such a system because bankruptcy costs would be lower.[5]

Fiduciary Duty and Conflicts of Interest. Option analysis can also illustrate when particular actions involve a conflict of interest. For example, a risky investment, normally a matter of unreviewable business judgment, may take on a different light when a company's ability to pay its debt is uncertain. By increasing the risk of default, the investment benefits stockholders at the expense of debtholders.

Judges have begun to appreciate the implications of option theory for the fiduciary duties of the directors. In a recent case, Delaware Chancellor William Allen explicitly used option theory to argue that directors of a firm at or near insolvency should maximize the value of the firm as a whole, rather than the value of its stock.

---

[5] See, e.g., Mark Roe, *Bankruptcy and Debt: A New Model for Corporate Reorganization*, 83 Colum.L.Rev. 527 (1983).

CREDIT LYONNAIS BANK NEDERLAND, N.V.
vs. PATHE COMMUNICATIONS CORP.
1991 WL 277613, at n.55 (Del.Ch.1991)

The possibility of insolvency can do curious things to incentives, exposing creditors to risks of opportunistic behavior and creating complexities for directors. Consider, for example, a solvent corporation having a single asset, a judgment for $51 million against a solvent debtor. The judgment is on appeal and thus subject to modification or reversal. Assume that the only liabilities of the company are to bondholders in the amount of $12 million. Assume that the array of probable outcomes of the appeal is as follows:

[Outcome]	Expected Value
25% chance of affirmance ($51mm)	$12.75 million
70% chance of modification ($4mm)	$ 2.8 million
5% chance of reversal ($0)	$ 0
Expected Value of Judgment on Appeal	$15.55 million

Thus, the best evaluation is that the current value of the equity is $3.55 million. ($15.55 million expected value of judgment on appeal − $12 million liability to bondholders). Now assume an offer to settle at . . . $17.5 million. By what standard do the directors of the company evaluate the fairness of [this offer]?

The creditors of this solvent company would be in favor of accepting . . . [the offer to] avoid the 75% risk of insolvency and default. The stockholders, however, . . . very well may be opposed to acceptance of the $17.5 million offer [even though] the residual value of the corporation would increase from $3.5 to $5.5 million. This is so because the litigation alternative, with its 25% probability of a $39 million outcome to them ($51 millon − $12 million = $39 million) has an expected value to the residual risk bearer of $9.75 million ($39 million × 25% chance of affirmance), substantially greater than the $5.5 million available to them in the settlement. . . .

[I]t seems apparent that one should in this hypothetical accept the best settlement offer available providing it is greater than $15.55 million, and one below that amount should be rejected. But that result will not be reached by a director who thinks he owes duties directly to shareholders only. It will be reached by directors who are capable of conceiving of the corporation as a legal and economic entity. Such directors will recognize that in managing the business affairs of a solvent corporation in the vicinity of insolvency, circumstances may arise when the right (both the efficient and the fair) course to follow for the corporation may diverge from the choice that the stockholders (or the creditors, or the employees, or any single group interested in the corporation) would make if given the opportunity to act. Thus, the option perspective can support a rule that gives directors' fiduciary duties to debtholders when a firm approaches insolvency.

A subsequent case, *Geyer v. Ingersoll Publications Co.*, 1992 WL 136,473 (Del.Ch.1992), relies on *Lyonnais Bank* in holding that directors owe fiduciary duties to creditors as soon as a firm becomes insolvent, even if the firm has not yet filed for bankruptcy. This, though, doesn't fully resolve the tension between maximizing value to the corporation, and maximizing value to the shareholders. Chancellor Allen's hypothetical, after all, involved a solvent corporation.

2. An Option Perspective on Management Incentive Compensation

An option perspective can also be useful in examining the conflict between managers and stockholders. It is commonplace to recognize that managers and stockholders have different incentives with respect to some firm decisions. Stockholders desire profit maximization. Managers, however, desire that combination of salary, perquisites, and profit maximization that yields *them* the most value. Absent corrective forces, managers will engage in less profit maximization than the stockholders would prefer.

Managers are also often more risk-averse than diversified shareholders. There are two principal reasons. First, managers typically have a large investment in firm-specific human capital. Taking more risk exposes this human capital to greater risk, since the managers are more likely to lose their jobs if the company gets into financial trouble. Second, managers' financial assets are often concentrated in the firm they manage. Thus, managers may be more risk averse than stockholders would prefer. The concentration of human and financial capital in a single firm also makes the managers averse to both systematic and firm-specific risk, while diversified stockholders care only about systematic risk.[6]

One way to make managers more interested in profits is to give them stock in the firm. Too little stock, and managers won't care enough about profits. Too much stock, though, will make the managers less financially diversified and may make them too risk averse.

Firms can also offer managers stock options, instead of or in addition to stock. Options will also enhance the profit incentive, and can make the managers more willing

---

[6] See Eugene Fama, *Agency Problems in the Theory of the Firm*, 88 J.Pol.Econ. 288 (1980).

to accept risk. Too many options, though, and the managers may develop too great an affinity for risk. This may partly explain why management stock options are often issued with an exercise price equal to the current market price, and a long time (often 10 years) until expiration, so the options are deep in the money in present value terms. This gives managers incentives that are something of a hybrid between stock and an out of the money option.

A further possibility is leveraging the firm, say through a leveraged buyout. This makes stock take on more of the characteristics of a call option. By reducing the fraction of invested capital that is in the form of equity, leverage also makes it feasible to give managers a larger percentage stake in the residual value of the firm.

Complexities like these make designing a good management compensation package a difficult task. But understanding the option characteristics of stock, and how options can be used as part of the compensation mix is an essential tool. Option theory is central to understanding managers' attitudes toward risk, and how manager and shareholder interests may diverge.[7]

---

[7] For a recent effort to incorporate some of these complications into the theory of managerial compensation, see M.P. Narayanan, *Compensation Contracts and Managerial Myopia* (U.Mich.Bus.Sch. working paper 92-10, 1992).

Problems to Accompany Chapter 7

1. Figure 7-1 shows the return at expiration to the *holder* of a call option on common stock, as a function of the value of the stock at expiration. Draw the return at expiration to the *seller* of a call option on common stock, with an exercise price of X, as a function of the value of the stock at expiration.

2. Draw the return at expiration to the seller of a put option on common stock, with an exercise price of X, as a function of the value of the stock at expiration.

3. In order to get your feet wet in the world of option finance you have decided to buy both a call and a put on the same stock. The stock sells for $40 per share. The call option has an exercise price of $45 and the put has an exercise price of $35. Both expire in 6 months. Draw a graph of the value at expiration of this package of options, as a function of the value of the stock at expiration. Label as many points as you can.

4. What beliefs about future changes in the price of the underlying common stock would lead an investor to adopt the strategy described in problem 3?

5. Draw the return at expiration to an investor who both (i) holds a call option on an asset with an exercise price of X, and (ii) has sold a put option on the same asset, with the same exercise price and expiration date, as a function of the value at expiration of the underlying asset.

6. Explain why holding the option position described in problem 5, and also having on hand enough money to pay the exercise price at expiration, is *equivalent* to owning the underlying asset, if there are no cash distributions on the underlying asset between now and the expiration date.

7. Alpha Company common stock currently sells for $40 per share. Alpha has just issued $100 million of 8% convertible debentures due in ten years at a price equal to their principal value of $1000. The debentures pay interest annually. Each debenture is convertible, on the maturity date of the debentures, into 20 shares of Alpha common stock. Describe the Alpha convertible debentures as a combination of nonconvertible debentures and a call option on Alpha common stock. Specify the exercise price and expiration date of the option.

8. You are a consultant to the Ministry of Finance of the newly democratized nation of Freedonia. The government is anxious to implement its new privatization program. Privatization of state owned companies will be conducted by distributing 20% of the shares in each company to its current employees, and selling the remaining 80% to the highest bidders. To attract investor interest, the shares will carry, for 10 years after issuance, a guaranteed minimum annual dividend of 4.5% of the initial price of the shares. There may also be a bonus dividend which will be set by the board of directors based on the success of each company and its need for new funds to invest in the business. Each share will be entitled to one vote on the election of directors and other matters on which shareholders are entitled to vote. To prevent disparities in personal wealth from appearing too quickly, the government will have the right to repurchase the shares within 10 years after issuance for three times the initial sale price. Holders of these "Freedonia shares" will have a claim on the firm's assets which is junior to that of all other creditors.

Break the Freedonia shares into two or more component parts, so that each part resembles a simple security -- common stock, preferred stock, debt, or option -- that is commonly traded in the U.S. That is, construct a bundle of component securities that offer the same expected payoff as the Freedonia shares.

9. Suppose, in Table 7-1, that the risky investment being considered by Firm X has a 30% chance of returning $250, and a 70% chance of being a total loss.

a) What is the expected return from this investment?

b) What is the expected gain for the stockholders of Firm X from making this investment?

c) What is the expected loss to the debtholders of Firm X from making this investment?

d) What is the expected value of Firm X if it makes this investment?